First World War
and Army of Occupation
War Diary
France, Belgium and Germany

8 DIVISION
23 Infantry Brigade
Devonshire Regiment
2nd Battalion
4 November 1914 - 19 April 1919

WO95/1712

The Naval & Military Press Ltd
www.nmarchive.com
Published in association with The National Archives

Published by

The Naval & Military Press Ltd

Unit 10 Ridgewood Industrial Park,

Uckfield, East Sussex,

TN22 5QE England

Tel: +44 (0) 1825 749494

www.naval-military-press.com

www.nmarchive.com

This diary has been reprinted in facsimile from the original. Any imperfections are inevitably reproduced and the quality may fall short of modern type and cartographic standards.

© **Crown Copyright**
Images reproduced by permission of The National Archives, London, England, 2015.

Contents

Document type	Place/Title	Date From	Date To
Heading	2nd Division 23rd Infy Bde 2nd Bn Devonshire Regt Nov 1914-Apl 1919		
War Diary	Hursley Park	04/11/1914	05/11/1914
War Diary	Havre	06/11/1914	09/11/1914
War Diary	Neuve Berquin	10/11/1914	11/11/1914
War Diary	Neuve de Line	12/11/1914	17/11/1914
War Diary	Estaires	18/11/1914	18/11/1914
War Diary	Trenches	19/11/1914	21/11/1914
War Diary	La Fleque	22/11/1914	24/11/1914
War Diary	Trenches	25/11/1914	27/11/1914
War Diary	Estaires	28/11/1914	30/11/1914
War Diary	Trenches	01/12/1914	03/12/1914
War Diary	La Flinque	04/12/1914	06/12/1914
War Diary	Trenches	07/12/1914	09/12/1914
War Diary	Pont Rirchon	10/12/1914	11/12/1914
War Diary	Trenches	12/11/1914	14/11/1914
War Diary	Red Barn	15/12/1914	16/12/1914
War Diary	Trenches	17/12/1914	19/12/1914
War Diary	Pont Rirchon	20/12/1914	24/12/1914
War Diary	Trenches	25/12/1914	27/12/1914
War Diary	La Flinque	28/12/1914	31/12/1914
Heading	23rd Inf. Bde. 8th Div. 2nd Battn. The Devonshire Regiment. January 1915		
War Diary	Trenches	01/01/1915	02/01/1915
War Diary	Pont Rirchon	03/01/1915	05/01/1915
War Diary	Trenches	06/01/1915	08/01/1915
War Diary	La Flinque	09/01/1915	11/01/1915
War Diary	Trenches	12/01/1915	14/01/1915
War Diary	Pont Rirchon	15/01/1915	17/01/1915
War Diary	Trenches	18/01/1915	20/01/1915
War Diary	La Flinque	21/01/1915	23/01/1915
War Diary	Trenches	24/01/1915	26/01/1915
War Diary	Pont Rirchon	27/01/1915	29/01/1915
War Diary	Trenches	30/01/1915	31/01/1915
Heading	23rd Inf. Bde. 8th Div. 2nd Battn The Devonshire Regiment. February 1915		
War Diary	Trenches	01/02/1915	01/02/1915
War Diary	La Flinque	02/02/1915	04/02/1915
War Diary	Trenches	05/02/1915	07/02/1915
War Diary	Pont Rirchon	08/02/1915	10/02/1915
War Diary	Trenches	11/02/1915	13/02/1915
War Diary	La Flinque	14/02/1915	16/02/1915
War Diary	Trenches	17/02/1915	19/02/1915
War Diary	Pont Rirchon	20/02/1915	22/02/1915
War Diary	Trenches	23/02/1915	25/02/1915
War Diary	La Flinque	26/02/1915	28/02/1915
Heading	23rd Inf. Bde. 8th Div. 2nd Battn. The Devonshire Regiment. March 1915		
War Diary	Le Corbet	01/03/1915	07/03/1915
War Diary	Estaires	08/03/1915	09/03/1915

War Diary	Vicinity Of Neuve Chapelle	10/03/1915	12/03/1915
War Diary	S.W. Pietre	13/03/1915	14/03/1915
War Diary	Pont Du Hem	15/03/1915	16/03/1915
War Diary	Trenches	17/03/1915	19/03/1915
War Diary	Billets	20/03/1915	25/03/1915
War Diary	Trenches	26/03/1915	28/03/1915
War Diary	Billets	29/03/1915	31/03/1915
Heading	Report on Part Taken by 2nd Bn. Devonshire Regiment in Operations 10th to 12th March		
Miscellaneous	Ref. Map Belgium. Sheet 36 1/40000 and Trench plan of Neuve Chapelle and German Trenches.		
Heading	23rd Inf. Bde. 8th Div. 2nd Battn. The Devonshire Regiment. April 1915		
War Diary	Trenches	01/04/1915	03/04/1915
War Diary	Billets	04/04/1915	06/04/1915
War Diary	Bac St Maur	07/04/1915	12/04/1915
War Diary	Trenches	13/04/1915	18/04/1915
War Diary	Billets	19/04/1915	24/04/1915
War Diary	Billets Doulieu	25/04/1915	30/04/1915
Heading	23rd Inf. Bde. 8th Div. 2nd Battn. The Devonshire Regiment. May 1915		
War Diary	Billets Trenches	01/05/1915	04/05/1915
War Diary	Trenches	05/05/1915	06/05/1915
War Diary	Billets	07/05/1915	08/05/1915
War Diary	Neighbourhood of Trenches	09/05/1915	10/05/1915
War Diary	Wangerie	11/05/1915	12/05/1915
War Diary	Billets	13/05/1915	13/05/1915
War Diary	Trenches	14/05/1915	18/05/1915
War Diary	Billets	19/05/1915	26/05/1915
War Diary	Trenches	27/05/1915	29/05/1915
War Diary	Billets	30/05/1915	31/05/1915
Heading	23rd Inf. Bde. 8th Div. 2nd Battn. The Devonshire Regiment. June 1915		
War Diary	Billets	01/06/1915	04/06/1915
War Diary	Trenches	05/06/1915	10/06/1915
War Diary	Billets	11/06/1915	16/06/1915
War Diary	Trenches	17/06/1915	22/06/1915
War Diary	Billets	23/06/1915	30/06/1915
Heading	23rd Inf. Bde. 8th Div. 2nd Battn. The Devonshire Regiment July 1915		
War Diary		01/07/1915	01/07/1915
War Diary	In Trenches	02/07/1915	06/07/1915
War Diary	In Billets	08/07/1915	12/07/1915
War Diary	In Billetsand Trenches	13/07/1915	13/07/1915
War Diary	In Trenches	14/07/1915	29/07/1915
War Diary	In Billets	30/07/1915	31/07/1915
Heading	23rd Inf. Bde. 8th Div. 2nd Battn. The Devonshire Regiment. August 1915		
War Diary	In Billets	01/08/1915	08/08/1915
War Diary	In Trenches	09/08/1915	17/08/1915
War Diary	In Billets	18/08/1915	24/08/1915
War Diary	In Trenches	25/08/1915	31/08/1915
Heading	23rd Inf. Bde. 8th Div. 2nd Battn. The Devonshire Regiment. September 1915		
War Diary	In Trenches	01/09/1915	01/09/1915
War Diary	In Billets	02/09/1915	30/09/1915

Heading	23rd Inf. Bde. 8th Div. 2nd Battn. The Devonshire Regiment. October 1915		
War Diary		01/10/1915	31/10/1915
Heading	23rd Inf. Bde. 8th Div. 2nd Battn. The Devonshire Regiment. November 1915		
War Diary		01/11/1915	30/11/1915
Heading	23rd Inf. Bde. 8th Div. 2nd Battn. The Devonshire Regiment. December 1915		
War Diary		01/12/1915	31/12/1915
Heading	23rd Inf. Bde. 8th Division 2nd Battalion Devonshire Regiment. January 1916		
War Diary		01/01/1916	31/01/1916
Heading	23rd Brigade 8th Division 2nd Battalion Devonshire Regiment February 1916		
War Diary		01/02/1916	29/02/1916
Heading	23rd Brigade 8th Division 2nd Battalion Devonshire Regiment. March 1916		
War Diary		01/03/1916	31/03/1916
Heading	23rd Brigade 8th Division 2nd Battalion Devonshire Regiment April 1916		
War Diary		01/04/1916	30/04/1916
Heading	8th Division 23rd Brigade 2nd Battalion Devonshire Regiment May 1916		
Miscellaneous	The D.A.G. 3rd Echelon	02/06/1916	02/06/1916
War Diary		01/05/1916	31/05/1916
Heading	23rd Brigade. 8th Division 2nd Battalion Devonshire Regiment June 1916		
War Diary		01/06/1916	30/06/1916
Heading	23rd Inf. Bde. 8th Div. 2nd Battn. The Devonshire Regiment July 1916		
War Diary		01/07/1916	31/07/1916
Miscellaneous	Report on The Part Taken By The 2nd Battalion Devonshire Regiment During The Attack On Pozieres of The 1st July 1916		
Heading	23rd Brigade. 8th Division 2nd Battalion Devonshire Regiment August 1916		
War Diary		01/08/1916	31/08/1916
Heading	23rd Inf. Bde. 8th Division. 2nd Battalion Devonshire Regiment. September 1916		
War Diary		01/09/1916	30/09/1916
Heading	23rd Inf. Bde. 8th Division. 2nd Battalion Devonshire Regiment. October 1916		
War Diary		01/10/1916	31/10/1916
Miscellaneous	Report On Raid		
Heading	23rd Brigade. 8th Division 2nd Battalion Devonshire Regiment November 1916		
War Diary	2nd Battalion Devonshire Regiment.	01/11/1916	30/11/1916
Heading	23rd Brigade. 8th Division 2nd Battalion Devonshire Regiment December 1916		
War Diary	2nd Battalion Devonshire Regiment.	01/12/1916	31/12/1916
Heading	23rd Brigade. 8th Division 2nd Battalion Devonshire Regiment January 1917		
War Diary	2nd Battalion Devonshire Regiment	01/01/1917	31/01/1917
Heading	23rd Brigade 8th Division 2nd Battalion Devonshire Regiment February 1917		
War Diary		01/02/1917	28/02/1917

Heading	23rd Brigade. 8th Division 2nd Battalion Devonshire Regiment March 1917		
War Diary		01/03/1917	31/03/1917
Heading	23rd Brigade. 8th Division 2nd Battalion Devonshire Regiment April 1917		
War Diary		01/04/1917	30/04/1917
Heading	23rd Brigade. 8th Division 2nd Battalion Devonshire Regiment May 1917		
War Diary		01/05/1917	31/05/1917
Heading	23rd Brigade 8th Division 2nd Battalion Devonshire Regiment June 1917		
War Diary		01/06/1917	30/06/1917
Heading	23rd Brigade. 8th Division 2nd Battalion Devonshire Regiment July 1917		
War Diary		01/07/1917	31/07/1917
Miscellaneous	Report on Raid by 2nd Devonshire Regt.	26/07/1917	26/07/1917
Miscellaneous		27/07/1917	27/07/1917
Heading	23rd Brigade. 8th Division 2nd Battalion Devonshire Regiment August 1917		
War Diary		01/08/1917	31/08/1917
Heading	23rd Brigade 8th Division 2nd Battalion Devonshire Regiment September 1917		
War Diary		01/09/1917	30/09/1917
Heading	23rd Brigade. 8th Division 2nd Battalion Devonshire Regiment October 1917		
War Diary		01/10/1917	31/10/1917
Heading	23rd Brigade 8th Division 2nd Battalion Devonshire Regiment November 1917		
Miscellaneous			
War Diary		01/11/1917	30/11/1917
Miscellaneous	G.97/2 C.T.	27/11/1917	27/11/1917
Miscellaneous	Report on Minor Operation carried out by this Battalion on night of 24th/25th November.	06/11/1917	06/11/1917
Map	Passchendaele		
Heading	23rd Brigade 8th Division 2nd Battalion Devonshire Regiment December 1917		
War Diary		01/12/1917	28/02/1918
Heading	23rd Inf. Bde. 8th Div. 2nd Battn. The Devonshire Regiment. March 1918		
War Diary		01/03/1918	31/03/1918
Heading	23rd Brigade. 8th Division 2nd Battalion Devonshire Regiment April 1918		
War Diary		01/04/1918	30/04/1918
War Diary	Boutillerie	01/05/1918	03/05/1918
War Diary	On the move	04/05/1918	04/05/1918
War Diary	Dravegny	05/05/1918	09/05/1918
War Diary	Romain	10/05/1918	11/05/1918
War Diary	Concevreux	12/05/1918	12/05/1918
War Diary	In Trenches	13/05/1918	20/05/1918
War Diary	Roucy	21/05/1918	31/05/1918
Miscellaneous	Day of Attack 24/4/18		
Miscellaneous			
War Diary	In The Field	01/06/1918	30/06/1918
Miscellaneous	23rd Inf. Bde. No. G. 12/1	08/06/1918	08/06/1918

Miscellaneous	Record of the 2nd Bn Devonshire Regiment on action 26th May to 12th June 1918 Soissons Rheims front. Ref Map Soissons 1/100000		
War Diary	Montieres	01/07/1918	15/07/1918
War Diary	Trenches	21/07/1918	27/07/1918
War Diary	Bourseville	16/07/1918	20/07/1918
War Diary	Monro St Eloy	21/07/1918	21/07/1918
War Diary	Trenches	28/07/1918	31/07/1918
War Diary		01/08/1918	31/08/1918
War Diary		01/09/1918	30/09/1918
Miscellaneous	Operations		
Heading	23rd Bde. 8th Division War Diary 2nd Bn Devonshire Regt October 1918		
War Diary		01/10/1918	31/10/1918
Miscellaneous	Diary of operations during the forcing of the passage of the River L'Escaut Night of 3d/1st October 1918		
Heading	O/C Historical Section Committee of Imperial Defence (Military Brigade) Public Record Office Chancery Lane London 22nd Brigade 2nd Devon. Vol I 4.11-31.12.14		
War Diary		01/11/1918	30/11/1918
War Diary	Tournai	01/12/1918	17/12/1918
War Diary	Barry	18/12/1918	18/12/1918
War Diary	Ath	19/12/1918	31/12/1918
War Diary		01/01/1919	31/01/1919
War Diary		01/02/1919	28/02/1919
War Diary	ATH	01/03/1919	31/03/1919
War Diary	ATH	01/04/1919	15/04/1919
War Diary	Dunkirk	16/04/1919	19/04/1919

8TH DIVISION
23RD INFY BDE

2ND BN DEVONSHIRE REGT
NOV 1914 - APL 1919

Army Form C. 2118.

WAR DIARY
or
INTELLIGENCE SUMMARY.
(Erase heading not required.)

Instructions regarding War Diaries and Intelligence Summaries are contained in F. S. Regs., Part II. and the Staff Manual respectively. Title pages will be prepared in manuscript.

Hour, Date, Place	Summary of Events and Information	Remarks and references to Appendices

1914.

6 a.m. 4 Nov/14 Hursley Park — Received orders from H.Q. 23rd Bde. to telephone to move for embarkation within 48 hours, at 2.30 p.m. received orders to march off at 2.30 a.m.

2.30 p.m. " " " — 5th to embark at Southampton

2.30 a.m. 5 Nov/14 Hursley Park — Batt⁰ paraded and marched off fully ordered in pouring rain. Strength 30 officers, including M.O. 983 other ranks, including 6 A.S.C. drivers and 4 clerures Sergts. Arrived at Southampton dock at 7 a.m. Embarked on S.S. Bellerophon. Blue funnel line. Also did H.Q. 1 Batt⁰ & details about 5.20 p.m. on leaving 10 draft horses below. Sea very calm

9.40 a.m. 6 Nov/14 Havre — Began to disembark at 9.40 a.m. Left Docks at 1 p.m. for Rest Camp at Granville, where pitched camp and stayed night.

7 Nov/14 " — Ads received about 7 p.m. that 23rd Bde would proceed by train to unknown destination. Batt⁰ to parade at 12 noon and march to station.

8 Nov " — Paraded at 12 m.d. and marched to station. (commenced to entrain transport at 6 a.m. Train left at 10 a.m. Left 2 men behind sick. Train stopped 1 hour at Rouen where Batt⁰ had coffee, stopped at Albeault, (Calais) Etaples and Steenwers, at Strazeele about

10 a.m. 9 Nov " — on March⁰ to Renes Berguin at 1 h.o.n. after Steenwers and went into billets. Lt. Featherston, Lt. At. Stanger, & 48 men about R.S.M. remained in billets. Officers of Bde. coul'd billet'd some at Haverbuen

10 Nov " Renes Berguin — to see trenches in afternoon.

12 m.d. 11 Nov " — on Brigadier (General Penny) brought us orders to march at 6 a.m. with 4 [?] ours, and he (Colonel Phillips) to Renes Eshir, about 13 miles.

Left billets 5.30 a.m. Arrived Renes Eshir about 10.30 a.m. Billeted in farms.

12 Nov " Renes & Esh — Received orders at 9 a.m. to take our trenches of K. Batt. W.O.Y. L. I [?] with 4 ours Batt⁰ paraded at 3 p.m. and marched to trenches at night

* Indian Army

WAR DIARY
or
INTELLIGENCE SUMMARY.
(Erase heading not required.)

Army Form C. 2118.

Instructions regarding War Diaries and Intelligence Summaries are contained in F.S. Regs., Part II. and the Staff Manual respectively. Title pages will be prepared in manuscript.

Hour, Date, Place	Summary of Events and Information	Remarks and references to Appendices.
13th Rest. Reserve Bellewaarde	We told over after dark. Had he (Wounded) 31 men (whom ankle P & SH on one night post & mustn in support. French on our left with Scots Guys in support.	
14th " "	In trenches all day. Heavy shelling on both sides. Relieved by K/Yorks between 7 p.m. and 12 a.m. Heavy fighting at Ypres.	
15th " "	Got back to billets about 2.30 a.m. all not through.	
16th " "	In billets all day. A & B Coy dinners from 5.30 p.m. to 9.30 a.m. (about). 4 Div. received at 11 a.m. for Battn. & 3 yds. to proceed to Querrieu in lorries at 11 F.	
17th " "	At 3 a.m. orders/movements cancelled and Battn ordered to proceed with Brigade, other 2 Battns of which had arrived. 15th L.F. entrained at 8.30 a.m. Battn (and 16th) at 8 a.m. and 1st Brigade Sert for all together en a school at Cassis where we arrived about 12 noon.	
18th " Estaires	Battn paraded at 3.30 a.m. and marched to trenches S. of Rue du Bacquerot in La Flinque where it took over the trenches of R.B. and fr. Irish of 4 London. Tail during relief. 1 N. I rest with our & 2 m. two wounded of same on S. coming two man killed and two wounded.	
19th " Trenches	In trenches all day. One man killed and two wounded.	
20th "		
21st "	Relieved by 2 Scottish Rifles between 5.30 & 9.30 p.m. 1st Battalion (killed) and 3 wounded during Day. Went into billets in Brigade reserve at La Flinque fizzing hard.	
22nd La Flinque	In billets. German aeroplane & Captain Hindman & Lingan laid	

(9 26 6) W 257—976 100,000 4/12 HWV 79/3298

Army Form C. 2118.

WAR DIARY
or
INTELLIGENCE SUMMARY.
(Erase heading not required.)

Instructions regarding War Diaries and Intelligence Summaries are contained in F. S. Regs., Part II. and the Staff Manual respectively. Title pages will be prepared in manuscript.

Hour, Date, Place	Summary of Events and Information	Remarks and references to Appendices
23 Nov. La Flinque	In billets. Local Reserve.	
24 " "	Batt. paraded at 4.30 and marched to trenches taking over from 2/Sco: Rif. Had 2 men wounded in taking over.	
25 " Trenches	In trenches all day. Several men suffering from frostbite, feet bad. None wounded.	
26 " "	One killed and 2 wounded. 2/R.B. attacked German trench on our left and an attempt made to blow up farm in front of us, 6 oils now in it. R.B. musketry having stored haven 1 off. missing. Farm was partly blown up. No casualties. 1 Cas: 2/Middlesex came down as support, if wanted, and returned at 2.30 a.m. artillery fire opened on both sides.	
27 " "	Lost 3 men killed and 2 wounded. Relieved between 7h and 9h. by 2/Sco: Rif and marched back to Estaires. Billets into billets about 11pm	
28 " Estaires	In billets all day as corps reserve. Church parade at 10 a.m.	
29 " "	Paraded at 4.30 h. m. for trenches. 54 men to Hospital, nearly all with frost bitten feet. Relieved 2/Sco: Rif. One man killed in taking over.	2/11
30 " "		
1st Dec. Trenches	Shelling on both sides (H.E.). The king visited Estaires with Prince Consort, Prince of Wales, General Joffre & staff.	
2 " "	Heavier sniping than usual. Two men wounded (Head Capt K) Roylance, & Batt/Sgt died of wounds.	
3 " "	Usual sniping during night. Relieved Shrewsbury dark, early 4th Dec. German on our hart of our trenches H.Q. of 57th Reg: Thirteen wounded During Day. Relieved in evening by 2/Sco. Rif. & went into billets at La Flingue. B. Dn. Reserve.	

Army Form C. 2118.

WAR DIARY
or
INTELLIGENCE SUMMARY.
(Erase heading not required.)

Instructions regarding War Diaries and Intelligence Summaries are contained in F. S. Regs., Part II. and the Staff Manual respectively. Title pages will be prepared in manuscript.

Hour, Date, Place	Summary of Events and Information	Remarks and references to Appendices
1914.		
4th Sept LA FLINQUE	In billets as Bde Reserve.	
5th " "	Much rain.	
6th " "	Battn took over trenches between 5.30 and 7 p.m. from 2/Scottish Rifles	
7th " Trenches	False alarm that Germans were attacking about 6 p.m. 2/Middlesex sent down 2 coys as support, which were sent back at 7 p.m.	
8th " "	Quiet Day.	
9th " "	Relieved by 2/Seaf: Rif: between 6 and 8 p.m. and went into billets at Pont Richou as Bde Reserve.	
10th " PONT RICHON	Whole Battn had baths & change of underclothing in ESTAIRES	?/"
11th " "	Relieved 2/Sea Rif in trenches about 5.30 p.m. very wet.	
12th " Trenches	Brigadier went round our trenches which were very wet and falling in many places. Our artillery very busy.	
13th " "	One man wounded. 50 R.m of 3rd Rif were conveyed went to transport lines	
14th " "	Relieved by Royal Berks about 6 p.m. The 2/4th Bde having somebad to retain the 23rd and 25th foot over whole lots of 5th Bde trenches	
15th " RED BARN	Went into Bde Reserve on LA BASSEE ROAD.	
16th " "	Billets.	
17th " Trenches	Relieved 2/West Yorks in line about 5.30 p.m.	
18th " "	One man killed and one wounded. 53 N.C.O.s and men of 1st Reinforcement joined at Transport lines. C.O. and 2nd in C. went to conference at H.Q. 23rd Bde. at 6.45 a.m.	

Army Form C. 2118.

WAR DIARY
or
INTELLIGENCE SUMMARY.
(Erase heading not required.)

Hour, Date, Place	Summary of Events and Information	Remarks and references to Appendices

Subject being proposed attack on German trenches at 6.30 p.m. Lieuts
Hooders, 2/Wyche in support and 2/Sco. Rif. and 2/Middlesex in reserve.
After short discussion conference broke up till 1/2 noon. At latter Brigadier
C.O.s. sgts again and attack was ordered to hold good as above.
C.O. and adjt hastened back to our H.Q. and N followed to trenches for
Cy commanders to whom orders were issued. D and C coys were to
lead supported by B coy. A coy was to continue in usual
and supplied upon coy. Commanders only 2 of back to their own Coys
called upon Coy. Commanders only 2 of back to their own Coys
about 10 or 15 minutes before operation were to commence.
C.O. and adjt repaired to trenches with party of N.C.O.s with lands
at M.M. 3 of latter wounded on way down. An artillery fire
heavy bombardment of trenches to be taken at 4.15 observed
began at 4.30 hrs. D Coy under Capt Lafone took German trench
C Coy under Major Good urging started but owing to latter being
covered at not and not having had time to explore scheme to
his officers apparently the right direction of the march to
left and were caught up in barbed wire being heavily shelled
it Coy with a few men finally joining D Coy. Capt R Spencer and
Capt F Pinkerton were killed Capt H Lees [?] many others killed

2/11

WAR DIARY
or
INTELLIGENCE SUMMARY.
(Erase heading not required.)

Army Form C. 2118.

Instructions regarding War Diaries and Intelligence Summaries are contained in F.S. Regs, Part II. and the Staff Manual respectively. Title pages will be prepared in manuscript.

Hour, Date, Place	Summary of Events and Information	Remarks and references to Appendices
19th Dec. Trenches.	2/Lt Radcliffe 2.S.O. Regt (attached 1st Rifle Brig) Andrews and Page wounded, and 121 R.B. O.Rs and in all 115 wounded and missing. We find 27 prisoners in trench and many Germans were killed and wounded.	
	Short early hours before enormous crowd of W. Yorkshiremen in German trench about 12 m.n. or 1 a.m. We retired to our own trenches, and came into action in twenty's.. Very into billets at PONT RIRCHON by 8 o'c. Reserve.	3/11
	2/Lt. Yards were landed out of trench as took on the morning and retired to our end of trench, as in security. Part of [illegible] [illegible]	
20th, 21st PONT. RIRCHON. In billets.	At [illegible]	
22nd " "	better. Very wet [illegible] the morning officers and armed [illegible] the [illegible]	
23rd Dec " "	[illegible] Xmas Day. (Com. Offr. went round, Dinners in each mess tables	
	Battalion) answered the cards of plum puddings etc.	
24th Dec " "	Relieved 2nd Scots. Rifle in trenches. During between 5+7 h.m. flag of	
25th " Trenches	Informal armistice during day by N.Germans standing out of their trenches and came towards our line. Our men went out there also they exchanged each other a merry Xmas, shook hands, exchanged souvenirs	
	etc. about 7.30 a.m. sniping began again. All had are marked dead. [illegible] are wounded. Handshaft	

WAR DIARY
or
INTELLIGENCE SUMMARY.
(Erase heading not required.)

Hour, Date, Place	Summary of Events and Information	Remarks and references to Appendices
1914.		
26th Trenches	Report received about 11 p.m. that German army was to make attack at 12.15 a.m. 27th. Every body warned and stood to arms.	
27th "	at 12 a.m. 26th-27th Our artillery opened fire & unfortunately stopped any attack — if such a mad contemplation[?] disposal infact came from Deserter. Turned in about 1.30 a.m.	
" "	Relieved in evening by 2/ Seo: Rif. & went into billets at La Flangue.	2/"
28th LA FLINQUE	Stood to arms at 6 a.m. [(1 Coy) moved into new billets. H Coy.]	
	Sades. very wet night of 28-29th.	
29th "	Quiet day [stand to arms as usual.]	
30th "	Reconnoitring[?] and day in billets.	
31st "	Relieved 2/ Seo: Rif. in trenches in evening.	

Jas. Sandes. Major
Adjt. 2 Seven Regt.

23rd Inf.Bde.
8th Div.

2nd BATTN. THE DEVONSHIRE REGIMENT.

J A N U A R Y

1 9 1 5

Army Form C. 2118.

WAR DIARY
or
INTELLIGENCE SUMMARY.
(Erase heading not required.)

Instructions regarding War Diaries and Intelligence Summaries are contained in F. S. Regs., Part II. and the Staff Manual respectively. Title pages will be prepared in manuscript.

Hour, Date, Place		Summary of Events and Information	Remarks and references to Appendices
1st Jan 1915	Trenches	One man killed. Five wounded. Attacks given of day.	
2nd "	"	Relieved by 2nd Seo. Rif. at evening and went into billets on Rue l'Ausnel at Pont Riches	
3rd "	PONT RICHON	Very wet. In billets as before. Russell Scraft[?] of R.E. As[?]me[?] journal mostly. Too old and some very young.	
4th "	"	[a billet of] Lt Belfield went to Hospital	
5th "	"	Relieved 2nd Seo Rif. in Trenches in evening	
6th "	Trenches	One man killed and one wounded. First field artillery rify in Trenches lines.	
7th "	"	Trenches very flooded. [Capt? Laforshatts, Lieut Lebby fog Holden] Palmer and 2 R.E.O.s went Home on 7 days leave.	2/11
8th "	"	Relieved by 2nd Seo Rif. and went into R.D.C Reserve at 9 rue LA FLINAUE [La billet?] 1st and 2nd as a maskast sent to Hospital	
9th "	LA FLINAUE	"	
10th "	"	Voluntary service.	
11th "	"	One man wounded in billets in RUE DUBACQUEROT in morning by a bomb that burst from our own guns. Relieved 2nd Seo Rif. in trenches in evening. Draft of 75 R.I.O.s on joined at Transport lines.	
12th "	Trenches	In Trenches. One man killed and one wounded. Great concentration with all cavity to typhoid causes to those who have been exposed to it. 5 officers and 2 R.E.O.s returned.	
13th "	"	Very wet. Three killed and two wounded. Trenches very bad and communication between coy and from heav[y] Trenches very bad hands of coys confused etc.	

WAR DIARY or INTELLIGENCE SUMMARY.

Army Form C. 2118.

Instructions regarding War Diaries and Intelligence Summaries are contained in F.S. Regs., Part II. and the Staff Manual respectively. Title pages will be prepared in manuscript.

(Erase heading not required.)

Hour, Date, Place		Summary of Events and Information	Remarks and references to Appendices
14 Jan/1915	Trenches	Relieved by 2nd Scot Rif in evening and went into Gen Reserve at PONT	
	PONT RIRCHON	RIRCHON. Casualties killed [Bustehez] 1 wounded.	
15th	"	In billets. Draft of 75 R.C. & 54 men joined Batt from Transport lines	
16th	"	" Greneciers of rank (eg firebrands) dumb pridgeons	
17th	"	" Funeral service Sunday evening 11th Reg at Fort Pinney	
	"	Relieved 2/ Scot Rif in Trenches between 5.0 & 7 pm Cast 1 killed and 2	
	"	wounded in taking over trenches	
18th	Trenches	Very wet & cold but trenches held. A frozen L Friendza leg was	
	"	broken. Off 9 2 R.C. & 63 men gas (in each Batt reg per R.C. & P.W.)	2/11
	"	but had provide serving any of them (killed 3 wounded)	
19th	"	Trenches over slightly. Few Casualties (wounded). It was cold	
	"	30 R.C & 63 men in reserve and joined at Transport lines at Gunning	
20th	"	Relieved by 2 Scot Rif and went into Billets Reserve at LA FLINQUE	
	"	No casualties. Capt Indrup, Lieut Tough, 2nd Lieut Lewis, Boulton, at 6.30pm	
	"	Wand Rive went Advance from 21st to 27th inclusive	
21st	LA FLINQUE	In Billets. Draft - joined from Transport lines (2/Lieut Watson & 54 men)	
22nd	"	In billets	
23	"	Relieved 2/ Scot Rif in trenches between 5.30 pm & 7pm. One man wounded day	
	"	"" and Scot Rif had 2 wounded. The moon badly wounded today (wounded)	
24	Trenches	Enemy unusually this held and sunk wounded	

WAR DIARY
or
INTELLIGENCE SUMMARY.
(Erase heading not required.)

Army Form C. 2118.

Instructions regarding War Diaries and Intelligence Summaries are contained in F.S. Regs., Part II. and the Staff Manual respectively. Title pages will be prepared in manuscript.

1915	Hour, Date, Place	Summary of Events and Information	Remarks and references to Appendices
25th Jan/1915	Trenches	1st Bays on right of our Bde. repulsed attack on imminent. Enemy attacked at La Bassée (a.m.) based heavily at junction of British and French lines. 1 officer and 17 N.C.O.s & men of 1st Bn. Grenadiers (reg. sent to H.Q.D. to stay night in case Bty. should be wanted. (None within 3 miles.) Finished wounded and 3 rank & file killed and 6 wounded.	
26th Jan?	Trenches	Relieved by 2nd Sco. Rif. 4 men wounded. G.O.C. Corps visited Trenches in evening. Went into billets as Divl. Reserve at Pont Richon. [11 Bde. went into 7 days leave]	
27th Jan?	PONT RICHON	C.O. Capt. R. Blunt (left Pont midnight 26/27th) was Gds pieces in a 7 days leave Bn. or L. Colonel Dyer in command and Lt. Bostock as adjut.] Maj? Jos. Lee Bryant as Russ. in billets.	
28th "	"	Resting day.	
29th "	Trenches	Resting day. Relieved 2nd Sco. Rif. in trenches in evening. Casualties in as warned.	
30th "	"	Quiet Day except for snipers. (2nd Lt Watkin Jones slightly wounded) Sergt Blakehus 7.R.C.O.s & men wounded.	
31st "	"	Quiet day except that enemy shelled B. Bay. & officers in evening. (Capt. Wilson died at 9.10 p.m. 2 or 6 others. Hospital section) 1/2 of [Remand] of B. Bay. killed in evening. No other casualties.	

J. Foster Bryan
Maj. 1/2 P.W.O.W. Russ.
1st Feb: 1915.

23rd Inf.Bde.
8th Div.

2nd BATTN. THE DEVONSHIRE REGIMENT.

FEBRUARY

1915

Army Form C. 2118.

WAR DIARY
or
INTELLIGENCE SUMMARY.
(Erase heading not required.)

Instructions regarding War Diaries and Intelligence Summaries are contained in F.S. Regs., Part II. and the Staff Manual respectively. Title pages will be prepared in manuscript.

Hour, Date, Place		Summary of Events and Information	Remarks and references to Appendices
1915.			
1st Feby.	Trenches	Relieved in trenches by 2nd Sco. Rif. (casualties 2 killed, 1 wounded).	
2nd Feby	LA FLINQUE	In billets. B.Dr. issued. One man wounded by stray fire.	
3 "	"	Shelled but no casualties. Half Battn. L.F. (strong) returned from leave.	
4 "	"	Relieved 2nd Sco. Rif. in trenches, casualties 3 wounded.	
5 "	Trenches	Enemy shooting aeronograph overhead shelled, 6 wounded.	
6 "	"	Very quiet day.	
7 "	"	Relieved by 2nd Sco. Rif - Casualties shelled, 4 wounded.	
8 "	PONT RIRCHON	In billets.	
9 "	"	In billets. Lieut Peake rejoined - Capton R.A.M.C. presented a team 10 to 16th	
10 "	"	Relieved 2nd Sco. Rif. in trenches [2 gun Indts + 2 sects Batn] on leave has returned from leave	
11 "	Trenches	Enemy fairly active in shooting line (casualties shelled 4 wounded)	
12 "	"	Considerable firing by day & night on H.Q. in mountain	
13 "	"	Relieved by 2nd Sco. Rif. Quiet day (casualties - killed 5 wounded).	
14 "	LA FLINQUE	In billets. B.Dr. issued. Enemy shelled Bldg. in RUE DU BACQUEROT	
15 "	"	Bldg. shelled but of billets in RUE DU BACQUEROT. One billet burnt down with considerable amount of equipment and about 70 men wounded.	
16 "	"	In billets Coy of men arrived yesterday 2nd Relieved 2nd Sco Rif in trenches. Draft of 1 offr (2nd Lieut Litt J.G. M. Shefit) & 75 O.R. Own journal at Rampart time very wet	

Army Form C. 2118.

WAR DIARY
or
INTELLIGENCE SUMMARY.
(Erase heading not required.)

Instructions regarding War Diaries and Intelligence Summaries are contained in F. S. Regs., Part II. and the Staff Manual respectively. Title pages will be prepared in manuscript.

Hour, Date, Place		Summary of Events and Information	Remarks and references to Appendices
1915			
17th Feby.	Trenches.	Quiet day. Two men wounded. 2nd Lieuts. [?] and Low [?] promoted from ranks of Cathds. Rifles, joined at transport lines. They not sent up.	
18th	"	Quiet day. Two men killed and two wounded.	
19th	"	Relieved by 2nd Geo. Rif. and went into billets as Div'l reserve	
20th	PONT RIRNON	Three officers and Draft (which joined transport lines on 18th) joined H.Q.	
21st	"	Church Parade at 9½ am followed by funeral of Pte [?] (Cathds. of Arg.) who was suffocated in his sleep by fumes from coke fire.	2/11
22nd	"	Relieved 2nd Geo. Rif. in trenches in evening. Four men wounded.	
23rd	Trenches	Draft of 90 men joined. Brigadier visits trenches before breakfast & inspected Draft after. Casualties —	
24th	"	Quiet day. Casualties one wounded.	
25th	"	" " killed one, wounded one. Relieved by 2nd Geo. Rif.	
26th	LA FLINQUE	B.Os. Russell, Wagon load of bombs delivered severely wounding 2 Ptes. McCarthy and Pike, both of whom died subsequently. They were carrying behind out trenches from B.H.R. to Battn H.Q.	
27th	"	Received orders to march into billets W of MERVILLE fr next [?]. Rest of B.D. to follow later.	

WAR DIARY
or
INTELLIGENCE SUMMARY.
(Erase heading not required.)

Army Form C. 2118.

Hour, Date, Place	Summary of Events and Information	Remarks and references to Appendices
1915 28th Feby.	Companies and H.Q. rendezvous at Transport lines LE DRUMEZ at 9.30 a.m. Battn marches off at 10 a.m. and starts billets about 2 miles W of MERVILLE about 4 h.m. No arrangements made for billets except an area marked out on map. This area had to be exceeded as the farms & barns had not sufficient room in them for Battn. J.D. Ingles Major adjt. 2/Devon Regt.	mont (K 15. W 37 2/11

23rd Inf.Bde.
8th Div.

2nd BATTN. THE DEVONSHIRE REGIMENT.

M A R C H

1 9 1 5

Attached:

Report on Operations
10th/12th March.

WAR DIARY or INTELLIGENCE SUMMARY.

Army Form C. 2118.
(Erase heading not required.)

Instructions regarding War Diaries and Intelligence Summaries are contained in F.S. Regs, Part II. and the Staff Manual respectively. Title pages will be prepared in manuscript.

Hour, Date, Place	Summary of Events and Information	Remarks and references to Appendices
1915.		
4th March LE CORBET.	In billets, resting. Informed that MERVILLE and HAVERSQUERRE conferences about manœuvres.	
5th March "	Conferences at Bde. H.Q. in morning. P.E.s afternoon, officers' baths.	
6th " "	" " as 1st & 4th.	
7th " "	Brigade church parade in the rain at 10 a.m. at LE SART. 23' Bde. marched to billets at ESTAIRES in evening, this Batt. passed at 5.45 p.m., marched at billets about 11 p.m. Bde. much cheered by inhabitants of Indian Division being on the way out & West of MERVILLE. Batt. at 5th Ghurkas billets (part empty)	
8th ESTAIRES.	In billets. Preparations made for attack on NEUVE CHAPELLE on 10th.	
9th "	Tris conference at Bde. H.Q. during day. Batt. paraded at 11.45 p.m. and marched to front from	
	which Bde. marched to Pt. of assembly for attack, one section of march A.B.C.D. & one M.G. section (4 guns)	
10 " Vicinity of NEUVE CHAPELLE	Left starting point 12 m. 9 – 10th. Reached Rendezvous 1.30 a.m. Halted for 1 hour when billets etc.	
2.30 a.m.	statd for positions of assembly. Bde. one side in following order: Rif. B, Middlesex, 2nd Seaforth, 2nd Middlesex	
5.0 a.m.	2nd Leaves, 2nd West Yorks. Arrived at position of assembly (behind breastworks, M.S. end of RUE TILLELOY	
	Some difficulty was experienced in finding way across country, inspite of guides having been reconnoitred	
	which pointed to necessity of placing men at intervals to direct troops moving to a given point	
	across country by night. The daylight dawn was over-cast in morning, it's passing of orders	
	passing but of march of Bde. and also to troops in rear. After a long time two parties arrived Bdes. Rainer 2nd West Yorks.	
	to become attenuated. The following was order for attack on 23rd Inf. Bde. – 1st line 2nd Scot Rif.	
	on right, 2nd Middlesex on left. In support 2nd Lances. Bde. Rainer 2nd West Yorks.	

WAR DIARY or INTELLIGENCE SUMMARY

Army Form C. 2118.

1915

Hour, Date, Place	Summary of Events and Information	Remarks and references to Appendices
10th March (continued) Jt. 300 hh	Were checked by field artillery and bombardment of enemy position (withdrawing of trenches) began	
8.0 a.m.	2nd Scots Guards began attack from our trenches advancing in rear of and in same manner as 1st Scots Guards	
8.15 a.m.	1/A and 1/B Coys began advance along SIGN POST LANE as right in support of 2nd Scots Rif. 1/A 1/B Battn.	
	C Coys along RUTLAND ROW in left in support to occupy trenches vacated by 2nd Rifle Brig. (2nd Lady was followed by every other unit). The men of B Battn. belonging to Bn. Grenadiers (ie. 1/4 of every Coy but themselves advanced as 1/4 of 2nd Bn. Gren. did)	
	were followed immediately by 1/2 half of A.B Coys, 2 Brethren Cos no follow of 1/2 half of A.B Coys;	
8.45 a.m.	Rest of 1/2 of A & B Coys in their turn advanced. These four advances when combined seemed that 2 Rifle Brigade turned out to advance, every man being shot down as he appeared over the parapet of B.Bn ...	
	and 3 attempts to cross to German trenches were unsuccessful, and on reaching 9 or 10 ft 76. all of which were found to be open, men all killed or wounded. Lt. R.B. Bates led the attack but all who were killed falling on German and front parapet before reaching the German line ...	
	on way of trench and both machine guns were put out of action before getting into position ... any further attempt to advance on Lt.B. was stopped on the L.b. was stopped by the movement and b.d. ... D coys to support of 1st Bn., which Walked German trench about	
	Jt 8-2. The attack came of a concentrated fire of 1 Rifles of A.B. (?) which had followed 2 Scots Rifle into trenches 74-17 and our losses were sent far and to clear enemy out of	
9.30 a.m.	Trenches running towards point 76. Enemy were already looking over men faltering (?) in bombing	

WAR DIARY or INTELLIGENCE SUMMARY

Army Form C. 2118.

(Erase heading not required.)

Instructions regarding War Diaries and Intelligence Summaries are contained in F.S. Regs., Part II. and the Staff Manual respectively. Title pages will be prepared in manuscript.

Hour, Date, Place	Summary of Events and Information	Remarks and references to Appendices
1915 March (continued) 7.30 A.M.	Wire broken by field artillery and bombardment of enemy's trenches (which forms his) began	
2.0 A.M.	2nd Scot: Rif: began attack from our trenches and were on verge of enemy trench of many lines	
8.15 A.M.	1/A and 1/B Coys began advance along SIGNPOST LANE on right in support of 2nd Sc: Rif: 2/A/B Battn followed by 2/C Coy: Rut LAND ROW on left to occupy trenches vacated by 2nd Sc: Rif: was held ready as reserve. The other 2 Coys of Battn belongs to Bde: Grenadier Coy: (Divisional Left) of A/B	
	by 1 company trenches. The remaining Batt: belongs to Bde: Grenade Coy:	
	2 platoons some followed 1/Half of A/B Coys	
8.45 A.M.	Head of 1/A + 1/B Coys on entering third line of our communication trench encountered that hostilities the enemy over the height of Bdy: then went unable to advance, every man being shot down as he appeared and eventually 2/Lt 7. B. made 3 attempts to cross to German trenches in rest of trenches and was killed with practically the men being all killed or wounded. 2/Lt P. B. also to this splendid attempt and was killed falling on German trench + 2/Lt Parker on crossing trench was wounded. All officers of A + B Coys of the right half of Battn were sufferings as were several others before getting into enemy before getting into position. Remainder of men thought to advance in rest of Kimmock was stopped by Kimmock. Other heavy casualties were further attempt to advance in the left was stopped by heavy German attack. R.O.O. and C.O. decided C. Coys to support the left Battn which attacked German trench 74-17 and our bullets were seen following over no: 82. This attack came up a mound at left of 1st Half of A/B Coy (supposed had followed)	
	2nd Sc. Rif: into trenches 74-17 and our bullets were sent forward to clear in enemy east of	
9.30 A.M.	French advancing towards front 76. Enemy were already bombing our own XVII bombers.	

Forms/C. 2118/10
(9 20 6) W 4141-463 100,000 9/14 HWV

WAR DIARY or INTELLIGENCE SUMMARY.

Army Form C. 2118.

(Erase heading not required.)

Instructions regarding War Diaries and Intelligence Summaries are contained in F.S. Regs, Part II. and the Staff Manual respectively. Title pages will be prepared in manuscript.

Hour, Date, Place	Summary of Events and Information	Remarks and references to Appendices
1915. 10th March (continued)	MOULIN DU PIETRE). But they did not advance far to our front. There were heavy shelling on our area east of line 79-78. Other Germans were seen on the run. It was said that PIETRE and BOIS DU BIEZ were actually occupied by the Warwicks and 2 battns Indian Troops but that fire had to get away to our own shell fire and late in evening. It became evident (conversation between 2 Brs of infantry on attack and to support — a telling certainty was expressed very much. Telephone wires appear to start at [?] station in front of 23 B.D. [?]	Apparently considerably have respectively westwards the Day they [?] to those remaining [?] a telling certainty was...
11th March Givenchy	... advanced practically unchanged throughout the day till the company when we captured an extra gun ([?] to p7. The [Orchard?] and seats disposed through our left). Battn were twenty-three [?] and telly Battn were sent [?] in the morning. The enemy appeared to discover reinforcements and artillery acting in and about 8 a.m. [?] and had several casualties. 2nd Lt Low was seriously wounded in [?] [?] Due on ambulance.	
12th March 5h.m.	Battn was again heavily shelled and 2nd Lay Ka[?] several casualties (left C.A. Peruicers killed by a bullet in head about noon). Fourth attacks at various points were repulsed Battn received orders to hold B.H. in station in line PIETRE-LA RUSSIE at 6.30 a.m. Battn was called to as quickly as possible and proceeded via ALT. 22-7-6-23-92 sitting up to [?] and to our own shells, no enemy [?] being any trench 87-92 with 2 Gr. Reg. in support. We knew nothing of the situation which we had never seen or drawn [?] attack was postponed till 11.30 and then till 1.30, about 1.45 a.m. we heard it had been cancelled.	

Forms/C. 2118/10
(9 29 6) W 4141—463 100,000 9/14 H W V

WAR DIARY
or
INTELLIGENCE SUMMARY.
(Erase heading not required.)

Army Form C. 2118.

Instructions regarding War Diaries and Intelligence Summaries are contained in F.S. Regs, Part II. and the Staff Manual respectively. Title pages will be prepared in manuscript.

Hour, Date, Place	Summary of Events and Information	Remarks and references to Appendices
1915 13th March 2.00 p.m. PIETRE S.W.	After attack was cancelled we took up line of trenches 87-92 with 2/West 2/[unit] on our left. Bty. which had advanced to within about 50 ft of buildings on our left. B[tt]y, which had advanced to within 50 ft of buildings on our left. Enemy fired even still[?] we and now[?] by which advance and support and any [?] wounded and officers. Enemy fired even still[?] us and now[?] by which [?] was had several casualties. They sent officers[?] one eight[?] but great day long in fight attack without having thoroughly reconnoitered ground and without having explained exactly what was expected of them was very firmly brought home to all.	A very heavy and fierce attack[?] was put up and in essence it was 50 men wounded and officer and advanced up too high ranks [?] and to all ranks exactly what
14th "	Trenches all day. Relieved in evening by 1st Lincolns. Went back into billets at [?] near PONT DU HEM & Mattias on about 11.30 p.m. (Capt. Dalziel was buried by shell and dug out. Coy of Batt on N.E. side of river accidentally injured about 274 R.C.B.s and one man killed wounded and missing.	Coy of Batt on N.E. side of river 3 officers killed, 9 wounded and
15th " PONT DU HEM	In billets. 2nd Lieut. Travers & I.F. went to hospital in evening with losses (app.) 1 Com. and 20 Lieut. Travers appears to be acting Capt.	Officers in batt Travers & app of B
16th "	Took over trenches. 3 hours from Leicesters and Northants On our extreme	(our battery)
17th " Trenches	2 men killed	
18th " "	About 2 coy	
19th " "	Relieved in evening by 2nd Sco. Rif. and went into billets as Bd. Res. on and near RUE DU BALGUEROT.	
20th " Billets	A draft of 4 officers (2/Lt Bolton, Bullock, Fraser and Roberts) and 42 other ranks joined.	

Army Form C. 2118.

WAR DIARY
or
INTELLIGENCE SUMMARY.
(Erase heading not required.)

Instructions regarding War Diaries and Intelligence Summaries are contained in F.S. Regs., Part II. and the Staff Manual respectively. Title pages will be prepared in manuscript.

Hour, Date, Place	Summary of Events and Information	Remarks and references to Appendices
1915		
21st March Billets	Voluntary service in morning. Brigadier inspected draft which joined yesterday. Route march & other drills.	
22nd "	In ESTAIRES in evening and remained in them on 23rd.	
23rd "		
24th "	Left ESTAIRES at 1.30 p.m. and marched into billets at BAC ST MAUR.	
25th "	Battn. remained in billets. C.O. and coy. commanders made inspection of trenches to be taken over on 26th.	
26th "	Took over trenches S. of BOIS GRENIER from 4th (Canadian) Regt.	
27th " Trenches	Very quiet day. 2 men wounded. Bois Grenier Rif. and 36th Res. had rather our 5 men wounded. No 1 Cov of "A" Res had — of 2 in hours.	
28th "	Enemy threw few shells into BOIS GRENIER. Withdrawn in reserve.	
	Very fine & frosty. Trenches dry in parts. 2 Lt. Gilson went to Hospital at 5 a.m. Enemy shelled BOIS GRENIER about 12 noon. Ten Trenches were shelled in afternoon. 2 Lieut. Radcliffe and 1 man dangerously wounded.	
	Battn. relieved in evening by 2nd Scs. Rif. and went into billets in Bois Grenier.	
29th and 30th Billets	Bois Grenier. Builds shelled but no damage done.	
31st March	Relieved 2nd Scs. Rif. in Trenches in evening.	
	J. L. Jackson Major	
	(Comdg. 2/ Queens Regt.)	

REPORT ON PART TAKEN BY 2ND BN. DEVONSHIRE
REGIMENT IN OPERATIONS 10TH TO 12TH MARCH.

Ref: map BELGIUM sheet 36. 1/40000
and numbered plan of NEUVE CHAPELLE and GERMAN TRENCHES.

Report on part taken by 2nd Bn. Devonshire Regt. in operations 10th to 12th March.
1915.

12 m.n. 9th–10th   Battn. left LA GORGUE to march to rendez-vous,
(in CAMERON LANE. Pt. M 15 d. 1.9.) of 23rd Bde:
2/Sco: Rif: in front followed by 2/Middlesex, ourselves and
2/ West Yorkshire Regt.

10th March.
1.30 a.m.   Reached rendez-vous, halted for an hour and had tea.

2.30 a.m.   Continued march to point of underground assembly.

4.30 a.m.   In position at pt. of assembly, 2/Sco: Rif and 2/Middle-
sex in trenches, ourselves in support behind breast-
work on RUE TILLELOY Quay M. 22. d.

7.30 a.m.   Bombardment of enemy's position began.

8.0 a.m.   2/Sco: Rif began advance from our trenches on
right of Bde: and 2/Middlesex on left. Latter failed owing to heavy fire.

8.15 a.m.   ½ A and ½ B Coys. (under Lt. Cobb) advanced along SIGNPOST LANE
in support of Sco: Rif: to occupy trench left by latter.
½ A and ½ B under Capt. Watts advanced along RUTLAND
ROW to occupy trench vacated by 2/Middlesex.
Lt Parker with 2 Machine Guns followed latter party.
All company bombing parties followed their coys:
and men of Bde: Grenadier Coy followed Battn.

8.45 a.m.   Arrived at head of RUTLAND ROW and found that
Middlesex had been prevented leaving trench by fire
and had suffered severely. "B" Coy: made 3 attempts
to advance on right of Middlesex but failed, losing
considerably, (1 killed, 21 wounded) Lt Bates being killed on reaching
wire entanglement and Lt. Bristowe also being
killed and Captain Watts wounded.
The machine guns were rendered useless before
coming into action and Lieut. Parker was wounded.

G.O.C.   × The C.O who saw we were held up on left decided to
send both C and D coys to support our right attack which

9.a.m.	which was on pt: about 82. This attack succeeded, the right half of A and B Coys came up on left of Sco: Rif: "A" Coy: Bombers under Lieut: Wright bombed the Germans out of trenches from which their left attack had been checked, in a most gallant manner 2 Lt. Wright being killed during the operation – not however before the left had been enabled to come on.
9.30 a.m.	The trench now occupied by us was 17-74-21. Between 9 a.m and 9.30 a.m Capt: Jenkins of B Coy: dislocated his knee 2 Lt. Jacob being then the only officer left with that Coy:
10.30 a.m.	A further advance was made by A and B Coys and ½ C and ½ D Coys to 82-21. remaining half of C and D being on north side of SIGNPOST LANE in rear and a delay ensued while our artillery bombarded trenches 22-78-77. We then advanced
12 noon. 1.0 p.m.	and reached these points but were prevented going on by our own shell fire only.
1.30 p.m.	Received orders to advance to 22-78-77. the fact of our being there evidently not having got back. Many prisoners were made during advance on last mentioned line and the Germans everywhere appeared to be well on the run. The rear ½ of C and D Coys: were now brought up
3.0 p.m.	and coys: were rearranged along line, and H.Q. were established at Point 18. We received orders to consolidate our position which we proceeded to do, with the 2/Sco: Rif: on our right about 19 and the 2/Middlesex at Point 6.
6 p.m.	21st Bde advanced, Royal Scots passing through our line, with orders to capture line BOIS DE BIEZ – MOULIN DU PIETRE. The advance however halted some 200 yds in front of our line.

3.

night of
10ᵗʰ–11ᵗʰ   Enemy's shells passing over us throughout night, but no harm done to us.

11ᵗʰ   Enemy had evidently brought up considerable amount of artillery and we were heavily shelled. Two shells falling in our H.Q. killed five signallers and orderlies and wounded six.
B Coy; to which Captn Tingy had been transferred was heavily shelled in afternoon and had several casualties, otherwise position remained the same till evening when we extended our left to pt. 7.

12ᵗʰ   Battn: again heavily shelled D Coy: had several casualties; 6 killed 26 wounded. Captn P.A. Lafone killed about noon by rifle bullet in head.

4-30 p.m.   Received orders to attack the line PIETRE – LA RUSSIE with remainder of Bde: Battn: was assembled and proceeded via 22.7.6.23.92 getting into position for attack on enemy side of trench 87-92, with 2/S co: Rif in support. The front was reconnoitred an an impenetrable fence was discovered about 150 yds in front of us. B Coy. got close to enemy on left and lost some thirty men wounded and missing. Captn Tingy and 2 Lt. Jacob bringing in remainder. ⁊ We heard the attack was cancelled about 1.45 a.m. and took up line of trenches 92 – 87 with 2/West Yorks on our right and 2/Middlesex on our left.

13ᵗʰ   Quiet day. In trenches and unable to leave them.

14ᵗʰ   Trenches all day. Relieved in evening by 1/2 inniskns arrived in billets at and near PONT DU HEM about 11.30 p.m. Total casualties for 5 days Officers 6 killed, 2 wounded. Other Ranks 52 killed
137 wounded
65 missing
Total 274.

× Col Travers?

× J.D. Ingles. Major
Ag O.C. 2/S.Wᵉˡˢ.

23rd Inf.Bde.
8th Div.

2nd BATTN. THE DEVONSHIRE REGIMENT.

A P R I L

1 9 1 5

Army Form C. 2118.

WAR DIARY
or
INTELLIGENCE SUMMARY.
(Erase heading not required.)

Instructions regarding War Diaries and Intelligence Summaries are contained in F.S. Regs., Part II. and the Staff Manual respectively. Title pages will be prepared in manuscript.

Hour, Date, Place		Summary of Events and Information	Remarks and references to Appendices
1915 April			
1st	Trenches	Cold bright day. Aeroplane active. 6th men [killed] and wounded. one man wounded.	
2nd	"	Lieut. Turner returned from Hospital. Quiet day. One man wounded.	
3rd	"	Quiet day. New section Bugaries [?] second attached in morning, the communication trench incomplete. Quiet night. Trees making at hospital very heavy and unhealthy from to N.E.	
		about 5 p.m. our own Bath was relieved by 2nd Seaforth [?] on leaving were sent into billets in	
		Brigade reserve.	
4th and 5th	Billets	Brigade reserve at and near LA TOURETTE.	
6th	"	Paraded at 3.5 p.m. and marched into billets at BAC ST MAUR on Divisional reserve. All 23rd Bde came back as Divl. reserve. Lt. [?] rejoined Battn from [?] Highlanders 3/Seaforth	
7th	BAC ST MAUR	Coys at disposal of Coy commanders. 200 men taken for digging in rear to R.E. [?] and in their R.E. b/s oven. Draft of 75 N.C.O.s & men arrived in evening.	
8th	"	Batt continued by Coys.	
9th	"	Coys at disposal of Coy commanders.	
10th	"	Batt route marched by Coys. N.C.O. Gun instrn billets in morning.	
11th	"	Church parade at 9.0 a.m. to approved offr [?] & N.C.Os instrn new trenches.	
12th	"	Battn paraded at 9.30 a.m. and was addressed by the Lieut. Genl Marshall [?]. Battn paraded again at 4.45 p.m. and marched down to [?]

(9 29 6) W 4141—463 100,000 9/14 H W V Forms/C. 2118/10

Army Form C. 2118.

WAR DIARY
or
INTELLIGENCE SUMMARY.
(Erase heading not required.)

Instructions regarding War Diaries and Intelligence Summaries are contained in F. S. Regs., Part II. and the Staff Manual respectively. Title pages will be prepared in manuscript.

Hour, Date, Place	Summary of Events and Information	Remarks and references to Appendices
1915.		
12th April BAC ST MAUR	Sector taken over from 1st London R.G.3 (regts in Trenches and in support Trenches) ANCIEN CHARTREUX	
13th " Trenches	Rev. Coms. sad - mostly waterlaid legs at much Kitchener Hse of heavy Jack/Jerries of parrapets	
" " "	(casualties 1 killed and 1 wounded)	
14th " "	Certain amount of rain. Took 2nd in command of West Yorks and officers sector our lines to	
" " "	see how situated, as they have to relieve us (one man killed). Such work done by R.E.s Engineers	
15th " "	B.D. Matthys visits Trenches in evening. Very fine day 1 man killed	
16th " "	Broadmeir visits Trenches in evening. Enemy very quiet. plenty aeroplanes over our own	
" " "	lines. Very fine day. No casualties.	
17th " "	Quiet day. Enemy placed a few shells in our neighbourhood in afternoon	
18th " "	Brigadier visits our Trenches] Relieved by 9/West Yorks in evening. went into Bde Reserve in	
" Rue Des Quesnoys near FLEURBAIX		
19th " BILLETS	Registrations, handing of arms took H.E. evening, warm, Le	
19-20 " "	do. 19"- 24" Conference at Bde H.Q. 11 a.m. to about 3 p.m. Aeroplanes very busy all day	
21st " "	do. 19"- 24"	
22nd " "	do. 19"- 24" Had conference with all officers in morning	
23rd " "	do. as in 19 - 24	
24th " "	Fine cold day. Batt. paraded out 3 p.m. and marched into billets near DOULIEU about 5 miles N.W. division very comfortable. Billets taken over from 4th West Ridings all in country.	

(9 29 6) W 4141-463 100,000 9/14 HWV Forms/C. 2118/10

WAR DIARY
or
INTELLIGENCE SUMMARY.
(Erase heading not required.)

Army Form C. 2118.

Hour, Date, Place	Summary of Events and Information	Remarks and references to Appendices
1915		
25 April BILLETS. DOULIEU	Coy retd. to billets (about 2h) which entered divisional reserve. Hands of several voluntary church parades	
"	evening at 6pm. Report to effect that enemy had broken through from BIXSCHOETE to N. of YPRES and had taken LIZERNE W. of canal: were ashy accelerators geril.	
26th "	Batt. bathed in batches of 50 at baths between SAILLY and BAC ST MAUR. General Reserve was issued to billets in afternoon. Brewers completing between A and B Coys between 4 and 6.30 p.m. as necessary.	
"	Hear of us in district of YPRES all day covering night	
27th "	Batt. sent marching by seqs. (have lorries) to YPRES but might [illegible] halt found 1800.	
28th "	Batt. without when reassembly by B.D.un. instruments. Complement of officers of Battn. is being	
"	to defend area from YPRES thence 7 Span. west to canal. On YPRES S. about last 2 Batts has been engaged and Maj. Radcliffe R.S.B. Lieut. Fish and Lieut. Parr had been wounded.	
29th "	Coys at disposal of Cog commander: Brigades composition confirm on position.	
30th "	Tom: recentenance in morning	

J.W. Jar. Fes. Major
Comdg. 2nd Leicester Regt.

23rd Inf.Bde.
8th Div.

2nd BATTN. THE DEVONSHIRE REGIMENT.

M A Y

1 9 1 5

WAR DIARY or INTELLIGENCE SUMMARY

Army Form C. 2118.

Hour, Date, Place	Summary of Events and Information	Remarks and references to Appendices
1915. Billets Nieppe 1st May	In billets near DOULIEU. Enemy bombarded NEUVE CHAPELLE and 6 am. Battⁿ ordered to stand to arms and be ready to move at moments notice. Transport sent in from Sof SAILLY. About 11 a.m. orders received for normal conditions to be resumed. Sent about 3 NCOs and men to Sections 1 and 2 of dressing in evening under their platoon officers for	Line very heavy between
2nd May "	Left our country billets near DOULIEU at 10.15 am and marched into billets (factory) at ESTAIRES. (arrived at Bd^e H.Q. at 5.30 p.m.) Voluntary church parade at 6 p.m. Arrangements made for Bd^e to take over C and D lines Tomorrow night.	
3rd May "	C.O. & Adjt. (Maj Fowers.) 2nd, 4th & 5th reported at H.Q. of Bn to relieve 1st R.F. on Rue TILLELOY at 7 a.m. and went round trenches. On return to Bd^e H.Q. at 12 noon heard that relief was cancelled owing that 23rd Bd^e. could succeed in present billets till further orders. About 9 p.m. orders received to take over E. and F. Section of Trenches from 2/Devonshire (when Tomorrow night).	Round hard during night
4th May "	(arrived at Bd^e H.Q. at 11.30 a.m.) Taken over F. Section of (?)	Trenches. Both flanks all not & 5/34 heavy working parties working
5th May Trenches	Battⁿ went to relieve 2/Devons in F and E Section of trenches about 9 p.m. (relieved amount of firing going on all night wire Casualties Sgt Tarr of 2/(?) killed.)	
5th May Trenches	Working in E and F trenches all day and night report of 2 Gen Bg? was visiting about 12 (?) until evening. Casualties heavy in morning through heavy trench mortar attack from Germans living?	
	Battⁿ fired 15 rounds rifle about 11.30 p.m. what our own (?) by(?) trench being shelled in (?)	
	7 or 8 enemy working parties of about 25 expected to be running.	

WAR DIARY or INTELLIGENCE SUMMARY.

Army Form C. 2118.

(Erase heading not required.)

Instructions regarding War Diaries and Intelligence Summaries are contained in F.S. Regs., Part II. and the Staff Manual respectively. Title pages will be prepared in manuscript.

Hour, Date, Place		Summary of Events and Information	Remarks and references to Appendices
1915:			
6th Aug.	Trenches	Artillery on active intelt. side all day. Our batt. H.Q. and dug-outs of Coy. shelled in afternoon about 5 p.m. but no harm done. The whole of area immediately behind trenches severely with enemy howitzers and rifles all day. Relieved by 2nd Middlesex Regt. in evening and went into billets in RUE DU BOIS.	
7th Aug.	Billets	Warned to hold ourselves in readiness to operate into assembly trenches on evening for attack following morning. This was however postponed for 24 hours. Spent day in billets.	
8th Aug.	"	Uneventful day. Batln. paraded at 8.30 p.m. and marched onto R. block of assembly trenches just S. of RUE DU BOIS. Cold night.	
9th Aug.	Neighbourhood of trenches	Cold. Few rifle shots	
	4.20 a.m.	British aeroplanes reconnaitre enemy position. Saw bichelren and heighton viens at about 4.10 a.m.	
	4.15 a.m.	Our guns began very ??? shots	
	4.30 a.m.	Heavy rifle fire broke out on our left flank in direction of ARMENTIERES.	
	5.0 a.m.	Artillery began bombardment of enemy's wire and trenches. The bombardment did not appear to be severe and although the wire was cut in places the enemy wire and all remained.	
	5.41 a.m.	The main assault began with 24 "K.2.5" R.Bn. Heavy rifle and machine gun fire	
	6.5 a.m.	Orders received to advance from assembly trenches. Batn. at once advanced to 2nd block of	

WAR DIARY or INTELLIGENCE SUMMARY

Army Form C. 2118.

1915

Hour, Date, Place	Summary of Events and Information	Remarks and references to Appendices
6.15 a.m.	Leaders reached just S. of RUE PETILLON avoiding [?] as if drawn [?] [?] evacuated him & others and that [?] was anxious on [Capt: had to move to right a file. RUE PETILLON having been ordered to pass to East of Black G (see plan) on reached 10 attack). It was here we suffered our first casualties, lower about 10 R.E. & 5 men from who [?] G. S. [?] inspection	
6.45 a.m. [?]	Shilfur Reserve advanced [?] 4 Camp supported by [?] att [?] R.G. Sulem and Batt leaders followed. A Coy in 2nd line and Batt reserve. A Coy (Lanes) (64) and R.S.M. followed in rear of Batt. The Batt continued advance followed by of London R.S. The latter were suffering so the Batt halted, have them making for out and of D. Coy Baux. A trenches during run advance we were subjected to a very heavy artillery fire and enfilade [?] fire from behind the enemy's trenches on our right, losing heavily. [?] Lieut Bowes-Lardlow 3/9 Sussex and Lieut: Tennant 3/8 Dorsets (attached) were both killed and #Lt Vaughan 2nd R. Berkshire 2nd Lieut Anderson 2nd Lieut (art.lt.wounded). The whole advance was very difficult owing to change of direction and trenches B. C and D not being at right angles to line of advance.	
7.30 a.m.	The lines during advance to front line trenches were about 200 R.E. & men killed & wounded & 2 [?] (both killed & wounded). Leaders Batt: arrived in trenches which were full of men of all Batt: of 25 Brigade. Scarcely an officer [?] knew. The order of [?] was well [?] by [?] [?] from Russia. and further orders awaited from Russia.	

WAR DIARY
or
INTELLIGENCE SUMMARY.
(Erase heading not required.)

Army Form C. 2118.

Hour, Date, Place	Summary of Events and Information	Remarks and references to Appendices
1915. 9th May (continued)	The C.O. went to H.Q. 25th Bde. to find out what they intended to do. General Joey-Pole had been killed and Bde Major's left. Bell received later. However continued to act in accordance and C.O. went to H.Q. 23rd Bde. with Major Carter (Campbell of 2nd Scot. Rif. The C.O. had Vandeleur having been wounded). Orders were received from a further bombardment of enemy's trenches would take place at four shoes and from 11.30 heavy front of Bn Rifle Bde. and some of trenches had scored enemy's trenches but owing to shell fire and enfilading rifle & M.G. fire they could not be supported.	
" to 9 a.m. 12.45 p.m.	During to our troops in and support of German trenches the bombardment was stopped. the remnants of 25th Bde were very few and withdrawn and the whole batln brought up into "Rue" trenches to replace them. Heavy shelled all the afternoon. The Battn of 2nd Scot. Rif. were told to hold themselves in readiness to assault enemy's trenches after dark but this was cancelled (while awaiting orders at Bde H.Q. the C.O. was wounded by a shell which burst in parapet of trench just outside — Lieut. Dodd & Tiny Vinne sent for to receive orders.	
10th May 12. Or. a. 2.30 a.m.	A heavy fire was kept out over troops in half of enemy trenches being bombarded an endeavour of our fire. Later the Rifle Bde. were counter attacked in force and forced to retire with heavy loss. This retirement as also enemy thousand with its attack between BOISGRENIER and LA BASSEE, this "cheyts and positive troops having failed to gain any advantage. Shelling continued in both sides during the day, however was of intermittent	

Army Form C. 2118.

WAR DIARY
or
INTELLIGENCE SUMMARY.
(Erase heading not required.)

Instructions regarding War Diaries and Intelligence Summaries are contained in F.S. Regs., Part II. and the Staff Manual respectively. Title pages will be prepared in manuscript.

Hour, Date, Place	Summary of Events and Information	Remarks and references to Appendices
1915		
11th May WANGERIE	Enemy) and ourselves shewed continued front was slightly intermittent shelling shell in afternoon of 4th (about intermittent) on 9th day. Left Sutton R.A. Inf. (sun 2nd D.) who is nearly a shell seriously ing [17] 2/g E. 10 P. We were relieved in afternoon by 1st Worcesters and 2/ Bedfords entering left and right respectively. On leaving trenches batta. was shelled losing 2 men wounded. We went into billets at WANGERIE, taking over from 1/ R. Scots Fusiliers, and reached.	
12th " "	Effort at 11.15 am. Our total casualties for two days were: One Officer killed, 6 wounded and 235 R.E.L. & 30 men killed, wounded or missing.	
	In billets refitting. Draft of 99 R.E. & 52 men arrived. 2/ R.E. did men sent to R.E. for ammunition 9 Bn. Sherwood Foresters took over from us in evening and In billets. Brigade marched into billets. 4 Bn Sherwood Foresters took over from us in evening and we arrived about 1½ miles east into billets. Sent out party to bury 2 Men Lieut. Tennant was R.E.L. & 9 men by night.	
13th " " BILLETS	At RUE DU QUESNE. Remained all day. Second Command Gun, Barnes, on the bath, is now.	
14th " " Trenches	We took over R.L. section of trenches in evening from 2/ Bedford Regt. Occasionally at 1 a.m. we bombarded enemy's position heavily for 7 minutes. Ready from trenches. Similar bursts took place at intervals all night. Gave the 2nd. Enemy replied. All guns try 1.15 am Brigadier visited trench H.Q. in morning. A repetition of bombardment took place at 2 p.m. and 12 noon. Enemy replied to both wire cbles were our trifles. Lent to trenches during latter. Communication to trenches also cut an man wounded by shell.	

Forms/C. 2118/10

Army Form C. 2118.

WAR DIARY
or
INTELLIGENCE SUMMARY.
(Erase heading not required.)

Instructions regarding War Diaries and Intelligence Summaries are contained in F. S. Regs, Part II. and the Staff Manual respectively. Title pages will be prepared in manuscript.

Hour, Date, Place	Summary of Events and Information	Remarks and references to Appendices
1915		
15th May. Trenches.	Artillery bombardment of enemy's position, & our trenches commenced at 5 a.m. and 9 a.m. calling forth replies. At 5 a.m. we cheered & our rifle fire/shots away from Panic sight of /R. and J. Dwr? a gun heard between 10 a.m. and 12 noon, but very few shell were fired. 2nd Lieut. Home went to hospital and 2 Lt. Tellit took over duties of actn: asst: all Platoon men in trenches were long burying dead and collecting arms equipment etc.	
16th May. "	2nd Lieut. E. G. Roberts joined.	
17th " "	A & B Coys relieved by 2/ West Yorks in subsections 1 P & 1 R and went into billets in RUE DU BACQUEROT. (Capt Sn Jenkins and 2 Lieut: Andrews rejoined at transport lines and 2 Lieuts Cawoer? joined for 1st time.	
18th " "	Relieved by 1/5th West Yorks in subsections 1 R v 1 S and Batt H.Q. and C & D Coys went into billets in RUE DU BACQUEROT.	
19th " Billets	Batt moved into fresh billets at & near ROUGE DE BOUT.	

WAR DIARY
or
INTELLIGENCE SUMMARY.
(Erase heading not required.)

Army Form. C. 2118.

Hour, Date, Place	Summary of Events and Information	Remarks and references to Appendices
1915		
20th May. Billets	Found 2 washing parties under R.E. at work (captains outright and ?) Every night from	
21st May. "	On 7 days leave.	
	Ordinary routine drills &c.	
22nd " "	Draft of 3 officers (Lieut. F.A. Byatt, Lieut. H. Archer & 2nd Lieut. R.R.K. Anderson) and 130 N.C.O.s & men arrived. Found 2 washing parties in evening under R.E.	
23rd " "	Voluntary church parade in morning. Brigade ordered the Regt. and detail joined officers at 12 noon. Relieved 2/ Welch Regt. in sections 1P & 4 in evening. A.B Coy's going into trenches and C & D Coy's into billets in support. Enemy killed & one Queen to trenches.	
24th " "	Two men wounded. Enemy artillery bombarded enemy in evening beginning at 8/10 and continuing at intervals all night.	
25th " "	Bombardment which commenced yesterday at eve about 5 a.m. this morning after	
26th " "	Enemy bombarded our left morning and afternoon with heavy artillery shells	

Army Form C. 2118.

WAR DIARY
or
INTELLIGENCE SUMMARY.
(Erase heading not required.)

Instructions regarding War Diaries and Intelligence Summaries are contained in F. S. Regs., Part II. and the Staff Manual respectively. Title pages will be prepared in manuscript.

Hour, Date, Place		Summary of Events and Information	Remarks and references to Appendices
1915.			
27th May	Trenches	Ordered to billet ourselves H/Q Ses Ref, close to Battn H.R.	
28th May	"	Very quiet day	
29th May	"	Enemy aeroplanes very active. A shaft of 25 men arrived.	
		Quiet by day. Enemy shelled houses & trenches but no damage. Relieved by 2/ Monmouths and went into billets near Rouge de Biut	
30th May	Billets	Lt SCOTT and Lt STEWART joined the Bn. Voluntary Church Parade in morning. Lt ARCHER left to take over command of 7. E. & W. C. O.s and men working under the R.E.	
31st May	"	Enemy shelled with heavy guns an anti-aircraft battery near our own billets & about 3pm killed one man and wounded another. 1½ Coys joined Divisional Commander Reserve. Remainder visited Bn. moved into fresh billets in the Rue du Quesnoy. Rouvroy, remainder Bn Hd with 1 Platoon.	

[signature] Capt for
O.C. 1/5 Berkshire Rgt

2nd June 1915

23rd Inf.Bde.
8th Div.

2nd BATTN. THE DEVONSHIRE REGIMENT.

J U N E

1 9 1 5

WAR DIARY
or
INTELLIGENCE SUMMARY.

(Erase heading not required.)

Army Form C. 2118.

Instructions regarding War Diaries and Intelligence Summaries are contained in F.S. Regs, Part II. and the Staff Manual respectively. Title pages will be prepared in manuscript.

Hour, Date, Place	Summary of Events and Information	Remarks and references to Appendices
1st June Billets	Ordinary routine drills &c.	
2nd June "	1 casualty - man accidentally wounded with rifle bullet.	
"	Worked under R.E. Enemy aeroplane reconnaissance. Enemy aeroplane over action Bn. furnished working parties of 250 men to work under R.E. 2nd Lieut. Truscott returned from hospital.	
3rd June "	Lieut. General Davies visited H.Q. 2nd Lt (a/g for Lieut. and 2nd Lieut. R. Jacob returned from leave	
"	Bn. relieved 2nd West Yorks in trenches in evening of that E. sub-sector and right sub-sector. Left T.G. Hilliard joined Battn.	
4th Trenches	Quiet day. Enemy aeroplane reconnaissance. Two men wounded.	
5th "	"	
6th "	"	
7th "	Very foggy morning. Indian Brigade a.e.s.c. Indian (who enquired re our trenches) between 6.30 a.m. and 9 a.m. Major Walter (10th Jats) of "J" Coy" arrived to be attached to Battn to see how French soldiers it. We carried out attack. Casualties 2 killed and 1 wounded in evening a/c.	
8th "	Very hot and quiet day. Enemy aeroplane at ...	
9th "	Quiet day. Enemy aeroplane (stood in evening and fired on one man wounded	
10th "	Quiet day. Relieved in evening by 1st West Yorks and went into billets in 2nd R Reserve took over	
11th Billets	Post H.Q. Major Walter 10th Jats attached left us. Routine work	

Forms/C. 2118/10

WAR DIARY
or
INTELLIGENCE SUMMARY.
(Erase heading not required.)

Army Form C. 2118.

Hour, Date, Place	Summary of Events and Information	Remarks and references to Appendices
1915.		
12 June. Billets	General Davis, G.O.C. Div. visits us in afternoon.	
13th March "	Batt. paraded and G.O.C. Div. presents D.C.M. ribbons to C.S.M. Kerr, Pte Self, March and Sergt Leacham & congratulates Batt. on work done. Airplanes active.	
14th " "	Church parade as usual. 2 G (new cond. n 7 days leave). Several 2 ammunition supports set as "Fowl?"/ "A" coy filling pits in every transport in rear of station at night.	
15th " "	Forwarded marching parties of 250 men.	
16th " "	Relieved 2nd O. Yorks in trenches. How! 15th Pel 5 men each of offices & 2 coy h.t attached to us to help in trenches. One seng? wounded.	
17th " Trenches	Enemy airplanes very active. Enemy shelled road in rear of trench H.Q. in morning	
18th " "	Quiet day. Two men killed. One wounded.	
19th " "	Trenches shelled with shrapnel but no damage done. Two men wounded.	
20th " "	Very quiet day. Enemy airplanes active in evening. One fatally shrapnel. Enemy transport which was heard moving at night heavily shelled was near??	
21st " "	Things a little more active in enemy's part. They shelled communication trench and part...	

(Erase heading not required.)

Army Form C. 2118.

WAR DIARY
or
INTELLIGENCE SUMMARY.
(Erase heading not required.)

Instructions regarding War Diaries and Intelligence Summaries are contained in F. S. Regs., Part II. and the Staff Manual respectively. Title pages will be prepared in manuscript.

Hour, Date, Place	Summary of Events and Information	Remarks and references to Appendices
1915		
21st June (contd)	without doing any damage. Lt Colonel Blaine 12th Durham LI attached to Bn for instructions on trench duties Te Kne now killed)	
22nd June Trenches.	Relieved in subsection F.3. by 2/ South Riff and remainder of Battn. by 2/ Welsh who Lt Cox returned from leave.	
23rd " Bellute	General Penney came to say "goodbye" of being promoted from Brigadier to command a Division. Lieut Tellit 2nd leaves Roberts and Batson proceeded on 7 days leave.	
24 " "	Battn officers & N.C.O & men of battn appeared in recent casualty lists (been awarded honours as follows. Lt Colonel J. C. Travers D.S.O. mentioned and awarded C.M.G. Mayor (Trophy killed) F.R. Jos (w mentioned and awarded Brevet Lt Colonel Capt. C.A. Lyons (killed) mentioned. Lieut F.R. Cotta (now Capt) mentioned and awarded Military Cross. Lieut R.A. F.E. Wright (killed) Bristow (killed) and H.J.H. Cox mentioned. Sgt Major Pritham mentioned & awarded Sgt Railton Military (now L/C Roberts and Pte L/C Middlement L/C Smith & L/C Wood mentioned Cpl Loch awarded D.C.M.	
25 "	Rose from work. Heavy thunderstorm and much rain.	

Army Form C. 2118.

WAR DIARY
or
INTELLIGENCE SUMMARY.
(Erase heading not required.)

Instructions regarding War Diaries and Intelligence Summaries are contained in F.S. Regs., Part II. and the Staff Manual respectively. Title pages will be prepared in manuscript.

Hour, Date, Place	Summary of Events and Information	Remarks and references to Appendices
1915.		
26th June. Billets.	Considerable number of troops on the move. 3rd W.Yorks. passed over lines in lorries moving east	
27th " "	Church parade in morning. 2/5th Bn. relieved in trenches by 1/5th W.Bn. and 1 Bn. of 1/4th B.D. We had to close up in our billets. Lieut. Archer and 72 men rejoined Batn. from 175th Coy. R.E.	
" " "	Major General Buring went through our position and Brigadier Genl Clark took over command of B.D....	
28th " "	Lt. Col. Onoly E. Iaccus (.A.G.Q.D.O. rejoined from sick leave and assumed command.	
29th " "	C.O. inspected all men in billets and wrong Infr Relinforcement of/r I/Oshna Battn unitary?	
30th " "	Orders received on evening for Bn. to take over trenches from 2nd R.U.S.S. and 3rd Inniski... men from Northampton and 5th Black Watch C.O. and 2 in command visited the of their Battm. and made necessary arrangements.	

1st July 1915.

J.B. Joyce Lieut Colonel
for O.C. of [reg't]

23rd Inf.Bde.
8th Div.

2nd BATTN. THE DEVONSHIRE REGIMENT.

J U L Y

1 9 1 5

Army Form C. 2118.

WAR DIARY
or
INTELLIGENCE SUMMARY.
(Erase heading not required.)

Instructions regarding War Diaries and Intelligence Summaries are contained in F.S. Regs, Part II. and the Staff Manual respectively. Title pages will be prepared in manuscript.

Hour, Date, Place	Summary of Events and Information	Remarks and references to Appendices
1 July 1915	In trenches. RELIEVED 2/Northampton Regt. and 5/Black Watch in trenches and posts No 2E and 3F about 9pm. A quiet night.	
2/7/15. In Trenches.	A quiet day Brigadier Genl. Clarke visited H'Q. 3 men wounded.	
3/7/15. In Trenches	The Brigadier visited the trenches during the morning. A quiet day. One man wounded.	
4/7/15. In Trenches	A quiet day. One man killed and one wounded.	
5/7/15. In Trenches	During the day a few shells were droped behind A Coy. and during the night a few trench mortar shells, neither did any damage. 2/Lt. FES Phillips (3rd.BN.) joined for the first time. He remained at H'Q. for the night and was posted to C Coy. He joined his Coy. in the trenches next day. No casualties.	
6/7/15. InTrenches	Germans shelled in rear of H.Q. during the morning and afternoon. No casualties.	
7/7/15. InBillets	Relieved by 2/W. Yorks Regt. Bn.moved into 2/Bde. Reserve Billets on the Rue due Quesnes and garrisoned posts 21,22, and 23. There were no casualties.	
8/7/15. In Billets	Foud working party of 400 men.	
9/7/15. In Billets.	Routine work. Found R.E. working party of 400 men.	
10/7/15. IN Billets	Received draft of 35 men. Routine work. Found R.E. working party of 400men.	
11/7/15. In Billets	There was a voluntary church parade in the morning.Found a R.E. working party of 300 men.	

Army Form C. 2118.

WAR DIARY
or
INTELLIGENCE SUMMARY.
(Erase heading not required.)

Instructions regarding War Diaries and Intelligence Summaries are contained in F.S. Regs, Part II. and the Staff Manual respectively. Title pages will be prepared in manuscript.

Hour, Date, Place	Summary of Events and Information	Remarks and references to Appendices
12/7/15 In Billets	2/ Lt. Neilson joined the Bn. for the first time with a draft of 12 machine gunners. 2/ Lt.Neilson was attached to A Coy. 2/ Lt. Carver proceeded to bombing school for course of instruc -tion in bombing. Furnished a R.E. working party of 400 men.	
13/7/15. In Billets and Trenches.	Relieved 2/ West Yorks Regt in the trenches. It was a very quiet night, there were no casualties.	
14/7/15 In Trenches.	Germans shelled a little behind our trenches but did no damage. There were no casualties.	
15/7/15 In TRENCHES	Enemy shelled behind our trenches but did no damage. There were no casualties.	
16/7/15. In Trenches:	A quiet day, one man wounded.	
17/7/15 In Trenches	Germans were very quiet during the day but after midnight became more active : they sent five trench mortar shells, which however did no damage. One man killed.	
18/7/15.	Lts. Andrews and Bryce left for England on leave. A quiet day.	
19/7/15.	Relieved by 2nd. West Yorks, and went to Billets, Rue de Bruges. Enemy took down some of their parapet. A quiet day. Two men wounded and one killed accidently.	
20/7/15.	In billets. Found R.E working parties. Brigadier visited H.Q.	
21/7/15.	In billets. Found R.E working parties. Brigadier and Bde. Major dined at Headquarters.	

Army Form C. 2118.

WAR DIARY
or
INTELLIGENCE SUMMARY.
(Erase heading not required.)

Instructions regarding War Diaries and Intelligence Summaries are contained in F.S. Regs., Part II. and the Staff Manual respectively. Title pages will be prepared in manuscript.

Hour, Date, Place	Summary of Events and Information	Remarks and references to Appendices
22nd July 1915.	In billets. Found R.E. Working Parties. Divisional Genl visited Headquarters.	
23/7/15	In billets. Found R.E. Working Parties.	
24/7/15	In billets. Found R.E. Working Parties.	
25/7/15	Moved into No 10 Bde Reserve. The battalion garrisoned Posts 26 and 27 with one platoon each and 1 Machine Gun. Posts 4 H and 3 F were also garrisoned with 1 Machine Gun and M.G. Detachment each. C Coy was in support to the 2nd Middlesex Regt, D Coy in support to the 2/ Sco Rifles. Both Coys and also B Coy being in billets near CROIX BLANCHE. "A" Coy was billeted at CROIX MARECHAL. Battalion Headquarters established at CROIX BLANCHE. Found R.E. Working Parties, and had Church during the morning.	
26/7/15	Found R.E. Working Parties. Brigadier visited Battn Headquarter	
27/7/15.	In billets found R.E. Working Parties. Capt Hawlett visited H.Q.	
28/7/15	Found R.E. Working Parties. Divnl Gen Davies left to take Comd of Corps in the DARDANELLES.	
29/7/15.	Found R.E. Working Parties. Brigadier visited H.Q. Lieut.Colonel Williams, Major Luxmore, Capt Blunt and Capt Llewellyn motored from the 1st Battalion and arrived at Battalion Headquarters about 5 pm and stayed about an hour.	

Army Form C. 2118.

WAR DIARY
or
INTELLIGENCE SUMMARY.

(*Erase heading not required.*)

Instructions regarding War Diaries and Intelligence Summaries are contained in F. S. Regs., Part II. and the Staff Manual respectively. Title pages will be prepared in manuscript.

Hour, Date, Place	Summary of Events and Information	Remarks and references to Appendices
29/7/15. (contd)	Captain J.R. Cartwright left to undergo a course of instruction in staff duties at the H.Q. 3rd Corps. Lieut. ~~illegible~~ J.A. Andrews took over command of C Coy.	
30/7/15. In Billets.	Brigadier visited H.Q. Furnished R.E. working parties.	
31/7/15. ~~In Billets.~~	The Bn. Moved into Divn reserve billets near Quatre Chemines.	

[signature]
Lt. Col.
O.C. 8/ Devon Regt.

2/8/15.

23rd Inf.Bde.
8th Div.

2nd BATTN. THE DEVONSHIRE REGIMENT.

A U G U S T

1 9 1 5

Army Form C. 2118.

WAR DIARY
or
INTELLIGENCE SUMMARY.
(Erase heading not required.)

Instructions regarding War Diaries and Intelligence Summaries are contained in F.S. Regs., Part II. and the Staff Manual respectively. Title pages will be prepared in manuscript.

Hour, Date, Place	Summary of Events and Information	Remarks and references to Appendices
1st August, 1915. In billets.	In billets. Had church parade during the morning.	
2nd -do- -do-	In billets. Furnished R.E. working party of 500 men.	
3rd	In billets. Routine. G.O.C. inspected the Battalion.	
4th	In billets. Furnished R.E. working party. Two men wounded.	
5th	In billets. Routine.	
6th	Received draft of 1 Officer and 45 O.R. Lieut C.G.Carson joined the battalion for the first time.	
7th	In billets. Routine.	
8th	Relieved 1/ Sherwood Foresters and 2/ East Lancs. in trenches and supporting posts. A quiet night, no casualties.	
9th In Trenches.	In trenches. A quiet day. One man wounded. T.E.Clarke	
10th -do-	In trenches. Divl General Hudson and Brigadier visited the trenches in the morning. Enemy sent about 6 H.E. shells behind C Coy but did no damage, otherwise a quiet day. One man wounded. 5 platoons of the Ox and Bucks L.I. were attached to the Battalion for instruction in trench duties (20th Division)	6th Bn (?) Ox and Bucks.
11th	In trenches. A quiet day. One man wounded. The 5 platoons were relieved by another 5 platoons Ox and Berks.	
12th	In trenches. Enemy shelled the trenches for a short time during the evening but did no damage. 5 platoons Of Oxs and Bucks were relieved by another 6 platoons. One man wounded.	

Army Form C. 2118.

WAR DIARY
or
INTELLIGENCE SUMMARY.
(Erase heading not required.)

Instructions regarding War Diaries and Intelligence Summaries are contained in F.S. Regs., Part II. and the Staff Manual respectively. Title pages will be prepared in manuscript.

Hour, Date, Place	Summary of Events and Information	Remarks and references to Appendices
13th Aug./15 In Trenches.	In the trenches. A quiet day. We successfully sniped the enemy during the day and burst 2 rifle grenades in their trenches. Other platoons of *Ox and Bucks relieved those in the trenches. One man wounded. *6th Battn:	
14th	In the trenches. The enemy were very quiet. We sniped the enemy with success and burst some rifle grenades over their trenches. One man wounded. Ox and Bucks relieved their platoons in the trenches.	
15th	In the trenches. Enemy little more active than on the previous day. One man wounded. Ox and Bucks relieved their platoons in the trenches.	
16th	In the trenches. Enemy very quiet. Ox and Bucks relieved their platoons in the trenches. One man killed and one wounded of the Ox and Bucks.	
17th	In billets.	
In Billets 18th	In billets. Furnished R.E. working party.	
19th	In billets. Furnished R.E. working parties.	
20th	In billets. Furnished R.E. working parties.	
21st	In billets. Furnished R.E. working parties. One man wounded outside Post 26 by a spent bullet.	
22nd	In billets. Furnished R.E. working parties. One man wounded	
23rd	In billets. Furnished R.E. working parties.	
24th	Relieved 2/Sco Rifles in trenches and posts.	

Forms/C.2118/10
(9 29 6) W 4141—463 100,000 9/14 H W V

Army Form C. 2118.

WAR DIARY
or
INTELLIGENCE SUMMARY.
(Erase heading not required.)

Instructions regarding War Diaries and Intelligence Summaries are contained in F. S. Regs., Part II. and the Staff Manual respectively. Title pages will be prepared in manuscript.

Hour, Date, Place	Summary of Events and Information	Remarks and references to Appendices
24th Aug/15. In trenches	It was a quiet night except that Germans fired about 6 Mortars at trenches. They did no damage, and 2 did not explode. One hit a man on the head and shoulder and fell into the trench but did not go off. On examination these shells appeared to be 77 m/m shell cases full of T.N.T.* m.m. Began work on trenches according to winter scheme.	
25th.	A quiet day. Our snipers were successful in bagging several germans. 2 men wounded.	
26th	Except for a little sniping by the enemy it was a quiet day Germans were seen working on their parapet. they were soon stopped by our rifle fire. Brigadier visited Headquarters.	
27th	A quiet day. The enemy were again stopped working by our rifle fire. Good work was done with the aid of sniperscop	
28th.	Our trench mortars successfully shelled the German trenches, they replied with trench mortars and howitzer shells, but did no damage, only knocking down a traverse and very slightly wounding two men.	
29th	In the trenches. During the night the enemy fired two trench mortar shells which did no damage, otherwise it was a very quiet day. Germans were seen revetting their parapet.	
30th	Several German working parties were seen at work and were dispersed by our fire. The enemy were more active than usual firing several bursts of fire with Machine Guns and rifles.	

(Continued) 31st

Army Form C. 2118.

WAR DIARY
or
INTELLIGENCE SUMMARY.
(Erase heading not required.)

Instructions regarding War Diaries and Intelligence Summaries are contained in F.S. Regs., Part II. and the Staff Manual respectively. Title pages will be prepared in manuscript.

Hour, Date, Place	Summary of Events and Information	Remarks and references to Appendices

31/8/15.
In the Trenches.
	At 5.30 pm the Germans exploded a mine just outside the parapet on the Kleft of 2.R. which was occupied by C Coy. As soon as the mine was exploded they bombarded the trenches on either side also the 70 yds line with shrapnel and high explosive; this lasted for about ten minutes. In reply we fired about 30 rifle grenades and the trench mortars fired about 20 shells; the supporting battery also opened fire. The Germans replied with trench mortars and rifle grenades. Our Field Howitzers opened fire on their trenches about 6.30 pm firing about 50 rounds. The enemy replied to this with 18 rounds from their howitzers.
	    Very little damage was done ; 3 men were slightly wounded; one or two dug-outs and the parapet smashed by the mine. The crater was about 40 yds in diameter.
	    Our bombardment appeared to be very successful, several breaches being made in their parapet.
	    During the night and next day the Germans were very quiet and were seen working hard on the breaches we had made.
	    2 Platoons less 2 Sections of A Coy who were in local reserve went up to support C Coy if required. The supporting Coy of the 2/ Sco: Rifles moved up to Trench Headqrs.
	    After standing to arms next morning, Coys returned to their original positions.
		4 men brought to notice i.e
		
		No 8439 Pte H.Hocking.
		No 8923 " F.Joint.
		No 9347 " E.Webber.
		No 14152 " W.Howells.
		
		All the above were men of C Coy.

[signature] Lieut-Colonel
Officer Commanding 2nd Devon Regt.

23rd Inf.Bde.
8th Div.

2nd BATTN. THE DEVONSHIRE REGIMENT.

SEPTEMBER

1915

Army Form C. 2118.

WAR DIARY
or
INTELLIGENCE SUMMARY.
(Erase heading not required.)

Instructions regarding War Diaries and Intelligence Summaries are contained in F.S. Regs., Part II. and the Staff Manual respectively. Title pages will be prepared in manuscript.

Hour, Date, Place	Summary of Events and Information	Remarks and references to Appendices
1st. September 1915 In Trenches.	Several mine experts visited the trenches during the morning also representives from the Divn. and Bde. C Coy. was relieved by 2/ Sco.Rifles about 5 pm., the remaining ¾ -er of the Bn. was relieved by 2/ Sco. Rifles about 9pm.	
2/9/15. In Billets	Furnished R.E. working parties .	
In Billets.3/9/15	Furnished R.E. working parties The Brigadier visited Bn. H.Q. Received a draft of 30 N.C.Os and men.	
4/9/15. In Billets	Furnished R.E. working parties . 2/ Lieuts. Lloyd and Wykes joined the Bn. for the first time and were posted to D.and C. Coys. respectively.	
5/9/15. In Billets	Church Parade during the morning . The Bn.was rilieved in posts and billets by 7/ K.O.Y.L.I, and 7/ Somerst L.I. On being releived the Bn. moved into billets North of the River Lays and was then in Divn. Reserve	
6/9/15. In Billets	Lieut.Col. Travers took temporary command of the Bde. Lt.Col. Ingles and the Company Commanders visited the ground in the vicinity of Bois Grenier during the day ,as the Bn. was in Divn. Reserve and might have to support the 24th.and 25th. Bds. should the proposed offensive in this prt of the line necessitate the Dvn. Reserve being brought up.	
6/9/15. In Billets	Routine Afternoon The Divn. band played at Bn. H.Q. during the after afternoon .	

Army Form C. 2118.

WAR DIARY
or
INTELLIGENCE SUMMARY.
(Erase heading not required.)

Instructions regarding War Diaries and Intelligence Summaries are contained in F.S. Regs., Part II. and the Staff Manual respectively. Title pages will be prepared in manuscript.

Hour, Date, Place	Summary of Events and Information	Remarks and references to Appendices
7/9/15. In Billets	The Bn. went for a route march in the morning. Brigadier General Tuson took over command of the Bde. Lt.Col. Travers returned to the Bn. Capt.Milne and Lt. Haynes of the 1st. Bn. visited H.Q.	
8/9/15. In Billets	Routine.	
9/9/15 In Billets.	Routine. The Brigadier visited Bn. H.Q.	
10/9/15.In Billets	Routine.	
11/9/15.In Billets	Routine.	
12/9/15. In Billets	Church Parade in the morning.	
13/9/15.In Billets.	Routine. Major E.G.Caffin 9/ Yorkshire Regt., who was attached to the 1st. Bn. during the siege of Ladysmith, visited Bn. H.Q.	
14/9/15. In Billets	Routine.	
15/9/15.In Billets	This day was observed as a holiday as far as possible .Bn. Sports were held during the afternoon in a field near Bn.H.Q.. the Dvn. Band played between 4pm.and 6pm. There were many visitors including the Dvn.General.	
16/9/15.IN Billets.	A detachment of about 500 men under the command of Lt.Col.Ingles was billeted on the Rue du Quesnoy till the 18th.This xxxxxxxxxxxxxxxxxxxxxxxxxxxxxxxxxxxxxxxxxxxxxxxxxxx this detachment was used for digging, finding working parties about 200 strong each day.	

Forms/C. 2118/10

(9 29 6) W 4141—463 100,000 9/14 H W V

Army Form C. 2118.

WAR DIARY
or
INTELLIGENCE SUMMARY.
(Erase heading not required.)

Instructions regarding War Diaries and Intelligence Summaries are contained in F. S. Regs., Part II. and the Staff Manual respectively. Title pages will be prepared in manuscript.

Hour, Date, Place	Summary of Events and Information	Remarks and references to Appendices
17/9/15. In billets.	Routine.	
18/9/15. In Billets	Routine. The detachment under Lt.Col. Ingles rejoined the Bn. The Brigadier visited Bn. H.Q.	
19/9/15. In Billets.	Church Parade during the morning; the Brigadier attended this service.	
In Billets. 20/9/15.	Routine.	
21/9/15. IN Billets.	Routine. Our guns began a four days bombardment of the German trenches in accordance with the proposed offensive operations.	
22/9/15. In Billets	Routine. Bombardment continued.	
23/9/15. In Billets	Routine. Bombardment continued. The Dvn. Band played at Bn. H.Q. between 4pm. and 6pm. Lt.Col. Travers received wire from the Bde. ordering him to proceed to the H.Q. 3rd. Corpsby "car" next morning at 8.30 am.	
24/9/15.	The whole of the 23rd Inf. Bde. was assembled in the vicinity of the Rue Biache and xxxxxxxxxxxxxxxxxxxxxxxx was in Div Reserve in preparation for the offensive movement which was to be undertaken next morning by the 8th Division. The 25th Inf. Bde was to xxxxxxt assault the German trenches on a front of about 1200 yards from N.6.d.1.6. to Le Bridoux Road (Bridoux Fort Inclusive). At day break next morning. The 24th Inf. Bde. was in support and the 23rd Inf. Bde. as before stated was in Divn: Reserve.	

(9 29 6) W 4141—463 100,000 9/14 H W V   Forms/C. 2118/10

Army Form C. 2118.

WAR DIARY
or
INTELLIGENCE SUMMARY.
(Erase heading not required.)

Instructions regarding War Diaries and Intelligence Summaries are contained in F.S. Regs., Part II. and the Staff Manual respectively. Title pages will be prepared in manuscript.

Hour, Date, Place	Summary of Events and Information	Remarks and references to Appendices
25/9/15.	After a short bombardment the 25th Inf.Bde. assaulted and captured the German trenches between Le Bridoux Road and N.6.d.1.6. but later had to vacate the captured trenches. The 23rd Inf.Bde. remained on the Rue Biache and did not assume any offensive movement.	
26/9/15.	The Brigade still remained in Divisional Reserve. The Battalion furnished a working party of 450 men.The foll- -owing casualties occured in this working party. No.8271 Pte Price. D.Killed. No.8600 Pte Baker.B. Wounded. No.9300 Pte Greenstreet.F.Wounded. No.9618 Bpl Knowles.E. ,, No.9297 Lc/Cpl Cooper.E. ,, No.9877 Pte Sumner.J. ,, No.8734 Pte Williams.A. ,, No.6856 Lc/Cpl Kingdom.A. ,, No.11340 Pte Litton. ,, No.8329 Pte Murray. ,, No.8453 Pte Warner. ,,	
27/9/15.	The Battalion remained at position of assembly. Lieut-Colonel Travers rejoined the Battalion.	
28/9/15.	The Battalion moved into billets on the Rue de Quesne and also garrisoned Croix Marechal Post with 1 Company. 1 Company was also in support to 2nd Battalion Middlesex Regiment and was in billets at Croix Marechal.	

Army Form C. 2118.

WAR DIARY
or
INTELLIGENCE SUMMARY.
(*Erase heading not required.*)

Instructions regarding War Diaries and Intelligence Summaries are contained in F.S. Regs., Part II. and the Staff Manual respectively. Title pages will be prepared in manuscript.

Hour, Date, Place	Summary of Events and Information	Remarks and references to Appendices
29/ 9/15.	In billets. Furnished R.E. Working party.	
30/ 9/15.	In billets. Furnished R.E. Working party.	

J.D. [signature]
Lieut-Colonel,
Officer Commanding 2nd Battalion Devon Regiment

23rd Inf.Bde.
8th Div.

2nd BATTN. THE DEVONSHIRE REGIMENT.

OCTOBER

1915

Army Form C. 2118.

WAR DIARY
or
INTELLIGENCE SUMMARY.
(Erase heading not required.)

Instructions regarding War Diaries and Intelligence Summaries are contained in F. S. Regs., Part II. and the Staff Manual respectively. Title pages will be prepared in manuscript.

Hour, Date, Place	Summary of Events and Information	Remarks and references to Appendices
1/10/15.	Relieved 2nd Middlesex Regiment in the trenches and Bottlery Post. A very quite night.	
2/10/15.	In the trenches a quite day. The following casualties occured:- No.8739 Pte R.Warne Killed No.9356 Lc/Cpl C.Mitchell Killed. No.15514 Pte C.Reekes. Wounded. Pte-J.Heyburn No.9997 -do-	
3/10/15.	In the trenches a quite day.	
4/10/15.	In trenches. Enemy shelled in vicinity of Trench H.Q.and also front trenches,one gun infaladed the trenches a shell going through the parados in "C" Coy's trench. C.S.M.Ward and Pte Monday were both wounded by rifle fire.	
5/10/15.	In the trenches. Divisional General Hudson visited the trenches A quite day.	
6/10/15.	Relieved by the 2nd Middlesex Regiment and moved into billets on the Rue de Quesne, 1 Company garrisoned CROIX MARECHAL POST and 1 Company was in support to the 2nd Middlesex Regiment and was in billets at Croix Marechal.	
7/10/15.	In billets. Furnished R.E. working party of 220 men.	
8/10/15.	In billets. Furnished R.E. working party of 200 men.	

Army Form C. 2118.

WAR DIARY
or
INTELLIGENCE SUMMARY.
(Erase heading not required.)

Instructions regarding War Diaries and Intelligence Summaries are contained in F.S. Regs., Part II. and the Staff Manual respectively. Title pages will be prepared in manuscript.

Hour, Date, Place	Summary of Events and Information	Remarks and references to Appendices
9/10/15.	In billets. Furnished R.E. working party of 200 men. No.14136 Pte E.Brown. Wounded.	
10/10/15.	In billets. The Battalion was relieved by the 2nd Worcester Regt and moved into fresh billets north of the River Lys.	
11/10/15.	In billets. Divisional Band played at Battalion Headquarters.	
12/10/15.	In billets. Routine.	
13/10/15.	In billets. Furnished R.E. working party of 200 men.	
14/10/15.	In billets. Furnished R.E working party of 250 men.	
15/10/15.	In Billets. Brigadier General visited Battalion Headquarters. Furnished R.E working parties.	
16/10/15.	In billets. Routine.	
17/10/15.	Relieved 1st Battalion Worcestershire Regiment in the trenches.	
18/10/15.	In trenches, a quiete day. Brigadier General visited Battalion Headquarters. 1 man wounded.	
19/10/15.	In Trenches. 8 Platoons of the 8th Battalion K.O.Y.L.I. Regiment relieved 8 platoons of the Battalion. The outgoing platoons were attached to the 8th Battalion K.O.Y.L.I.Regiment thus making two composite Battalions. Major 2nd in Command 8th Battalion K.O.Y.L.I.Regiment was OWEN	

Army Form C. 2118.

WAR DIARY
or
INTELLIGENCE SUMMARY.
(Erase heading not required.)

Instructions regarding War Diaries and Intelligence Summaries are contained in F. S. Regs., Part II. and the Staff Manual respectively. Title pages will be prepared in manuscript.

Hour, Date, Place	Summary of Events and Information	Remarks and references to Appendices
19/10/15. (contd)	attached to Battalion Headquarters. Lieut-Colonel J.D.Ingles left to take over Command of the 8th Battalion Devon Regiment.	
20/10/15.	In trenches. A quite day.	
21/10/15.	In trenches. Enemy opened very heavy rifle fire at one of our bi-planes during the afternoon otherwise enemy were very quite.	
22/10/15.	In trenches. The Battalion moved into billets. The platoons of the 8th Battalion K.O.Y.L.I.Regiment in the trenches remaining there, the remainder of the 8th Battalion K.O.Y.L.I.Regiment relieved our platoons in the trenches. The enemy shelled the right Coy with 16 - 4.2 H.E.Shells knocking down the parapet and wounding one signaller.	
23/10/15.	The Battalion moved into new billets at Bac St Maur.	
24/10/15.	In billets. Routine.	
25/10/15.	In billets. Routine. Captain Holdsworth joined 9th Battalion Devon Regiment.	
26/10/15.	In billets. Routine. Divisional Band played at "C"Coy's Headqrs.	
27/10/15.	The Battalion relieved 2nd Battalion Royal Berkshire Regiment in the trenches.	

Army Form C. 2118.

WAR DIARY
or
INTELLIGENCE SUMMARY.
(*Erase heading not required.*)

Instructions regarding War Diaries and Intelligence Summaries are contained in F.S. Regs., Part II. and the Staff Manual respectively. Title pages will be prepared in manuscript.

Hour, Date, Place	Summary of Events and Information	Remarks and references to Appendices
28/10/15.	In the trenches. The enemy shelled in rear of our trenches with Field guns but did no damage. Our Guns registered on German lines. 3 men wounded. The ground between the trenches was well reconoitered. Brigadier General visited the trenches.	
29/10/15.	In trenches. The enemy were quite. Our guns registered on German trenches during the day. The ground between the trenches was carefully reconoitered.	
30/10/15.	In the trenches. Our guns registered on German trenches, enemy replied with about 10 or 12 H.E. and Shrapnel shells from a Field gun but did no damage. Brigadier General visited the trenches. One man Killed.	
31/10/15.	In the trenches. About Stand-to Germans swept our trenches with Machine Gun fire, a powerful searchlight was played on our trenches at the same time and was used in conjunction with the guns. 1 Sgt counted 6 guns in what he estimated 600 yards. The ground was carefully reconoitered during the night, an enemy listening post was found, when discovered the 3 Germans in the post ran away. The Corps Commander General Pultney visited the trenches with Admiral Sir C. Gust during the afternoon.	

Officer Commanding 2nd Battalion Devon Regiment

Lieut-Colonel,

23rd Inf.Bde.
8th Div.

2nd BATTN. THE DEVONSHIRE REGIMENT.

NOVEMBER

1915

Army Form C. 2118.

2/4 Bn Berkshire Regiment

WAR DIARY
or
INTELLIGENCE SUMMARY.

(Erase heading not required.)

Instructions regarding War Diaries and Intelligence Summaries are contained in F.S. Regs, Part II. and the Staff Manual respectively. Title pages will be prepared in manuscript.

Hour, Date, Place	Summary of Events and Information	Remarks and references to Appendices
1/11/15.	The Battalion was relieved in the trenches by 1/7th Middlesex Regt and moved into billets near FLEURBAIX. One Man killed.	
2/11/15.	In Billets. Furnished working party of 50 men.	
3/11/15.	In Billets. Routine. 2nd Lieut Preedy joined the Battalion for the first time.	
4/11/15.	In Billets. The Battalion moved into Divisional Reserve, billets near Bac St Maur.	
5/11/15.	In billets. Routine. Coys practiced the attack on German trenches at BRIDOUX. Furnished R.E. working Parties.	
6/11/15.	In Billets. Routine. Coys practiced the attack. Lieut-Colonel J.O.Travers left to take over temporary Command of the 70th Infantry Brigade. Captain C.H.M.Imbert - Terry took over temporary Command of the Battalion.	
7/11/15.	In Billets. Routine . Practiced the attack. Brigadier-General visited the Battalion.	
8/11/15.	In Billets. Routine. Practiced the attack, the Brigadier-General was present at this parade.	
9/11/15.	In Billets Routine. Lieut-Colonel J.O.Travers C.M.G. D.S.O. proceeded on leave to England. Practiced the attack at night General Hudson and the Brigadier-General were both present. Furnished night working party of 25 men.	

Forms/C. 2118/10

Army Form C. 2118.

WAR DIARY
or
INTELLIGENCE SUMMARY.
(Erase heading not required.)

Hour, Date, Place	Summary of Events and Information	Remarks and references to Appendices
10/11/15.	In Billets. Routine. Practiced the attack. A party of R.Es and a digging party of 90 men from 1/5th Black Watch attended this parade Rugby Football was played during the afternoon against R.Es at the 8th Division - Result 3 points all. Divisional Band played at C Coy's billet during the afternoon.	
11/11/15.	Relieved the 8th Battalion York and Lancashire Regt in the trenches N/5.2., N/5.3., and N/5.4.	
12/11/15.	In the trenches. A quite day. Very wet.	
13/11/15.	In trenches. Very wet day. Trenches full of water, front trenches and communication trenches began falling in at many places Colonel Hayes 2nd Middlesex Regt, who was temporary in Command of the Brigade while Brigadier-General was on leave, visited the trenches. Enemy fired about 6 Shrapnel from a Field Gun and 6 4.2 H.E. Shells at Boutillerie otherwise a quite day. One man killed.	
14/11/15.	In the trenches. Enemy were more active during the night sweeping the parapet in C Coy with Machine Gun fire for about half-an-hour and firing nearly the whole night with rifles.	
15/11/15.	The Battalion was relieved in the trenches by 2nd Middlesex Regt and moved into billets in Brigade Reserve. A Coy garrisoned CROIX MARECHAL POST with one Company. B Coy was billeted at CROIX MARECH-AL and was in close support to 2nd Battn Middlesex Regt, the remaining two Companies were billeted near CROIX LECORNEX. 2nd Lieut's Wilson and Newton joined the Battalion for the first time.	

Army Form C. 2118.

WAR DIARY
or
INTELLIGENCE SUMMARY.
(Erase heading not required.)

Instructions regarding War Diaries and Intelligence Summaries are contained in F.S. Regs., Part II. and the Staff Manual respectively. Title pages will be prepared in manuscript.

Hour, Date, Place	Summary of Events and Information	Remarks and references to Appendices
16/11/15.	In Billets. Routine. Furnished R.E.Working Parties.	
17/11/15.	In Billets. Routine. Furnished R.E.Working Parties.	
18/11/15.	In Billets. Routine.	
19/11/15.	Relieved 2nd Battalion Middlesex Regt in the trenches, N/5.2.# N./5.3., and N/5.4., Quite night.	
20/11/15.	In Trenches. Artillery were active throughout the day and night - German trenches between N.10.c.2.2. and N.10.c.9.6. being bombarded in order "to destroy mine shafts and to cause as much damage as possible to personnel and material" Machine Guns and Trench Mortars co-operated - Enemy retaliated fairly vigorously - We lost one man wounded by shrapnel.	
21/11/15.	In Trenches. Fairly quite day. Our Field Guns shelled at intervals but the enemy made very little retaliation. Five men were wounded by splinters of bayonet which was hit by a rifle bullet, another man wounded himself in the hand with a Very Pistol.	
22/11/15.	In trenches. Quite day. Moved our line further to left and relieved the 8th Battalion Oxm and Bucks Regxx Light I.Regt. We now hold a length of trench more suitable for 2 Battalions. One man wounded when on sentry.	
23/11/15.	Relieved in the trenches by the 12th Battalion K.R.R.Regt and 5th Ox and Bucks Light I.Regt. Relief went off well, though very late. Sergt Dawe (A Coy) Killed whilst sniping. Battalion moved to bille--ts in Bac St Maur.	

Army Form C. 2118.

WAR DIARY
or
INTELLIGENCE SUMMARY.
(Erase heading not required.)

Instructions regarding War Diaries and Intelligence Summaries are contained in F.S. Regs., Part II. and the Staff Manual respectively. Title pages will be prepared in manuscript.

Hour, Date, Place	Summary of Events and Information	Remarks and references to Appendices
24/11/15.	Marched to VIEUX BERQUIN via SAILLY and ESTAIRES - Total distance about 10 miles. Arrived at new billets about 2.30.p.m.	
25/11/15.	Moved again to billets between HAZEBROUCK and MORBECQUE. Billets very scattered.	
26/11/15.	In Billets. Should have been inspected by the Commander-in-Chief weather very bad however and inspection indefinitely postponed. Fairly heavy fall of snow. Heavy Frost.	
27/11/15.	In billets. Training commenced.	
28/11/15.	In Billets. Church Parade. Weather very frosty.	
29/11/15.	In Billets. Parades in barns owing to bad weather. 2nd Lieut's Goodman, Vincent, Johns and Hill joined from the 3rd Battalion.	
30/11/15.	In Billets. Brigadier visited Headqrs. Training continued.	

LIEUT-COLONEL,
Officer Commanding 2nd Battalion Devonshire Regiment

23rd Inf.Bde.
8th Div.

2nd BATTN. THE DEVONSHIRE REGIMENT.

DECEMBER

1915

Army Form C.2118

WAR DIARY
or
INTELLIGENCE SUMMARY

(Erase heading not required.)

Instructions regarding War Diaries and Intelligence Summaries are contained in F. S. Regs., Part II. and the Staff Manual respectively. Title Pages will be prepared in manuscript.

Place	Date	Hour	Summary of Events and Information	Remarks and references to Appendices
	1/12/15.		In billets. Divisional Commander General Hudson visited "C" and "D"Coys in the morning – Training continued – R.E.Course for officers commenced	
	2/12/15.		In billets. Usual Training carried out – A.D.M.S. visited "A" and "C" Coys billets.	
	3/12/15.		In billets. Company training by Platoons.	
	4/12/15.		In billets. Company Training by Platoons. Lieut Tillett returned off leave.	
	5/12/15.		In billets. Church Parade.	
	6/12/15.		In billets. Company training by Platoons.	
	7/12/15.		In billets. Company training by Platoons. Lieut & Qr:Mr: Palmer proceeded on leave to England.	
	8/12/15.		In billets. Company training by Companies this included a route march by Companies. C.O. Adjutant and O.Cs.Companies attended a lecture at STEENBECQUE given by Major Hewlett on use of aeroplanes etc.,	
	9/12/15.		In billets. Company training by Companies this included a route march. Commanding Officer attended a lecture on use of gas.	
	10/12/15.		In Billets. Company training by Companies with route march. C.O. and O.Cs.Coys attended a lecture on the use of gas.	
	11/12/15		In Billets. Company training by Companies with route march.	

1875 Wt. W593/826 1,000,000 4/15 J.B.C. & A. A.D.S.S./Forms/C.2118.

Army Form C. 2118

WAR DIARY
or
INTELLIGENCE SUMMARY
(Erase heading not required.)

Instructions regarding War Diaries and Intelligence Summaries are contained in F. S. Regs., Part II. and the Staff Manual respectively. Title Pages will be prepared in manuscript.

Place	Date	Hour	Summary of Events and Information	Remarks and references to Appendices
	12/12/15.		In billets. Church Parade.	
	13/12/15.		In Billets. Training continued. Battalion Drill. Practice in the use of smoke helmets. Battalion Route march C.O. and Machine Gun Officer attended lecture on Machine Guns.	
	14/12/15.		In Billets. Battalion Drill and route march. C.O. and Machine Gun Officer attended lecture on Machine Guns.	
	15/12/15.		In Billets. Battalion Route March accompanied by "O" Battery R.H.A.	
	16/12/15.		In billets. Road march discipline by half Battalions. Field Engineering the C.R.E. attended this parade and gave professional advice. Divisional General Hudson visited Battalion Headquarters.	
	17/12/15.		In Billets. Outposts. Companies not on outposts practiced preliminary attack formations. Mayor of EXETER arrived on a visit to the Battalion.	
	18/12/15.		In Billets. The Brigade went for a route march during the morning. Order of march:- 2/Devon Regt., 2/Middlesex Regt., 2/West Yorks Regt., 2/Scottish Rifles., 1/7th Middlesex Regt.	
	19/12/15.		In Billets. Church Parade. Mayor of EXETER left.	
	20/12/15.		1st day of Divisional Manoeuvres. Order of March of the Brigade:- 2/West Yorks Regt., 2/Middlesex Regt., 2/Scottish Rifles., 1/7th Middlesex Regt., 2/Devon Regt. The Brigade moved as far as WARDRECQUES.. The Brigade billeted for the night being covered by the 25th Infantry Brigade. (contd)	

Army Form C. 2118

WAR DIARY
or
INTELLIGENCE SUMMARY
(Erase heading not required.)

Instructions regarding War Diaries and Intelligence Summaries are contained in F.S. Regs., Part II. and the Staff Manual respectively. Title Pages will be prepared in manuscript.

Place	Date	Hour	Summary of Events and Information	Remarks and references to Appendices
	20/12/15. (contd)		Battalions occupied billets as follows:- 2/West Yorks Regt at ECQUES. 2/Middlesex Regt at LE RONS & QUIESTEDE. 2/Scottish Rifles at BLAMBART-LA SABLAN GRAND-QUIESTEDE. 1/7th Middlesex Regt at RACQUINGHEM. 2/Devon Regt at WARDRECQUES. Brigade Headquarters were established at the CHATEAU at CLARQUES.	
	21/12/15.		Second day. The enemy having been driven back to the line RELY-AUCHEL. The 8th Division continued its march via THEROUANNE - COYECQUE - RADINGHAM. The 23rd Infantry Brigade(less 2 Battalions) Divisional Mounted Troops(less 2¾ platoons cyclists),5th Brigade R.H.A.(less 1 Battery and Ammunition Column),57th Battery R.F.A.,15th Field Company R.E., and No.1 Section 25th Field Ambulance,formed an advance guard under Brigadier General Tuson. The 1/7th Middlesex Regt and 2/Devon Regt marched at the head of the main body was about 1 mile outside COYECQUE when orders were received that the 23rd Infantry Brigade would attack on a front BOMY inclusive to and exclusive of Road Junction in N.W. corner of D.6., 1 mile due S. of ERNY St JULIEN. The 2/Middlesex Regt., 2/Scottish Rifles., and 1/7th Middlesex Regt deployed for attack. The 2/West Yorks Regt and 2/Devon Regt received instructions to remain at COYECQUE where they were to be in reserve. 2/Devon Regt billeted for the night at COYECQUE. Brigade Headquarters were established at BOMY.	the two battalions being under the command of Lt. Col.J.O.Travers,C.M.G.,D.S.O., Officer Cmdg. 2nd.Bn. Devon Regt. About 1 pm.when the head of the main body
	22/12/15.		The Brigade retired and moved into billets in the vicinity of BLARINGHEM. The Battalion was billeted at LE CROQUET.	
	23/12/15.		The Brigade moved to MORBECQUE where Battalions returned to billets.	

Army Form C. 2118

WAR DIARY
or
INTELLIGENCE SUMMARY
(Erase heading not required.)

Instructions regarding War Diaries and Intelligence Summaries are contained in F. S. Regs., Part II. and the Staff Manual respectively. Title Pages will be prepared in manuscript.

Place	Date	Hour	Summary of Events and Information	Remarks and references to Appendices
	24/12/15.		In billets. Routine.	
	25/12/15.		In Billets. Whole holiday. Church Parade in the morning. C.o.O. visited the men at dinner hour. All the officers dined at Battalion Headquarters. Christmas greetings sent & received from 1st Battalion	
	26/12/15.		In billets. Routine.	
	27/12/15.		In Billets. Routine. Company parades.	
	28/12/15.		In Billets. Routine. Company Parades.	
	29/12/15.		In Billets. Routine. Company parades. 2/Lieut H.K.Williams(3rd Battn) Joined for first time. Attached Excellent Officer	
	30/12/15.		In Billets. Routine. Battalion Route March combined with tactical exercises in the Field.	
	31/12/15.		In Billets. Routine. Company parades.	

10/1/xxxx
Lieut-Colonel,
Officer Commdg 2nd Battalion Devon Regt.

23rd Brigade.
8th Division.

2nd BATTALION DEVONSHIRE REGIMENT :: JANUARY 1916.

Army Form C. 2118

WAR DIARY
or
INTELLIGENCE SUMMARY
(Erase heading not required.)

Instructions regarding War Diaries and Intelligence Summaries are contained in F. S. Regs., Part II. and the Staff Manual respectively. Title Pages will be prepared in manuscript.

Place	Date	Hour	Summary of Events and Information	Remarks and references to Appendices
	1/1/16.		In Billets. at MORBECQUE. Routine. Company Parades.	
	2/1/16.		In Billets. Church Parade.	
	3/1/16.		In Billets. Routine. Company parades.	
	4/1/16.		In Billets. Routine. Company parades.	
	5/1/16.		In Billets. Routine. Company parades.	
	6/1/16.		In Billets. Routine. Battalion Route March.	
	7/1/16.		In Billets. Routine. Company parades.	
	8/1/16.		In Billets. Routine. Battalion Route March.	
	9/1/16.		In Billets. Church parade.	
	10/1/16.		In Billets. Battalion Route March.	
	11/1/16.		The Brigade marched to ESTAIRES. Order of march 2/Middlesex Regt, 1/7th Middlesex Regt, 2/Devonshire Regt, 2/Scottish Rifles, 2/West Yorkshire Regt. The Battalion was billeted in the vicinity of L.17.d.4.5. (Sheet 36A. France. 3rd Edition. 1/40,000.) for the night.	
	12/1/16.		The Brigade moved to SAILLY, there being half an hour interval between the time each Battalion passed the starting point (i.e., G.25d.8.7. Map Belgium and France Sheet 36. B series 1/40,000. 3rd Edition.) The Battalion moved into billets nearm DOULIEU.	
	13/1/16.		In Billets. Routine.	

(contd)

Army Form C. 2118

WAR DIARY
or
INTELLIGENCE SUMMARY

(Erase heading not required.)

Instructions regarding War Diaries and Intelligence Summaries are contained in F.S. Regs., Part II. and the Staff Manual respectively. Title Pages will be prepared in manuscript.

Place	Date	Hour	Summary of Events and Information	Remarks and references to Appendices
	14/1/16.		In Billets. Furnished R.E. working Parties. Routine. Received draft of 30 other ranks.	
	15/1/16.		In Billets. Routine.	
	16/1/16.		In Billets. Church Parade.	
	17/1/16.		In Billets. Routine.	
	18/1/16.		In Billets. Furnished working parties. The Battalion moved into billets at FLEURBAIX and was in Brigade Reserve. The Battalion occupied billets as follows:- Battalion Headqrs...PERGOLA HOUSE. H.22.d.4.4. "A"Company..........H.22.a.4.0. "B"Company..........H.28.a.6.3. "C"Company..........H.29.c.9.3. "D"Company..........H.21.d.6.4. Reference map Sheet 36. Belgium and France.	
	19/1/16.		In Billets at FLEURBAIX. Furnished R.E. working parties.	
	20/1/16.		In Billets. Furnished R.E. working parties.	
	21/1/16.		Relieved 2/Middlesex Regt in the trenches. N.6/1 to N.6/5 and supporting Posts.	
	23/1/16.		In Trenches. Brigadier visited the trenches in the morning. Artillery was fairly active during the day, about 20 77mm H.E.Shells were fired at Battalion Headquarters.(WYE FARM) 8 direct hits were obtained. Three men were wounded. One man was killed looking over parapet.	
	24/1/16.		In trenches. Enemy sniped a good deal during the morning but were very quiet during the night. The Division and Brigade Generals visited the lines during the morning.	
	25/1/16.		The enemy shelled a great deal during the day with Field and Heavy guns, (CONT'D)	

1875 Wt. W.593/826 1,000,000 4/15 J.B.C. & A. A.D.S.S./Forms/C.2118.

Army Form C. 2118

WAR DIARY
or
INTELLIGENCE SUMMARY
(Erase heading not required.)

Instructions regarding War Diaries and Intelligence Summaries are contained in F.S. Regs., Part II. and the Staff Manual respectively. Title Pages will be prepared in manuscript.

Place	Date	Hour	Summary of Events and Information	Remarks and references to Appendices
	25/1/16.	(contd)	little damage was done. 2 men were slightly wounded.	
	26/1/16.		The Battalion was relieved in the trenches by 2/Middlesex Regt and moved into billets at FLEURBAIX.	
	27/1/16.		In Billets. Routine. Furnished R.E. Working parties.	
	28/1/16.		In Billets. Routine.	
	29/1/16.		In Billets. Routine. Furnished R.E. Working Parties.	
	30/1/16.		The Battalion relieved the 2/Middlesex Regt in the trenches N.6/1 and N.6/5. One man was wounded in BOTTLERY Communication Trench during the relief. One Company 1/Tyneside Scottish was attached to the Battalion for instruction	
	31/1/16.		In Trenches. The enemy were active during the day and night especially on the left ("D"Company) firing a large number of shells chiefly 5.9 Hows and 77mm H.E.Shells. The enemy also fired several Rifle Grenades into this part of the line. One man was killed and another wounded by a sniper. The Company 1/Tyneside Scottish returned to their unit.	

10/xxxxx

Lieut-Colonel,
Officer Commdg. 2nd Bn. Devonshire Regiment.

23rd Brigade
8th Division.

2nd BATTALION

DEVONSHIRE REGIMENT

FEBRUARY 1916.

Army Form C. 2118

WAR DIARY

~~INTELLIGENCE SUMMARY~~

(Erase heading not required.)

Instructions regarding War Diaries and Intelligence Summaries are contained in F.S. Regs., Part II. and the Staff Manual respectively. Title Pages will be prepared in manuscript.

Place	Date	Hour	Summary of Events and Information	Remarks and references to Appendices
	1/2/16.		In Trenches. Enemy were again active on the left firing several 5.9 and 77mm shells and rifle grenades into the left Company. 2/Lieut A.W.F.Reed. joined Battalion for first time and remained at Transport Lines.	
	2/2/16.		In Trenches. The enemy were less active only firing a few 5.9 and 77mm shells and rifle grenades into the left Company. 2/Lieut H.C.Wilson was wounded in neck and knee by splinters from a rifle grenade. 2/Lieut A.W.F Reed was attached to "D"Company and joined the Company in the trenches.	
	3/2/16.		In Trenches. The enemy were very quiet all day. The Divisional and Brigadier Generals visited the trenches during the morning. The Battalion was relieved in thr trenches by 11th Battalion Sherwood Foresters and moved into billets on the RUE QUESNOY.	
	4/2/16.		In Billets. The Brigadier General visited Battalion Headquarters. Furnish -ed working parties.	
	5/2/16.		In Billets. Routine. Furnished R.E.Working Parties.	
	6/2/16.		In Billets. Church Parade. Furnished R.E.Working Parties.	
	7/2/16.		In Billets. Routine. Furnished R.E.Working Parties.	
	8/2/16.		In Billets. Routine. Furnished R.E.Working Parties.	
	9/2/16.		In Billets. Routine. Furnished R.E.Working Parties.	
	10/2/16.		In Billets. Routine. Furnished R.E.Working Parties. Regtl Sergt Major W. Pritchard left in the evening for HAVRE en route for England.	
	11/2/16.		In Billets. Routine. Furnished R.E.Working Parties.	
	12/2/16.		In Billets. Routine. Furnished R.E.Working Parties.	

Army Form C. 2118

WAR DIARY

INTELLIGENCE SUMMARY

(Erase heading not required.)

Instructions regarding War Diaries and Intelligence Summaries are contained in F.S. Regs., Part II. and the Staff Manual respectively. Title Pages will be prepared in manuscript.

Place	Date	Hour	Summary of Events and Information	Remarks and references to Appendices
	13/2/16.		In Billets. Furnished R.E.Working Parties. Church Parade.	
	14/2/16.		Battalion moved into billets near ESTAIRES. Major A.J.Sunderland rejoined the Battalion to take over Command Lieut-Colonel Travers having received orders to proceed to England for duty.	
	15/2/16.		The 23rd Infantry Brigade moved to LAVENTIE and relieved the 3rd Guards Brigade. 2/West Yorks Regiment and 2/Middlesex Regiment relieved the Guards in the Trenches. 2/Scottish Rifles and 2/Devonshire Regiment relieved the Guards in Billets in LAVENTIE and were in Brigade Reserve.	
	16/2/16.		In Billets. Routine. Major A.J.Sunderland took over Command.	
	17/2/16.		In Billets. Routine. Furnished R.E.Working Parties. Lieut-Col.Travers left early in the morning for England.	
	18/2/16.		In Billets. Routine.	
	19/2/16.		The Battalion Relieved the 2/Middlesex Regt in the trenches from Rotten Row inclusive to Bond Street inclusive and also garrisoned FIREWORKS POST with 1 section and A.1. and FLANK POST with 1 Platoon each. Battalion Headquarters were established at RED HOUSE.(M.6.d.2.0.) Reference Map Sheet 36. S.W.1. 6th Edition.	
	20/2/16.		In Trenches. A quiet day.	
	21/2/16.		In Trenches. A quiet day.	
	22/2/16.		In Trenches. The enemy were very quiet. One man wounded.	
	23/2/16.		The Battalion was relieved in the trenches by 2/Middlesex Regt and moved into Brigade Reserve in LAVENTIE.	

Army Form C. 2118

WAR DIARY

~~INTELLIGENCE SUMMARY~~

(Erase heading not required.)

Instructions regarding War Diaries and Intelligence Summaries are contained in F.S. Regs., Part II. and the Staff Manual respectively. Title Pages will be prepared in manuscript.

Place	Date	Hour	Summary of Events and Information	Remarks and references to Appendices
	24/2/16.		In Billets. Routine. Major General Pinney visited Battalion Headqrs.	
	25/2/16.		In Billets. Routine.	
	26/2/16.		In Billets. Routine.	
	27/2/16.		Church parade during morning. The Battalion relieved the 2/Middlesex Regt in the trenches. 2/Lieut J.G.W.A.Pinney A.D.C. to General Pinney was attached to "C"Company for instruction for 1 month. 2/Lieut R.N.K.Anderson. acted as A.D.C. to General Pinney during the absence of his A.D.C.	
	28/2/16.		In Trenches. 2 men were hit by snipers, 2/Lieut F.B.Lloyd and a Pte soldier were wounded by a bomb whilst on Patrol near German wire.	
	29/2/16.		In Trenches. Enemy were more active than usual, he fired about 10 4.2 How. shells and 20 77mm shells at Rotten Row, and 15 4.2 Howe shells into Bond street and Picantin avenue. The front line trench occupied by "A"Company was also shelled by about 50 5.2 shells. Very little damage was done only one man being wounded by a splinter in the jaw. The shelling was in retaliation to our own Artillery fire. One man was wounded while sniping.	

5/3/16.

[signature]

Major,
Officer Commanding 2nd Battalion Devonshire Regt

23rd Brigade.
8th Division.

2nd BATTALION DEVONSHIRE REGIMENT :: MARCH 1916.

Army Form C. 2118

Instructions regarding War Diaries and Intelligence Summaries are contained in F.S. Regs., Part II. and the Staff Manual respectively. Title Pages will be prepared in manuscript.

WAR DIARY

(Erase heading not required.)

Place	Date	Hour	Summary of Events and Information	Remarks and references to Appendices
	1/3/16.		In the Trenches. The enemy machine guns were active at night otherwise a quiet day. 2/Lieut R.A. Wykes appointed Instructor and Commandant 8th Division Trench Mortar School.	
	2/3/16.		The Battalion was relieved in the trenches by the 2nd Middlesex Regt and moved into billets at LAVENTIE. One man accidentally wounded.	
	3/3/16.		In Billets. Routine.	
	4/3/16.		In Billets. Routine.	
	5/3/16.		In Billets. Church parade.	
	6/3/16.		The Battalion moved into the trenches and relieved the 2nd Middlesex Regt. A quiet night.	
	7/3/16.		In the Trenches. Hostile machine guns were active at night. one man wounded.	
	8/3/16.		In the trenches. Between 1.50.p.m. and 5.p.m. enemy fired about 200 5.9 shells at old gun emplacements near Battalion Headquarters. One man accidentally wounded.	
	9/3/16.		In the Trenches. A quiet day. Furnished R.E. working parties. One man wounded on working party.	
	10/3/16.		In the trenches. Our Artillery bombarded the hostile trenches during the morning, the enemy replied by shelling our communication trenches with about 20 77mm shells. The enemy traversed our trenches at night with machine gun fire. Captain Jones R.A.M.C. was admitted to hospital sick and was relieved by Captain Blandy R.A.M.C. The Battalion was relieved by the 2nd Middlesex Regt and moved into billets at LAVENTIE. 2/Lieut S.T. Stephens joined the Battalion for the first time and was posted to "C" Coy.	
	11/3/16.		In Billets. Routine. Furnished R.E. Working parties. 2/Lieut F.B. Lloyd (contd)	

Army Form C. 2118.

WAR DIARY

(Erase heading not required.)

Instructions regarding War Diaries and Intelligence
Summaries are contained in F.S. Regs, Part II.
and the Staff Manual respectively. Title pages
will be prepared in manuscript.

Hour, Date, Place	Summary of Events and Information	Remarks and references to Appendices
(contd) 11/3/16.	rejoined from hospital.	
12/3/16.	In Billets. Church Parade. Furnished R.E. working parties. 2/Lieut H.Acomb, 11th Yorkshire Regt, joined the Battalion for the first time and was posted to "B"Company.	
13/3/16.	In Billets. Routine. Furnished R.E. working parties. Captain E.G. Roberts admitted to hospital sick. Captain G.L.Jones. R.A.M.C. returned from hospital.	
14/3/16.	The Battalion relieved the 2nd Battalion Middlesex Regt in the trenches. A quiet night. 2/Lieut C.W.Eales admitted to hospital sick. Each Company had one platoon 14th Hants Regt attached to them for instruction. One man wounded.	
15/3/16.	In the trenches. At 9.40.p.m. a hostile 4.2 Battery fired single shots at the ground just in rear of "A" and "B"Companies. No damage was done. Enemy fired several bombs during the night. One into the line held by "D"Company. No damage was done. ### ################################ The Brigade carried out a rocket test) at 10.p.m. The enemy took no notice of the rockets.	
16/3/16.	In the trenches. Very quiet day. The Brigadier visited the trenches.	
17/3/16.	In the trenches. During the morning enemy fired 3 77mm shells into the right communication trench. 4 77mm shells burst short of the wire in front of "C"Company during the afternoon. Enemy's machine guns were very active at night.	
18/3/16.	In the trenches. The Enemy shelled intermittently throughout the day in the vicinity of RUE TILLELOY tram base Gt CENTRAL and RED HOUSE (Battalion Headqrs) with 77mm shells. Captain J.A.Andrews was wounded in the leg when in front of his wire. The Brigadier visited Headqrs on his way to the trenches.	

Army Form C. 2118.

WAR DIARY
of
~~~~~~~~~~~~~~~~~~~~~~~~~~~~~~~~~~
~~~~~~~~~~~~~~~~~~~~~~~~~~~~~~~~~~
(Erase heading not required.)

Instructions regarding War Diaries and Intelligence Summaries are contained in F.S. Regs., Part II. and the Staff Manual respectively. Title Pages will be prepared in manuscript.

Place	Date	Hour	Summary of Events and Information	Remarks and references to Appendices
	18/3/16. (contd)		The Battalion was relieved in the trenches by 2nd Middlesex Regt and moved into billets at LAVENTIE.	
	19/3/16.		In Billets. Church Parade. 2/Lieut G.O.R.Jacob returned from the Base.	
	20/3/16.		In Billets. Routine. Furnished R.E. working parties. 2/Lieut G.W.Eales rejoined from hospital.	
	21/3/16.		In Billets. Routine. Furnished R.E. Working parties.	
	22/3/16.		Relieved the 2nd Middlesex Regt in the trenches. Each Company had 2 platoons of the 17th Sherwood Foresters attached to them for instruction. The enemy was unusually quiet hardly a shot being fired.	
	23/3/16.		In the trenches. The enemy was again extremely quiet. 2/Lieut G.Parker joined the Battalion for the first time. 2 Brigadiers and various other officers of the 105th Brigade visited the trenches during the day.	
	24/3/16.		In the Trenches. A very quiet day. The platoons of the 17th Sherwood Foresters attached to the Companies returned to their billets. Several officers of the 105th Brigade visited the trenches.	
	25/3/16.		In the trenches. A very quiet day. 2/Lieut R.A.Wykes rejoined from the 8th Divisional Trench Mortar School. One man wounded.	
	26/3/16.		The Battalion was relieved in the trenches by the 15th Battalion Cheshire Regt and moved into billets at Bac St Maur. Three Companies were billeted on the RUE BATILLE. Enemy were very quiet all day. Captain E.G.Roberts rejoined from hospital. 2/Lieut H.H.Goodman rejoined from 23rd Infantry Brigade Bomb School.	
	27/3/16.		The Battalion marched to Lestrem station where it entrained at 9.5.p.m. and proceeded to LONGUEAU detraining there at 6.30.a.m. on the morning of the 28th. 2/Lieut A.H.Smith, 2/Lieut R.J.Andrews, and 2/Lieut G.W.Dibble all joined the Battalion for the first time from the cadet school. (contd)	

Army Form C. 2118

WAR DIARY

(Erase heading not required.)

Instructions regarding War Diaries and Intelligence Summaries are contained in F.S. Regs., Part II. and the Staff Manual respectively. Title Pages will be prepared in manuscript.

Place	Date	Hour	Summary of Events and Information	Remarks and references to Appendices
	28/3/16.		2/Lieut A.H.Smith and 2/Lieut R.J.Andrews were posted to "A"Company and 2/Lieut G.W.Dibble to "D"Company.	
	28/3/16.		The Battalion marched to AMIENS after it had detrained at 6.30.a.m. and continued through that town to FREMENT where the Battalion was billeted with the exception of "D"Company who were billeted at VAUX.	
	29/3/16.		In Billets at FREMENT. "D"Company were brought back and billeted at FREMENT. The whole of the Battalion is now billeted at FREMENT.	
	30/3/16.		In Billets at FREMENT. Routine.	
	31/3/16.		In Billets at FREMENT. Routine.	

Major,
Commdg 2nd Battalion Devonshire Regiment.

23rd Brigade

8th Division.

2nd BATTALION DEVONSHIRE REGIMENT :: APRIL 1916.

Army Form C. 2118

WAR DIARY

~~INTELLIGENCE SUMMARY~~

(Erase heading not required.)

Instructions regarding War Diaries and Intelligence Summaries are contained in F.S. Regs., Part II. and the Staff Manual respectively. Title Pages will be prepared in manuscript.

Place	Date	Hour	Summary of Events and Information	Remarks and references to Appendices
	1/4/16.		In Billets, at Fremont. Routine. There was a conference at Bde Headqrs of all Commanding Officers.	
	2/4/16.		In Billets, at Fremont. Church parade at 11.30.a.m. for C of E. in village	
	3/4/16.		The Battalion moved into billets at St Gratien.(en route for ALBERT)	
	4/4/16.		The Battalion moved to billets in ALBERT and occupied left Bde. Reserve, relieving the 2nd Bn. Middlesex Regt. One platoon of "B"Company was occupying TARA REDOUBT.	
	5/4/16.		Billets at ALBERT. Routine.	
	6/4/16.		In Billets. Routine. Furnished R.E.Working parties.	
	7/4/16.		In Billets. Routine. Furnished R.E.Working parties.	
	8/4/16.		In Billets. Routine. Furnished R.E.Working parties.	
	9/4/16.		In Billets. Furnished R.E.Working parties. Church Parade. The Battalion was relieved in billets by the 2/Lincoln Regt and moved into new billets at ALBERT. The Battalion after relief went into Divisional Reserve but was under the orders of the 70th Infantry Brigade for working parties; half the Battalion working under the 15th Field Coy. R.E. and the other half Battalion under the 1st Home Counties R.E. Work was carried out on the Support and Reserve Lines daily.	
	10/4/16.		In Billets. Working Parties. Lieut R.N.K.Anderson was admitted to hospital	
	11/4/16.		In Billets. Furnished Working parties. The Brigadier visited Battalion Headquarters.	
	12/4/16.		In Billets. Furnished R.E.Working Parties. About 7.30.p.m. the Germans bombarded and raided the trenches held by the 1st Royal Irish Rifles. The Battalion stood to arms and was placed under the orders of the G.O.C.	

Army Form C. 2118

WAR DIARY
of
~~INTELLIGENCE SUMMARY~~

(Erase heading not required.)

Instructions regarding War Diaries and Intelligence Summaries are contained in F.S. Regs, Part II. and the Staff Manual respectively. Title Pages will be prepared in manuscript.

Place	Date	Hour	Summary of Events and Information	Remarks and references to Appendices
	12/4/16. (cont'd)		25th Infantry Brigade. Orders were received to stand down about 10.45.p.m.	
	13/4/16.		In Billets. Furnished R.E. Working parties.	
	14/4/16.		In Billets. Furnished R.E. Working parties.	
	15/4/16.		In Billets. Furnished R.E. Working parties.	
	16/4/16.		In Billets. Furnished R.E. Working parties. Captain M.R.M. McLeod proceeded to 4th Army Infantry School to take over the duties of Instructor.	
	17/4/16.		Relieved the ~~~~ 11th Battalion Sherwood Foresters Regt in the trenches during the morning. Enemy fired 6 77mm shells into our lines during the day and infiladed the right Company with machine Gun fire otherwise the enemy was very quiet.	
	18/4/16.		In the trenches. There was a little Artillery activity on both sides. A patrol from "C" Company tried to catch a German patrol which was seen near our lines but was ~~~~ unsuccessful. One of our wiring parties had to cease work owing to hostile machine gun fire. One man wounded. 2/Lieut H.K. Williams reported to 23rd Infantry Brigade for duty with Signals.	
	19/4/16.		During the morning our 4.5 Hows shelled the enemy's front line doing some damage. Enemy fired 16 77mm shells into our lines doing a little damage One shell fell into a dug out containing 5 men but all escaped untouched. About 7.p.m. the enemy bombarded our trenches with at least 8 guns, little damage was done. We suffered no casualties. Enemy machine guns and snipers were active throughout the night. The following appeared in the London Gazette of the 19th;-Major A.J.E.Sunderland to be Temp;Lt-Col;@ 17th March, 1916. Received a draft of 40 Other Ranks.	
	20/4/16.		Enemy fired 8 77mm shells into our trenches during the day doing no damage. Otherwise a quiet day.	

Army Form C. 2118

WAR DIARY

~~INTELLIGENCE SUMMARY~~

(Erase heading not required.)

Instructions regarding War Diaries and Intelligence Summaries are contained in F.S. Regs., Part II. and the Staff Manual respectively. Title Pages will be prepared in manuscript.

Place	Date	Hour	Summary of Events and Information	Remarks and references to Appendices
	21/4/16.		Enemy fired 18 77mm shells at our lines and 11 15cm shells. 3 of the latter were blind. One dug out was blown in burying 3 men. They were dug out uninjured. Enemy's machine Guns were active at night.	
	22/4/16.		Captain Preedy left to undergo a months course at the 4th Army School. The Division on our left carried out a successful raid on the enemy trenches roughly between the hours of 8.p.m. and 10.30.p.m. The enemy retaliated by heavily shelling our trenches, stoping about 11.p.m. damaging the trenches, killing One man, wounding 12 others and wounding Captain E.G.Roberts and Captain T.G.Hillyard. 2 men were killed during the morning by shell fire.	
	23/4/16.		The Battalion was relieved in the trenches by the 2nd Battalion Middlesex Regt and moved into billets in ALBERT.	
	24/4/16.		In Billets. Routine. Furnished R.E. Working parties.	
	25/4/16.		In Billets. Routine. Furnished R.E. Working parties.	
	26/4/16.		In Billets. Routine. Furnished R.E. Working parties.	
	27/4/16.		Relieved 2nd Battalion Middlesex Regt in the Trenches. A quiet day. Captain Fowler attached to Battalion during the abscence on leave of Captain Jones. R.A.M.C.	
	28/4/16.		In the Trenches. Enemy was very quiet. He was constantly seen at work on his front and Second Lines.	
	29/4/16.		In The Trenches. Enemy fired about 12 shells at our Trenches during the day otherwise it was a very quiet day. 2/Lieut L.A.Carey joined the Battalion on first appointment and remained at the Transport Lines.	

Army Form C. 2118

WAR DIARY

~~INTELLIGENCE SUMMARY~~

(Erase heading not required.)

Instructions regarding War Diaries and Intelligence Summaries are contained in F. S. Regs., Part II. and the Staff Manual respectively. Title Pages will be prepared in manuscript.

Place	Date	Hour	Summary of Events and Information	Remarks and references to Appendices
	30/4/16.		In The Trenches. About 2.30.a.m. the enemy bombarded the trenches of the Division on our right. The enemy also shelled our front line trenches very ???????? slightly and formed a barrage lasting about 10 minutes, hostile machine Guns were also very active. Our own Artillery replied some of the shells bursting short, some behind our trenches. The bombardment ceased at 3.25.a.m. Enemy again bombarded the trenches on our right at 7.p.m. Our Artillery replied. The bombardment ceased about 9.30.p.m. The enemy machine guns were very active. The enemy again shelled our front trenches and communication trenches doing little damage. One man wounded by our own shell fire. 2/Lieut L.A.Carey joined his Company in the trenches.	

4/5/16.

[signature]

Major for Lt.-Col;

Commanding 2nd Battalion Devonshire Regiment.

8th Division

23rd Brigade

2nd   BATTALION DEVONSHIRE REGIMENT ::: M A Y 1916.

The D.A.G.,

3rd Echelon.

Herewith War Diary for month of May 1916.

[signature]

Lt: Colonel,

3rd May 1916. Commanding 2nd Bn. Devonshire Regiment.

2 Devon Regt
Vol 18
5.V 5 sheet

WAR DIARY
or
INTELLIGENCE SUMMARY
(Erase heading not required.)

Army Form C. 2118

Place	Date	Hour	Summary of Events and Information	Remarks and references to Appendices
	1916 May	1st	The Battalion less 1 Coy was relieved in the trenches by the 2/K.R.R. Regt: and moved into Billets in ALBERT. "C" Coy was attached to 2/13th Essex Regt: in the trenches. One man was wounded.	
	"	2nd	In billets. Routine. Furnished R.E Working Parties.	
	"	3rd	The Battalion was relieved in the billets in ALBERT by the 2/Notts Regt:	
			HENENCOURT WOOD. "A" & "D" Coys moved into camp in the ALBERT BOUZIN— defenses for work under C.R.E. and were under the Command of O.O.C. 25th Infantry Brigade. This detachment was under the command of Lt: H. L. Sparkes.	
			One man wounded on R.E. working party.	
	"	4th	In camp. Routine. Furnished R.E. working parties.	
	"	5th	In camp. Routine. 2nd Lt: C.V. Eeles was accidentally wounded and Spr: K. was killed by a bomb accident at 25th Infantry Brigade Bomb School.	
	"	6th	In camp. Routine. Furnished R.E. H.Q. working parties.	
	"	7th	In camp. Church Parade. 2nd Lt: A.G.W. Dobbs proceeded to 8th School for a course of instruction.	
	"	8th	In camp. Routine. 2nd Lt: A.H.A.Phillips joined Battalion on return posted out from G.H.Q. Cadet School	
	"	9th	In camp. Routine. 2nd Lt: A.E.Cornell joined Battalion on return posted out from G.H.Q. Cadet School.	
	"	10th	Headquarters "B" & "C" Coys joined "A" & "D" Coys in the ALBERT BOUZIN-Court defences during the event.	

WAR DIARY
or
INTELLIGENCE SUMMARY

Army Form C. 2118

(Erase heading not required.)

Instructions regarding War Diaries and Intelligence Summaries are contained in F.S. Regs., Part II. and the Staff Manual respectively. Title Pages will be prepared in manuscript.

Place	Date	Hour	Summary of Events and Information	Remarks and references to Appendices
	May 11th		Relieved 2/Middlesex Regt: In the trenches during the morning. The enemy shelled "C" Coy between 3.50.p.m. and 4.50.p.m. with about 80 trench mortar shells doing a little damage to the trenches and wounding 2 men. One man was saved by his steel helmet. The enemy snipers and machine guns were more active than usual about 2.a.m. Our own artillery silenced the enemy's trench mortar batteries.	
"	12th		In the trenches. Enemy rather more active [struck through text] than usual about 54 77 m m shells 12 15 c.m shells and 100 light m.thrower, and rifle grenades were fired into our lines. The enemy Snomer heavy machine gun and rifle fire upon one of our patrols, one man being killed. Received a draft of 38 other ranks.	
"	13th		In the trenches. At 1.30.a.m. 3.30.a.m. 5.p.m. 9.30.p.m. 11.30.p.m. 12.30.a.m. and 1.25.a.m. enemy fired salvos of 12 shells (77 c m) at our trenches. At 11.p.m. & 12.30.p.m. enemy fired about 20 77 m m shells at our front line. Our artillery retaliated to the enemy's shelling.	
"	14th		In the trenches. Enemy was not very active during the day he fired 7 77 cm shells at Battalion headquarters, 8 77 m m shells, 5 trench mortar shells and 3 canisters about trenches, beyond killing one man with a canister little damage was done. The enemy machine guns were fairly active ene men was wounded whilst firing.	
"	15th		Relieved in the trenches by 2/Middlesex Regt. On completion of relief the Battalion moved into billets in ALBERT.	
"	16th		In billets. Routine. Furnished R.E.Working Parties, received draft of 28 other ranks. 2nd Lt: J.A.Rennie & 2nd Lt N.K.Gould joined the battalion on lst appointment.	

WAR DIARY
or
INTELLIGENCE SUMMARY

(Erase heading not required.)

Army Form C. 2118

Place	Date	Hour	Summary of Events and Information	Remarks and references to Appendices
	May	17th	In billets. Routine. Furnished R.E. working parties.	
	"	18th	In billets. Routine. Furnished R.E. working parties. Inspected C Coy. Lascage visited the billets with Major & Brigadier General Stockwell.	
	"	19th	The Battalion was relieved by 1st R.W.F. & moved into camp at HINGES COURT.	
	"	20th	In Camp. Routine.	
	"	21st	In Camp. Routine.	
	"	22nd	In Camp. R.C. Service. Captain J.A. Andrews rejoined. The following officers joined the battalion from a draft from 2nd Lines : 2nd Lieut : H.E. Hall, H.A. Jee, H.H. Jee, J.S. McGown, H.W. Jones.	
	"	23rd	In Camp. Routine. 2nd Lt. H.E. Morgan & 2nd Lieut. C.V. Bolton joined the battalion on relief from 2nd Lines.	
	"	24th	In Camp. Routine.	
	"	25th	In Camp. Routine. During the night there was a gas attack demonstration at which the C in C conducted by the present. No gas was used. Tributes to 2nd Middlesex Regt who made the demonstration.	
	"	26th	In Camp. 2nd Devon Regiment and Middlesex Regt practised the attack during the morning under the Brigadier. In the afternoon the battalion carried out a signal day, which was observed white tapes on the ground. C in C General ??? and Brigadier of the C.O. on the way in which was carried out and the condition of the battalion.	
	"	27th	In Camp. Routine. Moved into billets in HINGES COURT at 9 a.m.	
	"	28th	In billets. Church Parade. Furnished R.E. working party.	
	"	29th	In billets. Routine. Furnished R.E. working parties.	
	"	30th	In billets. Furnished R.E. working parties. All available officers and other ranks to FRANVILLERS where the German line is correctly over trenches taken over on the 6th of June by this R.C.	

WAR DIARY
or
INTELLIGENCE SUMMARY
(Erase heading not required.)

Army Form C. 2118

Place	Date	Hour	Summary of Events and Information	Remarks and references to Appendices
	May 31st		In billets. Routine. Furnished R.E. working parties. All available Officers were taken by bus to Brandhoek to study the ground marked out by flags to represent the German lines.	
	1st June 1916.			

W. Sutherland
Lieut. Colonel.
Commanding 2nd Bn. Devonshire Regiment.

23rd Brigade.

8th Division

2nd BATTALION DEVONSHIRE REGIMENT :: JUNE 1916.

Army Form C. 2118.

WAR DIARY
or
INTELLIGENCE SUMMARY. 2 Durm Regt
(Erase heading not required.)

Instructions regarding War Diaries and Intelligence Summaries are contained in F. S. Regs., Part II. and the Staff Manual respectively. Title pages will be prepared in manuscript.

6.V
6 sheet

Place	Date	Hour	Summary of Events and Information	Remarks and references to Appendices
	1916.			
	1st June.		In Billets. The Battalion moved off at 2.45 a.m. and marched to the ground near FRANVILLERS where the German Lines were marked out by white flags. Three Divisions practised the attack. The Army and Corps Commanders were present at this exercise. After the attack there was a conference of General Officers and O.C.Battalions.	
	2nd "		In Billets. Routine. Furnished R.E.Working Parties. 2/Lieut. E.M. Gould proceeded to 23rd Infantry Brigade Bomb School to undergo a Course of Bombing.	
	3rd "		In Billets. Routine. Furnished R.E.Working Parties. 2/Lieut. C.V. Beddow proceeded to LUCHEX to undergo a short Course of Sniping under Captain Hesketh Pritchard. A draft of 26 Other Ranks reported from 1st Entrenching Battalion. 2/Lieut. H.St Hill proceeded to 8th Divisional School of Instruction for a Course of Instruction.	
	4th "		Church parades were held during the morning. The Battalion relieved the 11th Battalion Sherwood Foresters in the right Sub-Section trenches during the afternoon. About 5.30 p.m. 6 5.9. shells fell near DONNETT PPST (Battalion H.Q.) No damage was done. There was considerable artillery and Trench Mortar activity between 5.45 p.m. and 9.45 p.m. in the Brigade on our right. Gas shells O2 could be slightly smelt at Battalion H.Q. Between 10 p.m. and 12 midnight a heavy bombardment could be heard in the vicinity of FRICOURT. The hostile Machine Guns were more active than usual at night, firing continually.	

T2134. Wt. W708—776. 500000. 4/15. Sir J. C. & S.

Army Form C. 2118.

WAR DIARY
or
INTELLIGENCE SUMMARY.
(*Erase heading not required.*)

Instructions regarding War Diaries and Intelligence Summaries are contained in F.S. Regs., Part II. and the Staff Manual respectively. Title pages will be prepared in manuscript.

Place	Date	Hour	Summary of Events and Information	Remarks and references to Appendices
	June 5th		In the Trenches. Our snipers claimed to have hit one of the enemy. At 3 p.m. our trench mortars opened fire on the enemy, who retaliated with Field Guns and Howitzers. This went on intermittently until 5.10. p.m. when fire from both sides ceased. About 5.30 p.m. our guns again open fire and the enemy retaliated. At 11.45 a.m. and 1 p.m. our guns retaliated for hostile shelling. Between 8 a.m. and 8.15 a.m. ten 77.mm shells fell at GROUCHY X.7.6. (D Coy)	
			At 11.45 a.m. six 77 mm shells were again fired at D Coy trenches 4 bursts in the wire and the remainder behind the front line trenches. During the afternoon the enemy shelled our trenches with minnenwerfer shells, Seventy 77.mm. shells and thirty seven 15 cm. shells. No serious damage was done but part of the trenches were knocked in.	
			Between 11 p.m. and 12 midnight the Divisions on our right and left carried out raids on the enemy's trenches. At 11 p.m. the enemy started a heavy bombardment on our front line, support and communication trenches employing Field Guns, Howitzers and minnenwerfer. At 12 midnight the bombardment slackened off a little but continued until 12.40 a.m. Considerable damage was done to our trenches.	
			During the bombardment the following casualties occured:-	
			2/Lieut. H.E.Marchant. Killed.	
			2/Lieut. S.D.Carver. Wounded.	
			3 other ranks. Killed.	
			14 other ranks. Wounded.	
			It was 2/Lieut. Marchants first tour in the trenches.	
			2/Lieut. Carver was buried by a shell.	
			"C" Coys Signaller's dugout was blown in one man escaped, but two others were buried and could not be dugout before they had died.	

Army Form C. 2118.

WAR DIARY
or
INTELLIGENCE SUMMARY.
(Erase heading not required.)

Instructions regarding War Diaries and Intelligence Summaries are contained in F.S. Regs., Part II. and the Staff Manual respectively. Title pages will be prepared in manuscript.

Place	Date	Hour	Summary of Events and Information	Remarks and references to Appendices
	June 5th (cont)		The worst of the casualties occured in the left Coy (D Coy) as this part of the line is enfiladed. During the bombardment heavy machine gun fire was kept up by the enemy. Two searchlights played in "No Man's Land" during the bombardment.	
	June 6th		In the trenches. The enemy were fairly quiet. Sixty-four 77.mm. shells and 12 15. cm. shells were fired. At night the enemy Machine Guns were active. Traversing our front line parapet. During the night, C and B Coys furnished a covering party to a party of about 600 men furnished by the South Wales Borderers and 2/Middlesex Regiments who under R.E. supervision constructed and advanced trench in front of our line, this work was superintended by Major Bebty R.E. We suffered no casualties. At the time the enemy were very busy repairing their front line and wire. Captain J.A. Andrews was in charge of our covering party. One man wounded.	
	7th		In the trenches. A comparatively quiet day. The enemy registered the new trench with a few 77 mm. shells. One man was wounded by shell fire. The following officers were struck off the strength of the Battalion Capt. M.R.M.McLeod on being appointed Assistant Instructor at 4th Army School 15/4/16. 2/Lieut. E.C.Gardiner on being ~~qqqqqqqqq~~ posted to 4th Field Survey Coy. 5/6/16. 2/Lieut. M.C.Ivey 3rd Battalion joined on first appointment and was posted to D Coy.	
Albert.	8th		In the trenches. ~~Thqqqqqqqqqqqqqqqqqqqqqq~~ During the morning the enemy fired about fifty 77 mm. shells at our trenches. The Battalion was relieved in the trenches during the morning by the 2/Middlesex Regt and on relief moved into Billets in Brigade Reserve in Albert.	

Army Form C. 2118.

WAR DIARY
or
INTELLIGENCE SUMMARY.
(Erase heading not required.)

Instructions regarding War Diaries and Intelligence Summaries are contained in F. S. Regs., Part II. and the Staff Manual respectively. Title pages will be prepared in manuscript.

Place	Date	Hour	Summary of Events and Information	Remarks and references to Appendices
	June 8th		One man was killed and 1 wounded. In addition one man was admitted to Hospital suffering from gas poisoning. This gas came out of the ground while deepening the new trench dug on the night 6/7th June. Two signallers attended a short course with R.F.C. in connection with communication with aeroplanes. One man killed and one wounded by shrapnel and another was wounded by an enemy sniper.	
	" 9th		In Billets. Routine. Furnished R.E. Working Parties.	
	" 10th		In Billets. Routine. Furnished R.E. Working Parties.	
	" 11th		In Billets. Routine. Furnished R.E. Working Parties. Church parades were held during the morning.	
	" 12th		The Battalion was relieved during the evening by 1st R.I.R. and moved into Camp at HENENCOURT WOOD. Furnished R.E. Working Parties.	
	" 13th		In Camp. 2/Lieut. G.S.D. Carver rejoined from Hospital. A Coy made up to 240 strong moved into the Albert-Bouzincourt Defences. This Coy was Commanded by Captain Preedy. A memorial service was held during the evening in memory of the late Lord Kitchener.	
	" 14th		In Camp. Routine. Furnished R.E. Working Parties.	
	" 15th		In Camp. Routine. Furnished R.E. Working Parties.	
	" 16th		Moved into the trenches. Received draft of 48 other ranks.	
	" 17th		In the trenches. Our artillery was fairly active. Between 9.15 a.m. and 10.50a.m. the enemy fired about twenty 15 cm. shells at out trenches killing one and wounding another man. About mid day the enemy fired several 77 mm shells at our trenches. The enemy Machine Guns fired throughout the night. Casualties 1 other rank killed and 4 other ranks wounded. The Coys were very busy carrying material required for the proposed offensive operations. 2/Lieut. R.A. Wykes proceeded to the 23rd Trench Mortar Battery for duty	

T2134. Wt. W708—776. 500000. 4/15. Sir J. C. & S.

Army Form C. 2118.

WAR DIARY
or
INTELLIGENCE SUMMARY.
(Erase heading not required.)

Instructions regarding War Diaries and Intelligence Summaries are contained in F.S. Regs., Part II. and the Staff Manual respectively. Title pages will be prepared in manuscript.

Place	Date	Hour	Summary of Events and Information	Remarks and references to Appendices
	June 18th		In the trenches. On two occasions our artillery silenced enemy Machine Gun fire. The enemy during the day fired about 60 77 mm. shells and several 15 cm. shells at our trenches. Enemy Machine Guns were again active at night. 3 men were wounded. The Coys were again hard at work carrying stores.	
	" 19th		In the trenches. The enemy fired about 40 77. mm. shells and a few 15 cm. shells at our trenches. One man was accidently killed in the trenches. One man was wounded. 2 men were accidently wounded at 23rd Infantry Brigade Bomb School. The Battalion was relieved in the trenches by the 2/Middlesex Regt and on relief moved into Camp at HENENCOURT WOOD. While in the trenches a great deal of stores were carried into the trenches. 2/Lieut. F.B.Coldwells and a draft of 31 other ranks joined the Battalion in Camp.	
	" 20th		2/Lieut. E.D.Hill proceeded to 23rd Trench Mortar Battery for duty. In Camp. ROUTINE. Furnished Working Parties. 2/Lieut. S.W.M.Neilson rejoined the Battalion from 23rd Inf. Bde. Trench Mortar Battery.	
	" 21st		In Camp. Routine. Furnished R.E.Working Parties.	
	" 22nd		The Battalion moved into LONG VALLEY V.24.h.2.2. (Map Sheet 57d 1st Edition, FRANCE.) where it bivouacked.	
	" 23rd		In LONG VALLEY. Routine. Furnished. R.E.Working Parties.	
	" 24th		In LONG VALLEY. ROUTINE. Received a draft of 43 O.R. First day of Bombardment preparatory to the attack on German trenches. D. Coy made up to 240 men from A. Coy moved into ALBERT DEFENCES. This detatchment was under the command of 2/Lieut. C.O.R.Jacob.	
	" 25th		In LONG VALLEY. Routine. 2nd day of Bombardment. Church parades held during the morning.	

T2134. Wt. W708—776. 500000. 4/15. Sir J. C. & S.

WAR DIARY
or
INTELLIGENCE SUMMARY.
(Erase heading not required.)

Army Form C. 2118.

Place	Date	Hour	Summary of Events and Information	Remarks and references to Appendices
	June 26th		In LONG VALLEY. 3rd day of Bombardment.	
	" 27th		In LONG VALLEY. Routine. 4th day of Bombardment. The Brigadier visited Battalion Headquarters. Temp. Captain. R.N.K.Anderson left to take up training duties with reserve Battalions at Home.	
	" 28th		In LONG VALLEY. 5th day of Bombardment. The Brigadier visited Battalion Headquarters.	
	" 29th		6th Day of Bombardment. The Commanding Officer addressed the Battalion on the forthcoming operations. The Battalion moved into the trenches. "D" Coy dug a new assembly trench during the night. 2/Lieut. G.W.Dibble and 1 other rank were wounded while digging this trench. One man wounded by shell fire.	
	" 30th		In the trenches. 7th day of Bombardment. The enemy shelled our trenches intermittently throughout the day with 5.9.cm, shells, 4.5.cm. shells and 77. mm. shells, there were few casualties and the trenches were knocked in, in several places, one shell going through the Batt'n. Fighting Headquarters which were to be occupied the next day. This damage was repaired by the Regimental Pioneers during the day. C.S.M.Turner was killed and two men wounded by Shell fire. "C" Coy completed the new assembly trench. The Battalion moved into its position of assembly. A and B Ceys moved into the new trench (front line and BORDER STREET. C and D Ceys moved into RYCROFT STREET and part of FURNESS STREET. Battalion H.Q. moved to the Fighting H.Q. in FURNESS STREET at Junction of CONISDON STREET. The 2/Middlesex Regt were on the right, 2/West Yorks Regt in support and 2/Scottish Rifles in Reserve.	

signature
Lieut. Colonel.
Commanding, 2nd Battalion Devonshire Regiment.

23rd Inf.Bde.
8th Div.

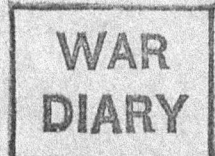

2nd BATTN. THE DEVONSHIRE REGIMENT.

J U L Y

1 9 1 6

Attached:

Report on Operations
1st July.

WAR DIARY
or
INTELLIGENCE SUMMARY.

(Erase heading not required.)

Army Form C. 2118.

Place	Date	Hour	Summary of Events and Information	Remarks and references to Appendices
	1916. July 1st		See attached report.	
	" 2nd		In Bivouacs at MILLENCOURT. About midday received orders to move at once to MERICOURT where the Brigade would entrain. The Battalion marched to MERICOURT and entrained about 8 p.m.	
	" 3rd		Arrived at AILLY about 12.30 a.m. and marched to LA CHAUSSEE arriving there about 4 a.m. and moved into Billets. The same evening orders were received from the Brigade to move to SOUES next morning.	
	" 4th		The Battalion fell in about 9.45 a.m. and marched to SOUES arriving there about 11 a.m. 2/Lieut. T.R.Johns rejoined the Battalion from 4th Army School of Instruction.	
	" 5th		In Billets at SOUES. Were informed by the Brigade that the G.O.C. would inspect the Battalion on the morning of the 6th. About 8 p.m. orders were received to be ready to move at a moments notice.	
	" 6th		About 2 a.m. received Operation Orders from the Brigade. The Battalion left SOUES at about 10.30 a.m. and marched to LONGEAU where the Battalion entrained about 6.45 p.m. for DIEVAL.	
	" 7th		Detrained at DIEVAL about 1.30 a.m. and marched to BARLIN where the Battalion moved into Billets about 8.30 a.m. Lieut. H.Archer rejoined the Battalion. Received draft of 92 Other Ranks, this included 20 men of the D.C.L.I.	
	" 8th		In Billets at BARLIN. Routine.	
	" 9th		In Billets at BARLIN. Routine.	

Army Form C. 2118.

WAR DIARY
or
INTELLIGENCE SUMMARY.
(Erase heading not required.)

Instructions regarding War Diaries and Intelligence
Summaries are contained in F.S. Regs., Part II.
and the Staff Manual respectively. Title pages
will be prepared in manuscript.

Place	Date	Hour	Summary of Events and Information	Remarks and references to Appendices
	1916. July 10th		In Billets at BARLIN. Routine. G.O.C. 8th Division inspected the Battalion and congratulated the Battalion on the splendid work it had done and the wonderful bravery shown by all Ranks on the 1st July 1916. Major C.H.M.Imbert Terry D.S.O. left to take over Temporary Command of 8th K.O.Y.L.I.	
	" 11th		In Billets. Routine.	
	" 12th		In Billets. Routine. 2/Lieut S.G.Blake and 2/Lieut. A.M.Rogers 15th Gloster Regt, joined the Battalion.	
	" 13th		In Billets. Routine. The C.O. and Company Commanders attended a Staff Tour.	
	" 14th		About 6.45 a.m. received orders from the Brigade that the G.O., O.C. Companys and Lewis Gun Officer were to report at Brigade Headquarters at 8.30 a.m. to go round trenches, and that the Battalion would move into the trenches that night. At 2.30 p.m. the Battalion was conveyed by Motor Busses to the Brigade Assembly position outside BETHUNE, arriving there about 4 p.m. At 8.30 p.m. the Battalion marched to the trenches and Relieved the 14th Hants. Regiment in the trenches near CUINCHY.	
	" 15th		In the trenches. About 11.15 p.m. six of the enemy attacked one of our Saps; they threw 3 bombs and were driven off. Later the enemy made another attempt to reach this Sap but was driven off suffering several Casualties. About 11.30 p.m. about 20 or 30 of the enemy attacked another of our Saps but were driven off by our Rifle Fire suffering several Casualties. The enemy fired a great number of aerial darts, rifle grenades, shells and trench mortars at our trenches damaging them badly in several places.	

Army Form C. 2118.

WAR DIARY
or
INTELLIGENCE SUMMARY.
(Erase heading not required.)

Instructions regarding War Diaries and Intelligence Summaries are contained in F.S. Regs., Part II. and the Staff Manual respectively. Title pages will be prepared in manuscript.

Place	Date	Hour	Summary of Events and Information	Remarks and references to Appendices
	1916. July 16th		In the trenches. Between 2 p.m. and 4.30 p.m. our artillery bombarded the hostile trenches. The effect of our bombardment could not be observed owing to the craters in front of our own line which entirely obscured the view. The enemy replied vigorously with shells of different calibre, minnenwerfer and rifle grenades doing considerable damage to our front, support and communication trenches, knocking in several dugouts. 2 men were killed and 5 others wounded. During the night our artillery carried out an intermittent bombardment of the hostile trenches.	
"	17th		In the trenches. From 12 noon until 10 p.m. the enemy were unusually quiet only firing a few rifle grenades at our trenches, doing very little damage. At 10.45 p.m. the enemy shelled our trenches and attacked 2 of our saps. Both these attacks were stopped by our fire and the enemy driven off, the enemy suffering some casualties. At 11.15 p.m. the enemy made another attack on one of our Saps, this was also unsuccessful. At 12.45 a.m. a party of the enemy advancing on our line were dispersed by our Lewis Gun fire. Hostile Trench Mortars and aerial torpedos were very active during the night causing serious damage to our trenches. Casualties 2 men killed 5 wounded. At 3.30 a.m. the enemy exploded a mine opposite the left Coy (A Coy)	
"	18th		The mine appeared to burst backwards, destroying the enemy's parapet and burying several of his garrison. 2/Lieut. R.J. Andrews at once pushed forward with one platoon and occupied the far lip of the crater, the enemy offered a vigourous resistance but was driven off with heavy losses. This platoon then retired to the near lip of the crater and immediately consolidated their position. The explosion of the mine caused considerable damage to our forward saps, four of the garrison of one sap were entombed. From 2.30 p.m to 5.30 p.m. @ our artillery bombarded the hostile trenches with good effect. The hostile retaliation was feeble and consisted mostly of 77 mm. Shells, Light Trench Mortars and Rifle Grenades doing no damage.	

T2134. Wt. W708-776. 500000. 4/15. Sir J. C. & S.

Army Form C. 2118.

WAR DIARY
or
INTELLIGENCE SUMMARY.
(Erase heading not required.)

Instructions regarding War Diaries and Intelligence Summaries are contained in F. S. Regs., Part II. and the Staff Manual respectively. Title pages will be prepared in manuscript.

Place	Date	Hour	Summary of Events and Information	Remarks and references to Appendices
	July 19		The enemy was much quieter, there was practically no artillery fire and the number of hostile rifle grenades fired was considerably less. Casualties 1 Officer Killed, 5 Other Ranks killed (4 of these were entombed) 13 Other Ranks wounded.	
	"	20	From 12 noon to 3.30 p.m. our artillery carried out a pre-arranged programme. The enemy retaliation was slight. A few 5.9 shells were fired at TOWER RESERVE Line, aerial torpedoes, Trench Mortars and Rifle Grenades were also fired in conjuction with 77. mm. shells, very little material damage being done. An enemy patrol of 12 men were caught by our bombers and driven back to their own lines. 2 Killed 1 Other Rank, wounded 1 Officer and 12 Other Ranks. In the trenches. A quiet day. There was very little firing by either side. During the night the enemy tried to enter one of our saps but was driven off by our rifle fire. Casualties. 3 Other Ranks wounded.	
	"	21	In the trenches. At 3 a.m. we successfully exploded a mine opposite the Left Coy (A Coy). The crater formed was commanded by us from Sap No 5. It was not found necessary to send anyone forward to deny the crater to the enemy who made no attempt to occupy it. On the explosion of the mine the enemy opened a heavy fire on our front line with Minnenwerfer, Rifle Grenades and Machine Guns. No damage was done. During the night we occupied and consolidated the near lip of the crater. During the day the enemy fired a certain number of Trench Mortars, Aerial Darts and Rifle Grenades, but it was noticed that he was much quieter than when we first took over the line. We appeared to have the upper hand. 2 Other Ranks wounded.	

Army Form C. 2118.

WAR DIARY
or
INTELLIGENCE SUMMARY.
(Erase heading not required.)

Instructions regarding War Diaries and Intelligence Summaries are contained in F.S. Regs., Part II. and the Staff Manual respectively. Title pages will be prepared in manuscript.

Place	Date	Hour	Summary of Events and Information	Remarks and references to Appendices
	July 22		The Battalion was relieved in the trenches by the 2/West Yorks Regt and moved into Supporting Posts and Keeps. Casualties 1 Other Rank wounded.	
	" 23		In support.	
	" 24		In support. Received draft of 26 Other Ranks. 2/Lieut. G.Law, 2/Lieut. W.H.L.Vesey Fitzgerald and 2/Lieut A.W.Harrison joined the Battn.	
	" 25		In support.	
	" 26		Relieved the 2/Scottish Rifles in the trenches. 2/Lieut. T.H.Trinaman 2/Lieut. E.C.Jacks, 2/Lieut. C.W.G.Hannah, 2/Lieut. G.P.Thuillier, and 2/Lieut. G.Hosegood joined the Battalion.	
	" 27		In the trenches. Between 12 noon and 1.45 p.m. the enemy fired a large number of 5.9 shells in rear of the right flank of the Battalion. The enemy were very active firing a large number of Rifle Grenades, Aerial Torpedoes and 77 mm. shells at our front, support and communication trenches doing very little material damage. We retaliated with Rifle Grenades, Stoke's Mortars and Field Guns. Hostile Machine Guns were very active during the night, our Lewis Guns retaliated.	
	" 28		In the trenches. Both ourselves and the enemy were very active firing a considerable number of Rifle Grenades, Trench Mortars and Field Guns. 1 Other Rank was wounded.	
	" 29		In the trenches. About 10 a.m. the enemy bombarded the Right Coy with MINNENWERFER and 10.5 cm. shells. At 3.48 p.m. a party of about 10 to 15 Germans raided one of our Saps, the raiding party with the exception of 1 man, believed to be an officer, were attired in shirt sleeves and wore no boots and were armed with revolvers, clubs and bombs. This party was attacked immediately attacked and were driven out, but managed to drag away one of our sentries who was cut off and had been clubbed.	

Army Form C. 2118.

WAR DIARY
or
INTELLIGENCE SUMMARY.
(Erase heading not required.)

Instructions regarding War Diaries and Intelligence Summaries are contained in F.S. Regs., Part II. and the Staff Manual respectively. Title pages will be prepared in manuscript.

Place	Date	Hour	Summary of Events and Information	Remarks and references to Appendices
	July 29.		The enemy heavily shelled the vicinity immediately afterwards. About 4.30 p.m. our 60 pounder Trench Mortars attempted unsuccessfully to cut the wire in front of one of the enemy's saps which it was proposed to raid that night. The enemy replied with 77 mm, and 10.5 cm. shells. The attempted wire cutting was continued until 8 p.m. but was not successful. At 8.45 p.m. the enemy started bombarding our trenches on the Right Company with Trench Mortars and 77 mm. shells, and after a while with 10.5 cm. shells. Little notice was taken of this bombardment at first as it was thought to be retaliation for our 60 pounder Trench Mortar Fire. This bombardment increased in intensity especially on the right, the enemy making use of shells of all calibre and a large number of heavy and light Trench Mortars. At 9.35 p.m. the Rifle Brigade asked our Machine Guns to open fire on the HOHENZOLLERN Flank. This request was complied with. About 10.30 p.m. an "S.O.S." message was received from the Battn. on our right (Rifle Brigade) and steps were at once taken to give any assistance that might be required. About 11.15 p.m. a party of the enemy advanced on our trenches but were dispersed by our Rifle and Lewis Gun fire. About 11.30 p.m. the hostile bombardment ceased. Patrols were sent to try and obtain indentification of the enemy but none of the enemy, either dead or alive, were seen.	
	July 30		About 2 a.m. another/hostile bombardment started on the left of the Battalion and lasted for about three quarters of an hour. About 6.15 a.m. the enemy rushed one of our saps which was unoccupied, we opened a heavy Lewis Gun fire on the enemy, who retired. During the afternoon the Battalion was relieved in the trenches by the 1st Northampton Regt and moved into Divisional Reserve Billets in ANNEQUIN. 2/Lieut. C.Law proceeded to the 23rd Infantry Brigade Bomb School for a Course of Bombing. Casualties for the 29th and 30th. Other Rank Killed 13 Other Ranks, 1 Other Rank taken prisoner, 1 Other Ranks wounded.	

T2134. Wt. W708—776. 500000. 4/15. Sir J.C. & S.

Army Form C. 2118.

WAR DIARY
or
INTELLIGENCE SUMMARY.
(Erase heading not required.)

Instructions regarding War Diaries and Intelligence Summaries are contained in F. S. Regs., Part II. and the Staff Manual respectively. Title pages will be prepared in manuscript.

Place	Date	Hour	Summary of Events and Information	Remarks and references to Appendices
	July	31	In Billets. Routine. Furnished R.E.Working Parties. 2/Lieut. A.E.Ruttledge and 2/Lieut.C.H.S.Buckley joined the Battalion on 1st appointment. 2/Lieut. A.C.G.Roberts promoted Lieut. and to date from 22/3/16.	

A.J.... [signature]
Lieut.-Colonel.
Commanding, 2nd Battalion Devonshire Regiment.

REPORT ON THE PART TAKEN BY THE 2ND BATTALION DEVONSHIRE
REGIMENT DURING THE ATTACK ON POZIERES ON THE 1st
JULY 1916.

It was a comparatively quiet night and there was little fire on either side until 6.30 a.m.

At 6.30 a.m. our artillery which consisted of artillery of all calibres opened an intense bombardment which lasted for one hour. The enemy front and support line came in for most of the shelling. The enemy's reply was not very vigourous, most of his fire being directed on our Support and Communication trenches.

During the last 7 to 10 minutes of the intense bombardment "A" and "B" Coys left the "NEW TRENCH" and advanced in open order to within about 100 yards of the enemy trenches, closely followed by "C" and "D" Coys, who moved down to the new line and advanced from there.

This advance was carried out in four successive waves in the most perfect order; the Casualties were not very heavy during this advance. Lieut. Temp. Captain E.G.Roberts who was in command of "A" Coy was badly wounded by shell fire while leaving our front line, 2/Lieut L.A.Carey also of "A" Coy was killed at the same time.

Just before the advance began a mist drifted over from the enemy's line towards our own and made observation very difficult. Captain J.A.Andrews was in Command of the Front Line and it was due to him, to a great extent, that the advance from our front line was carried out with such remarkable coolness and precision. At the same time as our Coys advanced towards the hostile trenches, the 2/Middlesex Regiment on our right and the 2/Royal Berks. Regiment on our left, advanced with remarkable coolness and order.

At 7.30 a.m. our artillery lifted from the enemy front line trenches on to the trenches in rear. During this pause the hostile artillery fire had gradually increased. As soon as the artillery lifted Captain J.A.Andrews got up and gave the order to advance, hardly had the order been given when he was killed by a hostile bullet which struck him in the head. As soon as the order to advance had been received, the four waves dashed for the German trenches opposite X.8.c.5.2. - X.8.c.8½.3½. - X.8.d.2.4.

Immediately the troops advanced the enemy opened a terrific machine gun fire from the front and from both flanks, which mowed down our troops, this fire did not deter our men from continuing to advance, but only a very few reached the German Lines alive. Some of these managed to effect an entry into the German Lines, where they "put up" a determined fight against enormous odds and were soon killed.

At first and for some little time owing to the mist and dust caused by our shell fire, it was difficult to realise exactly what had happened, although the heavy hostile Machine Gun fire told its own tale. The lines appeared at first sight to be intact, but it was soon made clear that the lines consisted of only dead or wounded, and that no one was there to support the few that had got in, and to carry on with the advance.

The cause of this was eventually discovered; the 2/ West Yorks. Regt who were in support had been caught by hostile Machine Gun and Shell fire as soon as they advanced from their assembly trenches, and had been cut to pieces.

The Brigade was informed as to what had happened to the Battalion but no information could be given to them as to what had happened to the supporting Battalion, as our runners were unsuccessful in getting in touch with them, neither could any accurate information be given as to what had happened to the 2/Middlesex Regt on our right and the 2/Royal Berks Regt on our left. From observation it was soon ascertained that the Battalions on either flank had also been caught by the hostile Machine Gun fire and had been unable to take the German trenches. This information was communicated to the Brigade. This information was shortly corroborated by our wounded who began to crawl back to our lines in small numbers. None of the runners sent by Companys reached Headquarters, they were all either killed or wounded.

No accurate information could be ascertained as to the exact number of casualties the Battalion had suffered, although it was clear that there were very few left who had not been hit; the enemy began to snipe our wounded When it was quite clear that we were not holding the front line the the barrage was brought back on the German front line trenches, and the 2/Scottish Rifles were moved forward to the "New Trench" and were told to hold themselves in readiness to advance.

(Contd)

(2)

During this time the hostile shelling had increased and the front line systems of trenches were very badly knocked about.

The enemy used a very high proportion of lachrymatory shells which caused a great deal of inconvenience to anyone not wearing gas goggles.

The enemy continued to confine his shelling practically entirely to our front line, support and communication trenches.

About mid.day orders were issued by the Brigade that no further advance would take place till further orders.

Our wounded still continued to crawl in to the "New Trench" but great difficulty was found evacuating the wounded to the Regimental Aid Post as the trenches were too narrow to allow a stretcher to pass and also the trenches had been so knocked about that in many places one was exposed to hostile Machine Gun and Shell fire.

The Medical Officer went down to the "NEW TRENCH" and bandaged all the wounded while the Stretcher Bearers and parties of Regimental Pioneers from Headquarters carried the wounded back to the Aid Post on their backs and in waterproof sheets. By this means all our wounded which it was possible to get at were removed to First Aid Post where the M.O. attended to them. The supply of Orderlies for removing the wounded from the Aid Post was not good. Several messages had to be sent asking for Orderlies to be sent up to remove the wounded.

About 4 p.m. all Adjutants were ordered to report at Brigade Head-quarters. The Brigade Major started to dictate orders to the effect that the Scottish Rifles would take over the front line and the remainder of the other Battalions of the Brigade would move into support trenches. While taking down the orders the 8th Division informed the Brigade that the whole Brigade would be relieved that night, and that orders for the relief would be issued. Adjutants then returned to their Battalions and C.Os were ordered to re-organise their Battalions.

About 4 p.m. the artillery fire on both sides slackened down considerably.

During the day wounded and unwounded crawled in, in small numbers. The unwounded were organised into parties by Companys.

About 8 p.m. orders were received that the Brigade would be relieved and that in the meantime the 2/Scottish Rifles would hold the line and the remainder of the Battalions were to move into dugouts in HODDER and HOUGHTON Streets, in the vicinity of Bde Headquarters and that the Brigade would later move to bivouacs in MILLENCOURT. By this time about 40 men not including Headquarters had been collected.

By 10 p'clock all the men had been placed in dugouts.

The C.O. and Adjutant then proceeded to Brigade Headquarters where a conference was held by the G.O.C. 23rd Infantry Brigade, on the operations and the best methods of overcoming the difficultys which had been met.

The remnants of the Battalion moved off for MILLENCOURT about 11 p.m. The C.O. and Adjutant left Brigade Headquarters for MILLENCOURT about 1.30 a.m. on the 2nd July and arrived at MILLENCOURT about 3 a.m.

The following Casualties were suffered during the action:-

Captain J.A.Andrews.	Killed.	(In Command of Front Line
Captain. A.Preedy.	-do-	O.C. "B" Coy.
2/Lieut. L.A.Carey.	-do-	
2/Lieut. E.M.Gould.	-do-	
2/Lieut. C.V.Beddow.	-do-	
2/Lieut. M.C.Ley.	-do-	
2/Lieut. E.A.Jago.	-do-	
43 Other Ranks.	-do-	
Captain E.G.Roberts.	Wounded.	O.C. "A" Coy.
2/Lieut. C.O.R.Jacob.	-do-	O.C. "D" Coy.
2/Lieut. A.R.Newton.	-do-	
2/Lieut. J.A.Rennie.	-do-	Since died of wounds
2/Lieut. G.Parker.	-do-	
2/Lieut. A.H.Cornell.	-do-	
194 Other Ranks.	-do-	
2/Lieut. J.S.McGowan.	Missing.	Since reported Killed.
2/Lieut. G.S.D.Carver.	-do-	
2/Lieut. F.B.Coldwells.	-do-	
178 Other Ranks.	-do-	

Two Lewis Guns were lost the remaining 4 were brought in during daylight under heavy fire, 2 of these by Privates who were the only men left of their teams.

The following Officers took part in the operations.

Lt. Col.	A.J.E.Sunderland.
Captain.	A.Tillett.
Captain.	J.A.Andrews.
Captain.	A.Preedy.
Captain.	E.G.Roberts.
2/Lieut.	C.O.R.Jacob.
2/Lieut.	L.A.Carey.
2/Lieut.	E.A.Jago.
2/Lieut.	G.Parker.
2/Lieut.	H.Acomb.
2/Lieut.	A.H.Smith.
2/Lieut.	A.H.Cornell.
2/Lieut.	M.C.Ley.
2/Lieut.	J.A.Rennie.
2/Lieut.	F.B.Coldwells.
2/Lieut.	A.R.Newton.
2/Lieut.	C.V.Beddow.
2/Lieut.	E.M.Gould.
2/Lieut.	F.B.Lloyd.
2/Lieut.	H.H.Goodman.
2/Lieut.	G.S.D.Carver.
2/Lieut.	J.S.McGowan.
2/Lieut.	G.W.Dibble.
2/Lieut.	A.E.A.Phillips. ATT. TO BRIGADE H.Q.

The undermentioned Officers were detailed to stay behind to replace Casualties:-

Major.	C.H.M.Imbert Terry D.S.O.
2/Lieut.	R.J.Andrews.
2/Lieut.	S.M.Neilson.
2/Lieut.	H.St Hill.
2/Lieut.	H.H.Jago.
2/Lieut.	J.H.Vincent.
2/Lieut.	H.W.Jones.

23rd Brigade.

8th Division.

2nd BATTALION DEVONSHIRE REGIMENT :: AUGUST 1916.

WAR DIARY

INTELLIGENCE SUMMARY.

(Erase heading not required.)

Army Form C. 2118.

Instructions regarding War Diaries and Intelligence Summaries are contained in F.S. Regs., Part II. and the Staff Manual respectively. Title pages will be prepared in manuscript.

Place	Date	Hour	Summary of Events and Information	Remarks and references to Appendices
	1/8/16.		In billets at ANNEQUIN. ROUTINE. Furnished R.E. Working parties. 2/Lieut. R.J. Andrews awarded the Military Cross for conspicuous gallantry CUINCHY on the 18th July, 1916. The enemy exploded a mine near No. 7 Sap completely filling in the sap and part of our front line trench. Lt. Andrews at once lead a party over the top and held the near lip of the crater. He succeeded in driving off the enemy and denying them the crater. He displayed quick grasp of the situation and great dash. No. 6588. C.S.M. Littlewood E. awarded the D.C.M. for conspicuous gallantry at CUINCHY, 18th July, 1916. When a mine exploded this W.O. was of great assistance to 2/Lieut. R.J. Andrews in organizing and leading the party which advanced to the lip of the crater. He showed great coolness and devotion to duty. No. 5456. R.S.M. King J.B. awarded the Military Cross for continuous devotion to duty and gallant conduct in the presence of the enemy from the commencement of the campaign in France to the 25th June, 1916. No. 6825. Sgt. E. Bowden, No. 8211. A/Sgt. E. Foster, No. 14206. L/Cpl. E. Budd. No. 14367. Pte. T. Pepperell, No. 15502. Pte. W. Sparkes, awarded the Military Medal for conspicuous gallantry and devotion to duty at CUINCHY on the 18th July, 1916. When a mine exploded these N.C.O's and men showed great courage and coolness in assisting in the capturing and holding of the crater which was denied the enemy.	
	2/8/16.		In billets at ANNEQUIN. ROUTINE. Furnished R.E. Working parties. 2/Lieut. L. Hollingsworth joined the Battalion on first appointment. During the afternoon the G.O.C. 1st Army inspected the 23rd Infantry Brigade near LA BOURSE. On the completion of the inspection he presented medal ribbons to 2/Lieut. R.J. Andrews, No. 5456. R.S.M. King J.B. No. 6588. C.S.M. Littlewood E. No. 8211. A/Sgt. Foster E. No. 14206. L/Cpl. E. Budd, No. 14367. Pte. Pepperell T. No. 15502. Pte. Sparkes W.	

Army Form C. 2118.

WAR DIARY
INTELLIGENCE SUMMARY.
(Erase heading not required.)

Instructions regarding War Diaries and Intelligence Summaries are contained in F. S. Regs., Part II and the Staff Manual respectively. Title pages will be prepared in manuscript.

Place	Date	Hour	Summary of Events and Information	Remarks and references to Appendices
	2/8/16. (Contd).		Before presenting the medal ribbons the G.O.C. addressed the Brigade congratulating the Battalion and the above Officer, W.O's, N.C.O's and men on their gallantry and devotion to duty. The Brigade then marched passed the G.O.C. in Column of Route and the G.O.C. granted those presented with medal ribbons the exceptional honour of standing by him as the Battalion marched past.	
	3/8/16.		In billets at ANNEQUIN. ROUTINE. Furnished R.E. Working parties. 2/Lieut. W.W. Drake joined the Battalion of first appointment.	
	4/8/16.		In billets. ROUTINE. Furnished R.E. Working parties. 2/Lieut. J.C. Patterson and 2/Lieut. W.M. Thomson joined the Battalion for the first time. Received a draft of 158 other ranks.	
	5/8/16.		The Battalion moved into Billets in FOUQUIERES.	
	6/8/16.		In billets at FOUQUIERES. ROUTINE.	
	7/8/16.		The Battalion relieved the 1/Royal Irish Rifles in the Right Sub-Section. About an hour after the relief the Brigade Major informed the Colonel that the enemy were reported to be working each night in FARMERS HOLE within 50 yards of one of our listening posts and that the Battalion must send out an offensive patrol under an officer to find out exactly what work was being carried out and that the 3" Stokes Mortars would co-operate. The C.O., Adjutant, and O.C. A and D Coys. went down to the line where the work was being carried out. It was found to be in D Coys. area and near the junction of A and D Coys.	

Army Form C. 2118.

WAR DIARY
or
INTELLIGENCE SUMMARY.
(Erase heading not required.)

Instructions regarding War Diaries and Intelligence Summaries are contained in F.S. Regs., Part II. and the Staff Manual respectively. Title pages will be prepared in manuscript.

Place	Date	Hour	Summary of Events and Information	Remarks and references to Appendices
	7/8/16. (Contd).		A raiding party was at once organized from D Coy, about 1.10 a.m. (8th) A patrol of 1 Officer and 18 other ranks examined this work and it was found to be an old disused trench on which no fresh work had been carried out. The party then crawled up to the enemy's lines and bombed one of his posts and returned without suffering any casualties. During the day our artillery and 60 lb trench mortars fired a few rounds. During the night the enemy was very quiet, but was very busy at work on his front line trenches, our Lewis Gun fire prevented him from mending his wire which he attempted to do.	
	8/8/16.		The Battalion was relieved in the trenches and moved into Brigade Reserve in Railway Reserve, Central Keep and Village Line, from Junction Keep inclusive to Gordon Alley. Casualties - 1 man wounded.	
	9/8/16.		In Reserve. Furnished Working parties. Enemy dropped a bomb from an aeroplane in the vicinity of Battalion H.Q. but did no damage. Casualties - 1 man killed and 2 wounded.	
	10/8/16.		In Reserve. Furnished Working parties. Casualties - 1 man wounded.	
	11/8/16.		The Battalion relieved the 2/Sco.Rifs. in the trenches from BOYAU 109 (exclusive) to MUD ALLEY (inclusive) A. B. & D Coys. in the front line and D Coy in Support in the Reserve Line. Our trench mortars and rifle grenade batteries were very active, doing a considerable amount of damage to his trench and causing his mortars to considerably moderate their activity. Our Lewis and Machine Gunners were also active, both sides sniped a great deal during the night. Patrols which were out inspecting our wire m	

T2134. Wt. W708—776. 500000. 4/15. Sir J. C. & S.

Army Form C. 2118.

WAR DIARY
INTELLIGENCE SUMMARY.
(Erase heading not required.)

Instructions regarding War Diaries and Intelligence Summaries are contained in F.S. Regs., Part II. and the Staff Manual respectively. Title pages will be prepared in manuscript.

Place	Date	Hour	Summary of Events and Information	Remarks and references to Appendices
	11/8/16. (Contd).		Patrols which were out inspecting our wire met none of the enemy. Casualties - 1 man killed and 2 accidentally wounded. Major H. de L. Sprye joined the Battalion for the first time.	
	12/8/16.		In the trenches. 2/Lieut. S.M. Neilson, 2/Lieut. S.G. Blake (15thGloucesters) 2/Lieut. L. Hollingsworth and 2/Lieut. J.C. Patterson left to join the 1st Battalion. Lieut. Archer took over command of "B" Coy. There was considerable trench mortar activity on both sides, our retaliation to the hostile mortar fire was very heavy. At 8.5 p.m. the enemy bombarded the right (B Coy) and the Battalion on our right (2/W. Yorks) with trench mortars and shells of all calibre, this was observed from Batt. H.Q. and the artillery who were communicated with, at once opened a heavy fire. At 9 p.m. the hostile bombardment ceased and a party of the enemy were seen advancing on our right. Lewis Gun fire and a heavy rifle fire was brought to bear on them and they swung off to the right and were not seen again. It was ascertained later that the enemy had raided the Batt. on our right and that 4 of the enemy had been taken prisoners. Our patrols which were out during the night met none of the enemy. 2/Lieut. J.C. Patterson was very slightly wounded (at duty) 4 other ranks wounded. 2/Lieut. C.W. Law was admitted to hospital "Sick".	
	13/8/16.		In the trenches. Field Guns and Trench Mortars were active on both sides. Our rifle grenade batteries were very active and carried out some very good work. Our bombers and snipers were particularly active and inflicted several casualties on the enemy. 2 parties of the enemy who were observed suffered heavy casualties from our rifle fire and bombs.	

Army Form C. 2118.

WAR DIARY

or

INTELLIGENCE SUMMARY.

(Erase heading not required.)

Instructions regarding War Diaries and Intelligence Summaries are contained in F.S. Regs., Part II. and the Staff Manual respectively. Title pages will be prepared in manuscript.

Place	Date	Hour	Summary of Events and Information	Remarks and references to Appendices
	13/8/16.		The bright moonlight prevented out patrols from going out. The enemy was noticed to be much quieter than usual. Casualties 1 other rank killed. 8 other ranks wounded. 2/Lieut. A.J.Snowden joined the Battalion on 1st appointment.	
	14/8/16.		In the trenches. Both sides were active with artillery and Trench Mortars the latter especially. The enemy trenches were knocked in in several places and he was prevented from repairing the damage owing to our Lewis Gun and Rifle fire. The enemy succeeded in knocking in one of our Communication Trenches and forced us to stop work on this part of the line for some time. The enemy made several attempts to mend his wire but ######## on every attempt he met with failure and suffered several casualties. Later the enemy tried to put wire out by means of long rods. Our snipers were active and met with considerable success, accounting for several of the enemy. Casualties. 2/Lieut. W.H.L.Vesey Fitzgerald killed (rifle fire) 2/Lieut H.Acomb (11th Yorks Regt) very slightly wounded (at duty) 1 man killed and 3 other ranks wounded, 2/Lieut. H.T.Marshall joined Battalion on 1st appointment.	
	15/8/16.		Relieved in the trenches by the 2/Scottish Rifles and moved into Bde. Reserve occupying the same trenches and posts as before. Furnished Working Parties. Casualties. 1 man killed, 8 other ranks wounded. Captain F.W.L.Bissett D.C.L.I. reported for attatchment to the Battalion.	
	16/8/16.		In reserve. 2 Officers and 125 other Ranks proceeded to SAILLY LABOURSE to be attached to 180th Tunnelling Coy R.E. for Spoils Party. Names of Officers, 2/Lieut. E.D.Hill and 2/Lieut. A.W.Harrison. Furnished Working Parties. Casualties 1 Other Rank wounded.	

Army Form C. 2118.

WAR DIARY
of
INTELLIGENCE SUMMARY.
(Erase heading not required.)

Instructions regarding War Diaries and Intelligence
Summaries are contained in F. S. Regs., Part II.
and the Staff Manual respectively. Title pages
will be prepared in manuscript.

Place	Date	Hour	Summary of Events and Information	Remarks and references to Appendices
	17/8/16.		In reserve. Furnished Working Parties. 2/Lieut. A.E.Rutledge and 2/Lieut C.H.S.Buckley granted leave to the United Kingdom from 18th to 24th August. Casualties. 3 other ranks wounded.	
	18/8/16.		In Reserve. Furnished Working Party. 2/Lieut. W.C.Jacks attached to 33rd Battery R.F.A. until 6 p.m. 19th inst as Liason Officer. Casualties. 1 other rank wounded.	
	19/8/16.		2/Lieut. G. Thuillier rejoined from 8th Divisional School of Instruction. Relieved the 2/Sco. Rifs. in the trenches from BOYAU 109(exclusive) to MUD ALLEY (inclusive). B. A. and C. Coys. in the front line and D Coy in Support in Reserve Trench. Our artillery was very active on hostile front at G. 4.2. and G.4.3. Retaliation was very weak. Throughout the night we sent over salvoes of rifle grenades and many Stokes Mortars. Hostile retaliation was very weak, except at G.4.5. where he replied with 8 Canisters and several Trench Mortars breaching the parapet in front line. Our snipers and bombers were very active. A patrol examined MUD CRATERS at BOYAU 116 and found them unoccupied. Enemy wire was inspected and found to be strong. We dispersed hostile working party at G. 4. b.7.3½. A connecting trench was dug between Saps No. 4 and 5 at G.4.a.5.5½.	
	20/8/16.		In the trenches. 2/Lieut. W.W.Drake, C Coy. attached to O Battery as Liason Officer for 24 hours. Throughout the day our artillery and Stokes Mortars were active upon enemy lines, but in the majority of cases met with no retaliation.	

Army Form C. 2118.

WAR DIARY
or
INTELLIGENCE SUMMARY.
(Erase heading not required.)

Place	Date	Hour	Summary of Events and Information	Remarks and references to Appendices
	20/8/16. (Contd).		We fired numerous rifle grenades and Mills' bombs, but the enemy made practically no reply. At 5 p.m. our Stokes Mortars in conjunction with those of Battalion on our left bombarded hostile lines. On this occasion enemy replied with Rum Jars, Trench Mortar Shells, Aerial Darts and Rifle Grenades, damaging our front line at G.4.4. and G.4.5. rather badly. During the night enemy fired a number of Rum Jars, accompanied at the same time with Aerial Darts into NORTHAMPTON TRENCH at BOYAU 114 and 116. Patrol examined MUD CRATERS, but none of the enemy were seen. Listening posts in gallery at G.4.4. report sounds of digging and same has been reported to Mining Officer. Casualties - 1 Other rank killed and 2 other ranks wounded.	
	21/8/16.		In the Trenches. Draft of 29 other ranks taken on strength. Morning very quiet. At 2.30 p.m. hostile bombardment of our front line with "Minenwerfers" and Trench Mortars doing some damage. Our Stokes and Medium Trench Mortars replied effectively, with artillery co-operation. At 4 p.m. we bombarded hostile trenches with Stokes and Medium Trench Mortars and rifle grenades. Enemy retaliated at 6.30 p.m. with minenwerfers, doing little damage. At 7 p.m. a hostile Mine was blown in existing Craters at G.2.a.4½.7. immediately in front of New Trench which joins Saps Nos. 3. and 4. None of our trenches were blown up and with the exception of filling up the New Trench and the adjoining Sap No. 3. thereby burying several men, no material damage was done and the conformation of front line trenches and Saps were not altered. The clearing of trenches began immediately after the explosion and several men, although buried were got out alive. All spare men of Reserve (D) Coy. with our own pioneers were immediately put upon the work.	

Army Form C. 2118.

WAR DIARY
or
INTELLIGENCE SUMMARY.
(Erase heading not required.)

Instructions regarding War Diaries and Intelligence Summaries are contained in F.S. Regs., Part II. and the Staff Manual respectively. Title pages will be prepared in manuscript.

Place	Date	Hour	Summary of Events and Information	Remarks and references to Appendices
	21/8/16. (Contd).		A party of 20 of the West Yorkshire Regiment also worked on the Clearing trenches was practically completed and with the aid of 1 Platoon from Reserve Coy. to replace casualties, all trenches and saps were garrisoned as before the explosion. Saps Nos. 1 and 2 and Lewis Gun (Right position) G.4.2. and Saps 3 and 4 and Lewis Gun (Left position) G.4.3. are all in use and intact. Immediately after the explosion the enemy bombarded the centre of Left Coys. (G.4.4. and G.4.5.) with Minenwerfers, Trench Mortars and Aerial Darts for 15 minutes and considerable damage was done to our trenches. It was observed that there was no hostile bombardment of the area effected by the Mine explosion. The enemy must have damaged his own trenches when the mine was blown as there was absolutely no action taken afterwards in this immediate section G.4.3., and although our men were forced to walk about in full view of the enemy not a single shot was fired over. Later the enemy was seen to be throwing earth over his parapet opposite this point. 2/Lieut. H. Acomb killed. 9 Other ranks killed. 16 O.R. wounded.	
	22/8/16.		In the Trenches. Our trench mortars were very active and our field artillery shelled intermittently during the day. During the night our heavy and light artillery carried out a pre-arranged shoot. During the afternoon the hostile trench mortars were active for 1 hour doing considerable damage to the centre Coy. (C Coy) trenches. We retaliated vigorously with trench mortars and field guns. During the night a large number of rifle grenades and bombs were thrown into the hostile trenches. Our snipers were active all day. It was noticed that the enemy was very quiet at night. Our patrols which were out at night met none of the enemy.	

Army Form C. 2118.

WAR DIARY
or
INTELLIGENCE SUMMARY.
(Erase heading not required.)

Instructions regarding War Diaries and Intelligence Summaries are contained in F.S. Regs., Part II. and the Staff Manual respectively. Title pages will be prepared in manuscript.

Place	Date	Hour	Summary of Events and Information	Remarks and references to Appendices
	22/8/16. (Contd).		2/Lieut. A.B.Kitson, 2/Lieut. H.F.Boyse and 2/Lieut. R.S.Holmes joined the Battalion for the first time. Casualties – 4 Other ranks wounded.	
	23/8/16.		The enemy were very quiet during the day. We fired the usual number of trench mortars and rifle grenades. During the afternoon the Batt. was relieved in the trenches and moved into Divisional Reserve billets in SAILLY LA BOURSE. 2/Lieut. T.L.Lewis and 2/Lieut. H.J.Skardon joined the Battalion for the first time. 2/Lieut. H.T.Marshall and 28 other ranks proceeded to 23rd Infantry Brigade Bomb School to undergo a course of Bombing. 2/Lieut. A.E.A.Phillips proceeded on a Sniping Course. 2/Lieut, H.H.Jago and 2/Lieut. T.H.Trinman and 5 N.C.O's proceeded on a course of Physical Training.	
	24/8/16.		In Billets. ROUTINE. Furnishing R.E. Working parties. 2/Lieut.A.C.Faulkener joined the Battalion for the first time. 2/Lieut.G.Thuillier and 8 other ranks proceeded on a course of Raiding. 1st Day of the Divisional Horse Show, the Battalion won the following prizes:– 1st & 3rd Prizes. Light Draught Pairs. 1st Prize. Chargers (Dismounted Units).	
	25/8/16.		In Billets. ROUTINE. Furnished R.E. Working parties. 2nd Day of Divisional Horse Show, the Battalion won the following prizes:– 1st Prize. Heavy Draught. Championship Class.	

T2134. Wt. W708—776. 500000. 4/15. Sir J. C. & S.

Army Form C. 2118.

WAR DIARY

Instructions regarding War Diaries and Intelligence Summaries are contained in F. S. Regs., Part II. and the Staff Manual respectively. Title pages will be prepared in manuscript.

INTELLIGENCE SUMMARY.
(Erase heading not required.)

Place	Date	Hour	Summary of Events and Information	Remarks and references to Appendices
	25/8/16. (Contd).		1st Prize, Best Light Draught Horse. Casualties. 5 Other ranks wounded. 1 Other rank killed, on Spoils Party.	
	26/8/16.		In Billets. ROUTINE. Furnished R.E. Working parties. Capt. G.L.Jones, R.A.M.C. proceeded on 7 days Special Leave. The undermentioned Officers promoted Temporary Captains whilst in charge of a company. Lieut. H. Archer. 7/7/16. 2/Lieut. A.H. Smith. 1/8/16. 2/Lieut. R.J. Andrews. 2/8/16. 2/Lieut. J.H. Vincent. 2/8/16.	
	27/8/16.		In Billets. ROUTINE. Furnished Working parties. 2 Signallers, No. 2. Squadron R.F.C. for practice in co-operation with aeroplanes. During the morning there was a Brigade Divine Service on the completion of which the Corps Commander presented medal ribbons to Officers and men of the Brigade who had not previously been presented with them. Included amongst these No. 8827. Sgt.C.Lock, No. 9917. Pte.G.Costello and No. 6759. Pte.P.Parker, who received the Military Medal Ribbon. 1 Other rank proceeded on an Anti-Gas Course. One man wounded on Spoils Party.	
	28/8/16.		In Billets. ROUTINE. Furnished Working parties. 2/Lieut. G.Hosegood and 4 other ranks proceeded on Sniping Course.	

Army Form C. 2118.

WAR DIARY

INTELLIGENCE SUMMARY.

(Erase heading not required.)

Instructions regarding War Diaries and Intelligence
Summaries are contained in F.S. Regs., Part II.
and the Staff Manual respectively. Title pages
will be prepared in manuscript.

Place	Date	Hour	Summary of Events and Information	Remarks and references to Appendices
	29/8/16.		In Billets. 2/Lieut. A.J. Snowden and 2 other ranks proceeded on course of Lewis Gun. ROUTINE. Furnished Working parties. 2/Lieut. E.C. Jacks, proceeded to 23rd Infantry Brigade Trench Mortar Battery for duty.	
	30/8/16.		In Billets. ROUTINE. Furnished Working parties. 7 Other ranks proceeded to 253rd Tunnelling Company to be permanently attached, but not struck off strength of Battalion.	
	31/8/16.		In Billets. ROUTINE. Furnished Working parties. 7 Other ranks proceeded to 23rd Infantry Brigade Bomb School to undergo a course of Bombing. 2 Other ranks proceeded to 1st Army School of Mortars to undergo a course of Instruction in Trench Mortars.	

[signature]
Lieut. Colonel.
Commanding 2nd Battalion Devonshire Regiment.

23rd Brigade.

8th Division.

2nd BATTALION DEVONSHIRE REGIMENT :: SEPTEMBER 1916

WAR DIARY
or
INTELLIGENCE SUMMARY
(Erase heading not required.)

2nd Battalion Devonshire Regiment.

Place	Date	Hour	Summary of Events and Information	Remarks and references to Appendices
	1/9/16.		The Battalion relieved the 2nd Royal Berkshire Regiment in the Reserve Trenches, QUARRIES SECTION. 5.30 p.m. Furnished Working Parties.	
	2/9/16.		In RESERVE. (BRIGADE). Considerable amount of work done in improving Reserve Trenches and Battalion Headquarters.	
	3/9/16.		In BRIGADE RESERVE. 2/Lieut. C.Law, "A" Coy. having embarked for England (sick) struck off strength from 24/8/16. 1st Corps Commander awarded Military Medals for Acts of Gallantry and Devotion to Duty to :- No 7193 Pte W.Raymont "B" Coy. No 16442 Pte D.J.B.Rees "B" Coy. No 9438 Pte J.Woolacott "B" Coy. No 11785 Pte A.G.Dickson "A" Coy. 138 other ranks transferred to the Battalion from 1/7th Cyclists Batt. Devon Regt. 2 other ranks rejoined from Base.	
	4/9/16.		In BRIGADE RESERVE. 11 other ranks qualified as trained Bombers. 3 other ranks evacuated (sick) and struck off strength.	
	5/9/16.		Battalion relieved the 2nd Scottish Rifles in the trenches from BOYAU 94 (exclusive) to BOYAU 100a inclusive of HULLUCH ALLEY. "B" Coy. Right Coy. "C" Coy. Left Coy. "D" Coy. Centre Coy. "A" Coy. Support Coy. 2/Lieut. Snowden and 2 other ranks rejoined from Course of Lewis Gun Instruction. Our Artillery fairly active. Stokes and Heavy T.M. very busy and did good work.	

WAR DIARY or INTELLIGENCE SUMMARY

(Erase heading not required.)

Army Form C. 2118

2nd Battalion Devonshire Regiment.

Place	Date	Hour	Summary of Events and Information	Remarks and references to Appendices
	5/9/16. (Contd).		Enemy retaliation on NORTHERN CRATER did no damage. Two of our patrols were out during the night with the object of capturing a prisoner, but none of the enemy were seen. Several bodies were found out in "No Man's Land" having been there for some months. Pocket books and shoulder straps brought in identifying them as ROYAL SCOTS. CASUALTIES:- 1 O.R. Killed. 1 O.R. Wounded.	
	6/9/16.		In the TRENCHES. Lieut. Palmer proceeded to BOULOGNE for dental treatment. 2/Lieut. H. St. Hill acting Quartermaster. 2/Lieut. A.B.Kitson attached to 32nd Battery R.F.A. for 24 hours as Liason Officer. 2 Other Ranks transferred to Machine Gun Coy. During the night our Artillery was very active shelling hostile front system. Stokes and 60 lbs. T.M. also very active. Enemy retaliated with several Minenwerfers, which did no damage. 3 Officers patrols went out during the night, but none of the enemy were encountered. CASUALTIES:- 1 O.R. Wounded.	
	7/9/16.		In the TRENCHES. 2/Lieut. W.M.Thomson and 1 O.R. rejoined from 8th Divisional School. Our Artillery was fairly active during the day and enemy replied with a few Minenwerfers, doing little damage. Our Stokes and 60 lbs. T.M. very active, receiving practically no reply. We sent several patrols during the night with a view of capturing a "Bosch", but none of the enemy were encountered. CASUALTIES:- 1 O.R. Killed. 2 O.R. Wounded.	

Army Form C. 2118.

WAR DIARY
or
INTELLIGENCE SUMMARY.
(Erase heading not required.)

Instructions regarding War Diaries and Intelligence Summaries are contained in F.S. Regs., Part II. and the Staff Manual respectively. Title pages will be prepared in manuscript.

Place	Date	Hour	Summary of Events and Information	Remarks and references to Appendices
			2nd Battalion Devonshire Regiment.	
	8/9/16.		In the TRENCHES. Our Artillery was fairly active firing in rear of HAIR PIN CRATERS but a large proportion of the shells were blind. They appeared to be 4.5 Hows. and a good many of them fell in "No Man's Land". The enemy was also active with his Artillery and Minenwerfers and did a considerable amount of damage to ourtrenches, especially in HIGHLAND TRENCH and ST. ELIE TRENCH. Our Lewis guns dispersed several hostile working parties during the night. Considerable amount of transport was heard in rear of hostile lines during the night. CASUALTIES:- 1 O.R. Killed. 1 O.R. Wounded.	
	9/9/16.		In the TRENCHES. The enemy was fairly active with his Minenwerfer, doing considerable damage again to HIGHLAND TRENCH in his attempt to find our T.M. positions. Our Stokes were very active and caused a great amount of damage to enemy trenches. This he attempted several times during the night to repair, but was prevented from so doing by our Lewis guns. CASUALTIES. 1 O.R. Killed. 2 O.R. Wounded.	
	10/9/16.		In the TRENCHES. 2/Lieut. C.H.Buckley "B" Coy. proceeded to 8th Divisional School of Instruction. Hostile Artillery very active. During the morning he bombarded G.11.5. with Minenwerfers and T.Ms. Completely filling in HIGHLAND TRENCH for 30 yards. Our Artillery retaliated and our Stokes Mortars continued to do good work. Our snipers accounted for 4 of the enemy. We sent several patrols out during the night, but none of the enemy were met. One of these patrols under 2/Lieut.G.Hosegood was unfortunately observed by the enemy, this Officer after getting right up to the enemy saps, was killed by machine gun fire. CASUALTIES:- 1 Offr. Killed. 1 O.R. Wounded.	

T2134. Wt. W708—776. 500000. 4/15. Sir J. C. & S.

Army Form C. 2118.

WAR DIARY
or
INTELLIGENCE SUMMARY.
(Erase heading not required.)

Instructions regarding War Diaries and Intelligence Summaries are contained in F. S. Regs., Part II. and the Staff Manual respectively. Title pages will be prepared in manuscript.

Place	Date	Hour	Summary of Events and Information	Remarks and references to Appendices
	11/9/16.		**2nd Battalion Devonshire Regiment.** In the TRENCHES. Our Stokes and 60 lbs. T.M. have been very active and are causing the enemy considerable annoyance, having damaged his wire and front trench badly. The enemy retaliated with several Minenwerfers and heavy T.Ms. again filling in HIGHLAND TRENCH in two places. He commenced to enfilade our front trenches with 77 mm. firing from the direction of ST. ELIE. During the night he attempted to repair his wire and trenches, but was prevented by our Lewis gun fire. Hostile sniping appears to have ceased. CASUALTIES:- Nil.	
	12/9/16.		In the TRENCHES. Our Artillery has not been very active, but the Stokes and 60 lbs. continue to do some good shooting. We have been very aggressive with our rifle grenades and our snipers have done good work penetrating all known hostile loopholes. Enemy sniping seems to have ceased on this front. The enemy again enfiladed our lines with 77 mm. from ST. ELIE, but did very little damage. CASUALTIES:- 5 O.R. Wounded.	
	13/9/1916.		In the TRENCHES. 2/Lieut. A. Winch "A" Coy. 2/Lieut. C.B. Rodd "B" Coy. 2/Lieut. E.L. Walters "C" Coy. 2/Lieut. L.N.L. Tindal "C" Coy. joined the Battalion and taken on strength. Our Artillery has been very inactive, firing only about a dozen 18 lb. shells. Nearly all of which were blind. Our Stokes and 2" Mortars continue to be very active, but hostile retaliation with Minenwerfer has been heavy. Our snipers appear to have completely subdued hostile sniping.	

Army Form C. 2118.

WAR DIARY
or
INTELLIGENCE SUMMARY.
(Erase heading not required.)

Place	Date	Hour	Summary of Events and Information	Remarks and references to Appendices
			2nd Battalion Devonshire Regiment.	
	13/9/16. (Contd).		The enemy retaliated to our Stokes Mortars by again shelling HIGHLAND TRENCH with his Minenwerfer, blocking up "B" Coys. Headquarters and damaging the trench considerably. The enemy was repeatedly prevented from repairing his trenches during the night by our rifle grenades. The night was too light to send out patrols. CASUALTIES:- 1 O.R. Killed. 2 O.R. Wounded.	
	14/9/16.		In the TRENCHES. A Draft of 4 Other Ranks joined the Battalion and taken on strength. Our Heavy Artillery shelled the Minenwerfer emplacements in the hostile JAEGER TRENCH apparently with good effect. Enemy has not fired from it since. We continue to be aggressive with our Stokes Mortars and rifle grenades, receiving little retaliation. The enemy fired a good number of 16ᵗʰ T.Ms. which were nearly all blind, several good specimens being obtained. Two of our patrols were out, but owing to the brilliant moon were forced to come in early. CASUALTIES:- 1 O.R. Wounded.	
	15/9/16.		In the TRENCHES. Our Artillery continues to be inactive. Our Stokes and 60 lb. T.Ms. have been very busy and much good shooting has been done. We also fired many salvoes from our rifle grenade batteries, receiving practically no reply. The enemy fired 6 minenwerfers from JAEGER TRENCH, but generally he has been very quiet.	

Army Form C. 2118.

WAR DIARY
or
INTELLIGENCE SUMMARY.
(Erase heading not required.)

Instructions regarding War Diaries and Intelligence Summaries are contained in F.S. Regs., Part II. and the Staff Manual respectively. Title pages will be prepared in manuscript.

Place	Date	Hour	Summary of Events and Information	Remarks and references to Appendices
			2nd Battalion Devonshire Regiment.	
	15/9/16. (Contd).		A hostile patrol was observed moving in the direction of SAP 98a and was immediately dispersed by our Lewis gun fire. Several small bodies of the enemy have been observed moving in the direction of their front line. A cyclist orderly was also seen and it is thought that a relief has taken place. CASUALTIES:- 1 O.R. Killed.	
	16/9/16.		In the TRENCHES. Temp. 2/Lieut. J.H.Vincent relinquishes the Temporary rank of Captain on ceasing to Command a Company. Our Artillery still very inactive. The Stokes and 60 lbs. T.Ms. have been causing the enemy great annoyance and our rifle grenade batteries also have been busy. The enemy still continues to fire Minenwerfer from JAEGER TRENCH, doing a fair amount of damage to HIGHLAND TRENCH. In retaliation for our Stokes the enemy fired a good number of trench mortars into CAMPBELL CUT, a large number of which were blind. Hostile sniping has ceased. Two of the enemy were accounted for by our snipers. At 2.30 p.m. the enemy fired a Camouflet opposite G.11.1. No damage was caused to our front line, but the entrance of a mining gallery at junction of BOYAU 93 and 94 was shaken in. Capt. A.H.Smith rejoined from Hospital and resumed Command of "C" Coy. CASUALTIES:- 2 O.R. Killed. 4 O.R. Wounded.	
	17/9/16.		In the TRENCHES in the morning. Our Artillery still inactive. Our Stokes and 2" Mortars bombarded hostile lines intermittently. Our snipers accounted for 2 of the enemy during the morning. The enemy still continues firing his Minenwerfer from JAEGER TRENCH to HIGHLAND TRENCH and he is beginning to retaliate more with rifle grenades.	

WAR DIARY
or
INTELLIGENCE SUMMARY.

(Erase heading not required.)

Army Form C. 2118.

2nd Battalion Devonshire Regiment.

Place	Date	Hour	Summary of Events and Information	Remarks and references to Appendices
	17/9/16. (Contd)		At 2.30 p.m. the Battalion was relieved in the trenches by the 1st Sherwood Foresters and we moved into billets at FOUQUIERES, being in Divisional Reserve. The Commanding Officer, Lieut-Col. A.J.E. Sunderland, proceeded to Brigade Headquarters, taking over Temporary Command vice Brig.Gen. Fagan on leave. Capt. A. Tillett proceeded on leave until the 25th inst. Capt. A.H.Smith, 2/Lieut. T.R.Johns, 2/Lieut. E.L.Walters and 45 other ranks proceeded to 8th Divisional School to practise as a Raiding Party. During this last period of 12 days in the trenches a very large amount of good work and many improvements have been made in the trenches by the Battalion; especially at Battalion Headquarters where several excellent dugouts were built and the trenches strengthened and improved. It was afterwards appropriately named EXETER CASTLE. CASUALTIES :- 5 O.R. Wounded.	
	18/9/16.		In Billets at FOUQUIERES. Very wet day. Battalion attended a FLAMENWERFER Demonstration in the morning at VERQUIN. Furnished Working Parties. A Draft of 6 other ranks arrived from the Base and taken on strength. 2/Lieut. A.W.Harrison and 53 O.R. rejoined the Battalion from Spoils Party.	
	19/9/16.		In Billets at FOUQUIERES. Furnished Working Parties. 2/Lieut. T.M.Lewis "C" Coy transferred to "D" Coy. 2/Lieut. C.W.C.Hannah and 1 O.R. rejoined from 1st Army School. 7 other ranks rejoined from Bombing School.	

WAR DIARY
or
INTELLIGENCE SUMMARY.
(Erase heading not required.)

Army Form C. 2118.

Place	Date	Hour	Summary of Events and Information	Remarks and references to Appendices
			2nd Battalion Devonshire Regiment.	
	20/9/16.		In Billets at FOUQUIERES. Furnished Working Parties. 2/Lieut. A.B.Kitson granted 5 days Leave to ROUEN. Received orders late in the night that the Battalion would relieve the 4th Royal Fusiliers in Brigade Reserve at PHILOSOPHE to-morrow morning.	
	21/9/16.		The Battalion relieved the 4th Royal Fusiliers in the Brigade Reserve of the HULLUCH Section at Midday. 2/Lieut. H.F.Boyce and 1 other rank rejoined from Anti-Gas Course. 6 other ranks rejoined from Spoils Party.	
	22/9/16.		In BRIGADE RESERVE, PHILOSOPHE. Furnished Working Parties. Lieut. Col. A.J.E. Sunderland returned from Brigade and resumed Command of the Battalion.	
	23/9/16.		In BRIGADE RESERVE, PHILOSOPHE. Furnished Working Parties.	
	24/9/16.		In BRIGADE RESERVE, PHILOSOPHE. Furnished Working Parties.	
	25/9/16.		In BRIGADE RESERVE. Furnished Working Parties. Lieut. A.C.G. Roberts, Transport Officer, proceeded on Leave until 3rd October, 1916. In the evening the Battalion relieved the 2nd Scottish Rifles in the trenches from ESSEX LANE exclusive to BOYAU 77 and WINGS WAY both inclusive A very quiet night.	

Army Form C. 2118.

WAR DIARY
or
INTELLIGENCE SUMMARY.
(Erase heading not required.)

Instructions regarding War Diaries and Intelligence
Summaries are contained in F. S. Regs., Part II.
and the Staff Manual respectively. Title pages
will be prepared in manuscript.

Place	Date	Hour	Summary of Events and Information	Remarks and references to Appendices
			2nd Battalion Devonshire Regiment.	
	26/9/16.		In the TRENCHES. Throughout the night and early morning the enemy were very quiet until 7 a.m. when he bombarded our front line and saps from BOYAU 70 to 72a with Minenwerfer and heavy trench mortars, doing a good deal of damage. In spite of retaliation by our Artillery the hostile shelling did not cease until 9.15 a.m. Our retaliation did not apparently trouble the enemy and most of our shells were blind. Considerable movement of transport was heard during the night in rear of hostile lines. CASUALTIES:- 1 O.R. Wounded.	
	27/9/16.		In the TRENCHES. Our Artillery generally inactive. Our Stokes and 60 lbs. T.Ms. at intervals shelled the hostile front system and caused him considerable annoyance and he retaliated with Minenwerfer and 77 mm. doing little damage, however. An Officers patrol went out during the night, but none of the enemy were encountered. A Draft of 44 O.R. arrived from the Base and taken on strength. CASUALTIES:- Nil.	
	28/9/16.		In the TRENCHES. A quiet morning. In response to Minenwerfer and T.M. fire, our Artillery fired several rounds at 3.45 p.m. Our Stokes shelled enemy front line and saps with apparent good effect and he retaliated with T.Ms. doing no damage. Hostile working parties were dispersed by our Lewis gun fire during the night.	

Army Form C. 2118.

WAR DIARY
or
INTELLIGENCE SUMMARY.
(Erase heading not required.)

Instructions regarding War Diaries and Intelligence Summaries are contained in F. S. Regs., Part II. and the Staff Manual respectively. Title pages will be prepared in manuscript.

Place	Date	Hour	Summary of Events and Information	Remarks and references to Appendices
			2nd Battalion Devonshire Regiment.	
	28/9/16. (Contd)		In spite of our Artillery fire the enemy still continues to use his Minenwerfer emplacement at H.13.c.7.9. A large amount of work was done to front line during the night to permit of a daylight relief with Scottish Rifles. CASUALTIES:- 2/Lieut. C.W.C. Hannah killed.	
	29/9/16.		In the TRENCHES. Morning very quiet. At 3 p.m. the Battalion was relieved in the trenches by the 2nd Scottish Rifles and moved into Brigade Reserve. Billets in PHILOSOPHE. "C" Coy proceeded to GOSNAY for Special Training. A Draft of 45 other ranks joined the Battalion and taken on strength.	
	30/9/16.		In BRIGADE RESERVE. ROUTINE:- Furnished Working Parties. Commanding Officer inspected new Draft. 2/Lieut. A.C.Faulkner and 2 other ranks rejoined from Lewis Gun Course.	

[signature]
Lieut. Colonel.
Commanding 2nd Battalion Devonshire Regiment.

23rd Brigade.

8th Division.

2nd BATTALION DEVONSHIRE REGIMENT :: OCTOBER 1916.

WAR DIARY
or
INTELLIGENCE SUMMARY

(Erase heading not required.)

Army Form. C. 2118

2nd Battalion Devonshire Regiment.

Place	Date	Hour	Summary of Events and Information	Remarks and references to Appendices
	1/10/16.		In Brigade Reserve Billets at PHILOSOPHE. ROUTINE. Furnished R.E. Working Parties. The C.O. and Adjutant rode to GOSNEY to inspect "C" Coy training for raid.	
	2/10/16.		In BILLETS. ROUTINE. Furnished Working Parties. The Brigadier, C.O. and Adjutant motored to GOSNEY at night to inspect "C" practising a raid.	
	3/10/16.		The Battalion relieved the 2/Scottish Rifles in the trenches & during the afternoon. Our Artillery, trench mortars, Lewis and machine guns fired according to programme doing considerable damage to hostile wire and trenches. The enemy were very quiet and replied very feebly to our bombardments and wire cutting. One chance 77 mm. shell killed 2/Lieut. F.B. Lloyd and wounded 2/Lieut. R.A. Wykes and A.J. Snowden. 2/Lieut. A, E.A. Phillips took over Command of "D" Coy.	
	4/10/16.		In the TRENCHES. We continued our bombardments and wire cutting. The enemy was again very quiet. 2 O.R. accidently wounded in a bomb store.	
	5/10/16.		In the TRENCHES. We attempted a raid on hostile trenches, preceded by a gas attack on the night of the 5/6th. (See report).	

Army Form. C. 2118

WAR DIARY
or
INTELLIGENCE SUMMARY
(Erase heading not required.)

2nd Battalion Devonshire Regiment.

Place	Date	Hour	Summary of Events and Information	Remarks and references to Appendices
	5/10/16. (Contd).		Casualties: Capt. A.H.Smith killed. 12 O.R. killed. 3 O.R. Died of Wounds. 21 O.R. wounded during 5/6th. During the day the hostile artillery was not very active, most of his fire was directed on the front and support lines.	
	6/10/16.		Our trench mortars fired at intervals during the day, good shooting was observed. The enemy fired a few 77 mm. shells, but was otherwise very quiet. 4 of our men went out in broad daylight and brought in 2 of our wounded from near the hostile trenches.	
	7/10/16.		The Battalion was relieved in the trenches during the afternoon and moved into Brigade Support Trenches in German Switch and 10th Avenue. Furnished Working Parties. 2/Lieut. H.T. Marshall rejoined from Hospital.	
	8/10/16.		In BRIGADE SUPPORT. The C.O. proceeded on Leave to England. Major H.F. Hardman, Somerset Light Infantry, joined the Battalion and remained at Transport Lines for the night. Furnished Working Parties.	
	9/10/16.		In SUPPORT. Furnished Working Parties.	
	10/10/16.		In SUPPORT. Furnished Working Parties. 2/Lieut. H. St Hill struck off strength, having embarked for England "sick" on the 1st inst. A draft of 6 O.R. joined and posted to "C" Coy.	
	11/10/16.		In SUPPORT. Furnished Working Parties.	

Army Form. C. 2118

WAR DIARY
or
INTELLIGENCE SUMMARY

(Erase heading not required.)

Instructions regarding War Diaries and Intelligence Summaries are contained in F. S. Regs., Part II. and the Staff Manual respectively. Title Pages will be prepared in manuscript.

Place	Date	Hour	Summary of Events and Information	Remarks and references to Appendices
			2nd Battalion Devonshire Regiment.	
	12/10/16.		The Battalion was relieved in the Support Trenches by the 14th Bn. Argyle and Sutherland Highlanders during the morning, and marched to HOUCHIN CAMP. 2/Lieut. A.E.A.Phillips granted leave to U.K. until 20th instant.	
	13/10/16.		In CAMP. The Battalion marched to LAPUGNOY and spent the night in billets. Capt. R.J.Andrews proceeded to England on duty and struck off strength.	
	14/10/16.		The Battalion marched to CHOCQUES and entrained for PONT-REMY arriving there during the evening. From PONT-REMY the Battalion marched to HUPPY and moved into Billets at midnight.	
	15/10/16.		In Billets at HUPPY. Church Parade. The Battalion was inspected by the O.C. Major H.F.Hardman.	
	16/10/16.		In billets at HUPPY. Information having been received that the Battalion would probably move this day, the programme of work was cancelled and everyone stood by ready to move in the afternoon. We did not however move until following morning.	
	17/10/16.		The Battalion formed up at 3 a.m. and marched to SOREL, where motor lorries were waiting and conveyed us to VILLE. From VILLE the Battalion marched to MEAULTE and moved into billets.	
	18/10/16.		In billets at MEAULTE. Furnished R.E. Working Parties. ROUTINE. Very wet day.	

Army Form. C. 2118

WAR DIARY
or
INTELLIGENCE SUMMARY
(Erase heading not required.)

Instructions regarding War Diaries and Intelligence Summaries are contained in F.S. Regs., Part II. and the Staff Manual respectively. Title Pages will be prepared in manuscript.

2nd Battalion Devonshire Regiment.

Place	Date	Hour	Summary of Events and Information	Remarks and references to Appendices
	19/10/16.		In Billets at MEAULTE. ROUTINE. Furnished R.E. Working Parties. Very wet day.	
	20/10/16.		The Battalion formed up add marched into "G" Camp at MONTAUBAN.	
	21/10/16.		In Camp at MONTAUBAN. Furnished Working Parties. Casualties: 3 O.R. wounded.	
	22/10/16.		In Camp at MONTAUBAN. Furnished Working Parties. Casualties: 1 O.R. wounded. Orders were received that the 8th Division and 4th Division on the Right would attack the German trenches in conjunction with an advance by the French Army on the 23rd October, 1916. The 1st Objective of the 23rd Infantry Brigade was as follows :- 1st Objective N.35.a.5.4½. to N.28.d.6.7. 2nd Objective N.35.a.9½.8. to N.28.d.9½.9. The attack was to be carried outby the 2nd Middlesex Regt. and 2nd Scottish Rifles, the 2nd West Yorks being in Support and the 2nd Devons in Reserve. The Battalion moved out of Camp at 12.15 a.m. on 23rd inst. and occupied the position of assembly in GAP TRENCH and PUNCH TRENCH. Lieut. Col. Sunderland who had been on leave returned about 12 noon on the 22nd and took over Command.	

WAR DIARY
or
INTELLIGENCE SUMMARY.

(Erase heading not required.)

Army Form C. 2118.

Place	Date	Hour	Summary of Events and Information	Remarks and references to Appendices
	22/10/16. contd.		**2nd Battalion Devonshire Regiment.**	
			The following Officers accompanied the Battalion into action.	
			Lieut. Col. A.J.E. Sunderhand. Commanding.	
			Temp. Capt. Lieut. A. Tillett. Adjutant.	
			do H. Archer.	
			2/Lieut. C.H.S. Buckley. O.C. "B" Coy.	
			2/Lieut. A.W. Winch. O.C. "C" Coy.	
			Major H. del. Sprye. O.C. "A" Coy.	
			2/Lieut. H.T. Marshall. O.C. "D" Coy.	
			2/Lieut. G.F. Thuillier.	
			2/Lieut. J.H. Vincent. 2/Lieut. C.B. Rodd.	
			2/Lieut. L.N.L. Tindal. 2/Lieut. E.L. Walters.	
			2/Lieut. W.M. Thomson. 2/Lieut. A.E. Rutledge.	
			2/Lieut. H.J. Skardon. 2/Lieut. H.H. Goodman.	
			2/Lieut. A.C. Faulkner. Capt. G.L. Jones. R.A.M.C.	
			2/Lieut. E.D. Hill was attached to 25th Brigade H.Q. as Liason Officer.	
			The following Officers remained at Transport Lines to replace Casualties.	
			Major H.F. Herdman (Som.L.I.). 2/Lieut. H.F. Boyce.	
			2/Lieut. A.B. Kitson. 2/Lieut. E.H. Jago.	
			2/Lieut. A.W. Harrison. 2/Lieut. W.W. Drake.	
			Lieut. A.C.xG. Roberts. Transport Officer.	
			Lieut. & Qr. Mr. G. Palmer.	
	23/10/16.		The morning of the 23rd broke with a thick fog which did not lift until about noon.	
			The C.O. went to Advanced Brigade H.Q. at 9 a.m. and returned about 11 a.m.	

WAR DIARY
or
INTELLIGENCE SUMMARY.
(Erase heading not required.)

Army Form C. 2118.

Place	Date	Hour	Summary of Events and Information	Remarks and references to Appendices
	23/10/16. (Contd).		**2nd Battalion Devonshire Regiment.**	
			In consequence of the fog the attack which should have taken place in the morning was put off until the afternoon. During the morning we furnished a carrying party which worked under cover of the fog. The Colonel returned to Advanced Brigade H.Q. after lunch. The attack was successfully carried out by the 23rd Infantry Brigade. The enemy did not fire any shells in the vicinity of the Battalion. The C.O. returned from Advanced Brigade H.Q. about 7 p.m. About 11 p.m. orders were received that the Battalion was to move at once to NEEDLE TRENCH and that Battalion H.Q. were to be established at the German Dump, which was Advanced Brigade H.Q. Some difficulty was found in getting the Battalion into this trench as the ground was wet and sodden and it was an extremely dark night. Casualties. 2 O.R. Wounded.	
	24/10/16.		When it was light a considerable number of wounded were discovered near H.Q. which it had been impossible to move further in owing to the state of the ground and lack of stretcher bearers. The Battalion assisted as far as possible in getting these men away. The Brigadier returned to Brigade H.Q. during the morning. The C.O. visited the trenches occupied by the 2/Middlesex Regt. during the morning and attended a conference later at Brigade H.Q. The Brigadier returned to Battalion H.Q. in the evening and remained there for the night. During the night 24/25th, "A" Coy was employed carrying wounded. "B" and "D" Coys carried stores from Brigade H.Q. to the Battalion H.Q. in the line during the night. Casualties. 4 O.R. Wounded.	

WAR DIARY
or
INTELLIGENCE SUMMARY.
(Erase heading not required.)

Army Form C. 2118.

Place	Date	Hour	Summary of Events and Information	Remarks and references to Appendices
			2nd Battalion Devonshire Regiment.	
	25/10/16.		During the morning orders were recived that as a result of the operations on the 23rd and early morning of the 24th October, the Division held ZENITH TRENCH from about N.34.b.9.5. to about N.28.d.5.5. and a line of shell craters running from the Northern end of ZENITH TRENCH (N.28.b.0.1½) to about MISTY TRENCH (N.28.a.6.4.). and that the portion of ZENITH TRENCH lying between N.28.d.5.5. and N.28.b.0.1½. however was still in the hands of the enemy.	
			This part of ZENITH TRENCH was to be taken by the 25th Brigade and that the 2/Devon Regt. had been placed at the disposal of the G.O.C. 25th Infy. Brigade to assist in this attack. The attack was to be carried out as soon as possible after the necessary arrangements had been made, as the weather offered a reasonable prospect of success.	
			The C.O. attended a conference at the H.Q. 25th Infantry Brigade.	
		6.30 p.m.	received orders to the effect that the Battalion was under the orders of the 23rd Infantry Brigade and that the Battalion was to be prepared to deliver a counter attack if required to do so, at a moment's notice.	
			Furnished carrying parties.	
			Major Sprye was admitted to Hospital.	
	26/10/16.		Orders were received that the Battalion was now under the orders of the 25th Infantry Brigade.	
			Furnished carrying parties.	
			C.O. attended Conference.	
	27/10/16.		The C.O. accompanied by the Adjutant, Coy Commanders and Coy St Majors visited the trenches the Battalion would occupy prior to the attack. It was found that owing to the bad condition of the trenches and the bad weather, also the fact that there were no Battalion H.Q. and that sufficient stores had not been taken down, the attack for the moment was not feasible.	

Army Form C. 2118.

WAR DIARY
or
INTELLIGENCE SUMMARY.
(Erase heading not required.)

Instructions regarding War Diaries and Intelligence Summaries are contained in F. S. Regs., Part II. and the Staff Manual respectively. Title pages will be prepared in manuscript.

Place	Date	Hour	Summary of Events and Information	Remarks and references to Appendices
			2nd Battalion Devonshire Regiment.	
	27/10/16. (Contd).		Furnished carrying parties. "C" Coy and 2 platoons of "B" Coy relieved the 2nd Royal Berkshire Regiment in LARKHILL and SPIDER TRENCHES during the night. These platoons came under fairly heavy shell fire during the relief (killed wou 2/Lieut. C.H.S. Buckley was wounded. 3 O.R. wounded and 5 O.R. wounded. 2/Lieut. E.L. Walters was admitted to Hospital sick. It was decided that the attack be carried out at 3 p.m. on the 29th October, 1916, and that the 1st Sherwood Foresters who were to take part in the attack would not do so, the whole attack to be carried out by the 2nd Devon Regt. The attack was to be carried out as follows:- "A" "D" and ½ "B" Coy were to attack the hostile trenches from the front; ½ "B" Coy under Capt. H. Archer posted on the left of the 23rd Infantry Brigade was to attack the enemy from the rear. "C" Coy was to be held in reserve. Battalion H.Q. to be established in the front line.	
	28/10/16.		Orders were received that the Battalion was to relieve the 1st Sherwood Foresters in the front line MISTY TRENCH, arrangements for relief to be made between O.C. Battalions concerned. The relief commenced at 9 p.m. Coys were ordered to occupy the trenches as follows:- Right Coy. "B". Centre "A". Left "D". "C" Coy in Support, in RAINBOW TRENCH. Casualties. 5 O.R. Wounded.	
	29/10/16.		Owing to the Guides supplied by the 1st Sherwood Foresters not being able to lead the Coys into the positions they were to occupy it was discovered that "D" Coy "C" Coy 2 platoons of "B" Coy and 2 platoons of "A" Coy only were in position at 4.50 a.m. 29th and that all these troops were greatly fatigued owing to the fact that they had been marching in waterlogged trenches since 9 p.m. 28th instant.	

Army Form C. 2118.

WAR DIARY
or
INTELLIGENCE SUMMARY.
(Erase heading not required.)

Instructions regarding War Diaries and Intelligence Summaries are contained in F. S. Regs., Part II. and the Staff Manual respectively. Title pages will be prepared in manuscript.

Place	Date	Hour	Summary of Events and Information	Remarks and references to Appendices
	29/10/16. (Contd).		**2nd Battalion Devonshire Regiment.**	
			The C.O. informed the 25th Infantry Brigade that he would be unable to carry out the attack at 3 p.m. on the 29th, but that he would do so at 3 p.m. on the 30th.	
			At 11 a.m. the missing four platoons were in position but in a very exhausted condition. The artillery on both sides was very active The enemy directed most of his energy in shelling the Support line only. During few shells burst near our front line. It rained at intervals during the day and the trenches soon became very bad. The Brigadier 25th Infantry Brigade sent the Brigade Major to see the C.O. at 9 a.m. to ascertain if the C.O. still considered it inadvisable to carry out the attack, informing him at the time that it would not be possible to carry out the attack on the next day as the Division was being relieved. The C.O. informed the Brigadier that the missing platoons were still absent and that the remainder of the men were too fatigued and that under the circumstances it was out of the question to carry out the attack.	
			Ration parties bringing up the rations were shelled by the enemy several animals being injured, one man killed and two others wounded. "B" Coy's rations were destroyed.	
			Casualties. 7 killed. 11 Wounded.	
	30/10/16.		It continued to rain throughout the day and night. The artillery was again active on both sides, the enemy again shelling the Support line only. One German deserter gave himself up during the night.	
			Orders were received that the Battalion would be relieved in the trenches by the 10th Sherwood Foresters and that the Battalion would move to "C" Camp S.23.b.3.3. Relief to be comleted by 5.30 a.m.	
			Owing to the Communication trenches being impassable the last Coy did not leave the trenches until 7.30 a.m. on the 30th. "A" Coy and 2 platoons of "B" Coy came out over the top in broad daylight.	

Army Form C. 2118.

WAR DIARY
or
INTELLIGENCE SUMMARY.
(Erase heading not required.)

2nd Battalion Devonshire Regiment.

Place	Date	Hour	Summary of Events and Information	Remarks and references to Appendices
	30/10/16. (Contd).		2/Lieut C.B.Rodd and two men were killed and nine men wounded.	
	31/10/16.		The Battalion arrived at "C" Camp in a muddy and exhausted condition Tea was issued to the troops and rifles, equipment, etc. cleaned. At 2 p.m. the Battalion fell in and marched to MANSEL CAMP and again came under the orders of the 23rd Infantry Brigade. Casualties - 2 men wounded. Two men who took shelter in a shell hole whilst leaving the trenches stuck in the mud near Brigade Headquarters and it took over an hour to dig them out.	

Lieut. Colonel.

Commanding 2nd Battalion Devonshire Regiment.

WAR DIARY
or
INTELLIGENCE SUMMARY
(Erase heading not required.)

Summary of Events and Information

REPORT ON RAID.

I have questioned the three Officers and Coy Sergt Major Radford as to what occurred. The party reached the position of assembly in the front trench without a hitch. There was some difficulty in laying out the tape owing to Stokes Mortars dropping short and also some misunderstanding about cutting our own wire, but the result was not effected thereby as the parties were lined up in front of the gaps at 2 a.m. 2/Lieut. Tindal noted the time.

Some of our 18 pdrs+ were falling short on and in front of the hostile line. The enemy threw bombs and when the men got up to dash in their machine guns opened. One from the base of the sap about H.13.c.5¾.¼., one firing straight down the tape and one from the left. One of the Officers thought there was a machine gun in the sap about H.13.c.5.¼. and this is confirmed by Capt. Tillett who went out afterwards to bring in wounded.

Army Form. C. 2118

WAR DIARY
or
INTELLIGENCE SUMMARY

(Erase heading not required.)

Instructions regarding War Diaries and Intelligence Summaries are contained in F. S. Regs., Part II. and the Staff Manual respectively. Title Pages will be prepared in manuscript.

Place	Date	Hour	Summary of Events and Information	Remarks and references to Appendices
			The leader of the raid, Capt. Smith, was killed at once and most of the leading men were knocked out. The party then became disorganised and withdrew.	
			I attribute the failure of the enterprise to the fact that Capt. Smith was killed at once and that the enemy were thoroughly alert and prepared.	
			The gas does not appear to have damaged the enemy or his machine gun.	
			Capt. Tillett and 2/Lieut. Tindal went out and brought in 3 wounded men, despite a heavy fire.	
			This morning at 8.30 a.m. &C/pl Dickeon and L/Cpl Wilson went out in broad daylight and carried in two wounded men from close to the hostile wire.	
			I wish to bring their names to notice.	
			Casualties were, killed, Capt. Smith, other ranks 12. 3 O.R. Died of Wounds, and 19 O.R. were wounded.	

23rd Brigade.

8th Division.

2nd BATTALION DEVONSHIRE REGIMENT:: NOVEMBER 1916.

Army Form C. 2118.

WAR DIARY
or
INTELLIGENCE SUMMARY.
(Erase heading not required.)

2nd Battalion Devonshire Regiment.

Place	Date	Hour	Summary of Events and Information	Remarks and references to Appendices
	1/11/16.		The Battalion moved from Mansell Camp to Meaulte, where the Battalion was billeted.	
	2/11/16.		In billets at MEAULTE. Routine.	
	3/11/16.		Moved from MEAULTE to CITADEL CAMP during the morning. During the evening received orders to the effect that the 23rd Infantry Brigade was at the disposal of the 33rd Division to assist in carrying out certain contemplated operations and that the Battalion should be prepared to move in fighting order at short notice. About 10 p.m. received orders that Brigade would probably have to move at 4 a.m. the 4th. About 11 a.m. received orders to the effect that the Brigade would not move before 9 a.m. 4th.	
	4/11/16.		About 10 a.m. received orders to the effect that the Battalion would move to GUILLEMONT, leaving Camp at 1 p.m., and that a general attack would be carried out on the 5th by the 6th French Army and our 4th and 5th Armies. The 23rd Brigade would be in reserve in COW and OX line and in the FLERS LINE by ZERO hour, probably 11 a.m. on the 5th. About 11 a.m. the Battalion was informed that all previous orders were cancelled and that the Battalion was to "stand by". About 1 p.m. informed that the situation was normal and that the Battalion need not "stand to".	

WAR DIARY
or
INTELLIGENCE SUMMARY.
(Erase heading not required.)

Army Form C. 2118.

2nd Battalion Devonshire Regiment.

Place	Date	Hour	Summary of Events and Information	Remarks and references to Appendices
	5/11/16.		CITADEL CAMP. Routine.	
	6/11/16.		Moved to BRIQUTERIE CAMP.	
	7/11/16.		Received a Draft of 20 other ranks. 2/Lieut. J.D. Harcombe and 2/Lieut. H.B. Brooman joined the Battalion from Cadet School, G.H.Q. The Battalion moved into the trenches during the night and relieved the 2nd Battalion Royal Welsh Fusiliers. There was not a great deal of shelling, although the rear Coy (D Coy) had a rather unpleasant journey. Casualties :- 3 wounded and 1 missing. The following Officers remained at the Transport Lines. Major H.F. Hardman. 2/Lieut. W.M. Thomson. 2/Lieut. L.N.L. Tindal. The trenches were found to be in a fair condition, but very waterlogged.	
	8/11/16.		In the Trenches. There was considerable artillery activity on both sides. The trenches were greatly improved. Casualties:- 2 Killed, 1 Wounded and 1 Missing.	
	9/11/16.		In the Trenches. Artillery was active throughout the night.	

WAR DIARY
or
INTELLIGENCE SUMMARY.
(Erase heading not required.)

Army Form C. 2118.

2nd Battalion Devonshire Regiment.

Place	Date	Hour	Summary of Events and Information	Remarks and references to Appendices
	9/11/16. (Contd).		About 2 p.m. the following message was received from the Brigade:- Can you arrange to advance the whole of your two front Coys. now in AUTUMN TRENCH on to the crest line in front to-night and dig in. If not the whole line could you arrange for short lines of trenches to be made on same position, prior to joining up later. This is most urgent and G.O.C. considers it imperative. Wire your views at once. AAA. A line dug close up to the crest would be sufficient. G.O.C. suggests a covering party with Lewis Guns on the crest line AAA. The C.O. wired to the Brigade to the effect that the whole line would be advanced and dug in during the night. The necessary orders were issued to Coys to assist the 2 Coys in AUTUMN TRENCH in this work, two platoons were allotted to each of these Coys; the whole operation was carried out under the direction of 2/Lieut. E.D. Hill. This operation was most successfully carried out during the night in spite of the fact that the troops were spotted and heavily fired on by the enemy as soon as they started work. By dawn next day the trench was completed, with fire steps, etc. and the communication trenches joined this new trench, later, named FALL TRENCH, to AUTUMN TRENCH. The enemy during the night made a small bombing attack on the new trench, but were easily dispersed. Casualties:- 2 Killed and 11 Wounded. The Battalion was congratulated by the Brigadier on the work done	
	10/11/16.		Artillery again very active. The Battalion was relieved in the trenches by the 2/West Yorks R.	

Army Form C. 2118.

WAR DIARY
or
INTELLIGENCE SUMMARY.
(Erase heading not required.)

Instructions regarding War Diaries and Intelligence Summaries are contained in F. S. Regs., Part II. and the Staff Manual respectively. Title pages will be prepared in manuscript.

2nd Battalion Devonshire Regiment.

Place	Date	Hour	Summary of Events and Information	Remarks and references to Appendices
	10/11/16. (Contd).		and on relief moved into Brigade Reserve in the FLERS LINE, less "C" Coy who moved into Camp in TRONES WOOD. Casualties:- 2 Killed, 6 Wounded.	
	11/11/16.		In Brigade Reserve in the FLERS LINE. H.R.H. The Prince of Wales visited the Battalion and remained for some time. During the night a field battery on the right of the Battalion was heavily shelled with gas shells and considerable damage done. Only a few shells were fired on the Battalion front and no damage was done beyond cutting the barbed wire. Furnished Working Parties both by day and night. Casualties:- 1 man wounded.	
	12/11/16.		FLERS LINE. Routine - Furnished Working Parties by day and night.	
	13/11/16.		The Battalion moved to CARNOY Camp during the morning. Received draft of 5 other ranks. 2/Lieut. L. Pertwee and 2/Lieut. F.R. Brocman joined the Battalion from the Cadet School.	
	14/11/16.		CARNOY Camp. Routine.	
	15/11/16.		Moved to CITADEL Camp.	
	16/11/16.		CITADEL Camp. Routine - Furnished Working Parties. Received Draft of 6 Signallers.	

Army Form C. 2118.

WAR DIARY
or
INTELLIGENCE SUMMARY.
(Erase heading not required.)

2nd Battalion Devonshire Regiment.

Place	Date	Hour	Summary of Events and Information	Remarks and references to Appendices
	17/11/16.		CITADEL Camp. Routine – Furnished R.E. Working Parties. Casualties:- 3 O.R. Wounded on Working Party	
	18/11/16.		CITADEL Camp. Routine. Received Draft of 37 other ranks.	
	19/11/16.		Entrained at GROVE TOWN about 5 p.m.	
	20/11/16.		Detrained at OISEMONT about 4.30 a.m. and marched to billets at VERGIES.	
	21/11/16.		In Billets at VERGIES. Coy Training. Received Draft of 32 O.R. 2/Lieut. L. Vinnicombe joined Battalion from Cadet School.	
	22/11/16.		In Billets. Coy Training. Received Draft of 6 other ranks.	
	23/11/16.		In BILLETS. Coy Training.	
	24/11/16.		In BILLETS. Coy Training.	
	25/11/16.		In BILLETS. Coy Training. Received Draft of 8 other ranks.	

Army Form C. 2118.

WAR DIARY
or
INTELLIGENCE SUMMARY.
(Erase heading not required.)

Instructions regarding War Diaries and Intelligence Summaries are contained in F. S. Regs., Part II. and the Staff Manual respectively. Title pages will be prepared in manuscript.

Place	Date	Hour	Summary of Events and Information	Remarks and references to Appendices
			2nd Battalion Devonshire Regiment.	
	26/11/16		In Billets. Coy Training.	
	27/11/16		In Billets. Coy Training.	
	28/11/16		In Billets. Coy Training.	
	29/11/16		In Billets. Coy Training.	
	30/11/16		In Billets. Coy training. At 10.30 a.m. the Brigadier inspected the Batt. in marching order. At 11.15 a.m. the Divisional Commander presented MILITARY MEDAL Ribbons to the following:- No. 8258 Sgt. M.Hobbs. For displaying great keeness and intelligence on patrol for which he has frequently volunteered. No. 8826 Sgt. Crispen. For devotion to duty. Has frequently shown great courage in mending telephone wires under heavy fire. This N.C.O. was wounded mending wire. No. 12608 Cpl. A.Holmes. For devotion to duty and showing great daring and resource on Patrol. Always volunteers for any dangerous work. No. 9937 L/Sgt. R.Roberts. For conspicuous courage and daring on patrol, and readiness to volunteer at all times for work in front of our lines. No. 9428 L/Cpl. W.Kirby. For devotion to duty on the night of 22/23 April 1916 near ALBERT when the telephone wires were being continually cut, he showed great promptitude in mending them in spite of heavy shell-fire. No. 6795 Pte. D.Greenslade. For devotion to duty. He has been Hd.Qr. Orderly throughout the Campaign and has frequently carried messages under heavy shell-fire.	

Army Form C. 2118.

WAR DIARY
or
INTELLIGENCE SUMMARY.
(Erase heading not required.)

Place	Date	Hour	Summary of Events and Information	Remarks and references to Appendices
	30/11/16 (contd)		2nd Battalion Devonshire Regiment.

8923 Pte. F.Joint. For showing great coolness and devotion to duty on the 31/5/16, when a German Mine was exploded in our lines, he manned the first available bay and carried on.
14152 Pte. W.Howells. For showing great coolness and devotion to duty on the 31/5/16 when a German Mine exploded in our lines, he manned the first available bay and carried on.

After the Medal Ribbons had been presented the Battn. marched past the Divisional Commander in Column of route. The men who had been presented with Medal Ribbons were drawn up beside the Divisional Commander as the Battalion marched past. | |
| | 2/12/16. | | Lieut. Colonel. Commanding, 2nd Battalion Devonshire Regiment. | |

23rd Brigade.
8th Division.

2nd BATTALION DEVONSHIRE REGIMENT ::: DECEMBER 1916.

Army Form C. 2118.

WAR DIARY
or
INTELLIGENCE SUMMARY.
(Erase heading not required.)

Instructions regarding War Diaries and Intelligence Summaries are contained in F.S. Regs., Part II. and the Staff Manual respectively. Title pages will be prepared in manuscript.

Vol 25

Place	Date	Hour	Summary of Events and Information	Remarks and references to Appendices
			2nd Battalion Devonshire Regiment.	
	1/12/16.		In billets at VERGIES. Coy Training.	
	2/12/16.		In Billets. Coy Training.	
	3/12/16.		In Billets. Church Parade. Received Draft of 46 O.R.	
	4/12/16.		In Billets. Coy Training.	
	5/12/16.		In Billets. Coy Training. Lieut. J. O'Bayle proceeded to England on termination of his engagement. Lieut. D. Mackinnon R.A.M.C. took over the duties of Regimental Medical Officer.	
	6/12/16.		In Billets. Coy Training. 2/Lieut. J.L.H.Richards joined Battn. for first time.	
	7/12/16.		In Billets. Coy Training.	
	8/12/16.		In Billets. Coy Training.	
	9/12/16.		In Billets. Coy Training.	
	10/12/16.		In Billets. Church Parade. The C.O. took over Temporary Command of the Brigade during absence of G.O.C.	
	11/12/16.		In Billets. Battalion Training.	

T2134. Wt. W708—776. 500000. 4/15. Sir J. C. & S.

Army Form C. 2118.

WAR DIARY
or
INTELLIGENCE SUMMARY.
(Erase heading not required.)

Instructions regarding War Diaries and Intelligence Summaries are contained in F. S. Regs., Part II. and the Staff Manual respectively. Title pages will be prepared in manuscript.

Place	Date	Hour	Summary of Events and Information	Remarks and references to Appendices
			2nd Battalion Devonshire Regiment.	
	12/12/16.		In Billets. Battalion Training. Draft of 123 O.R. joined the Battalion.	
	13/12/16.		In Billets. Battalion Training.	
	14/12/16.		In Billets. Battalion Training.	
	15/12/16.		In Billets. Brigade Field Day.	
	16/12/16.		In Billets. Battalion Training.	
	17/12/16.		In Billets. Church Parade. "A" Coy proceeded to 8th Divisional School of Instruction Lieut. Col. A.J.E. Sunderland was admitted to Hospital "sick". Major A. Tillett took over Temporary Command of the Battalion.	
	18/12/16.		In Billets. Battalion Training. 2/Lieut. P.Gay and 2/Lieut. A.R.Slater joined the Battn.	
	19/12/16.		In Billets. Battalion Training.	
	20/12/16.		In Billets. Battalion Training. Received Draft of 11 other ranks.	
	21/12/16.		In Billets. Battalion Training.	

T2134. Wt. W708—776. 500000. 4/15. Sir J. C. & S.

Army Form C. 2118.

WAR DIARY
or
INTELLIGENCE SUMMARY.
(Erase heading not required.)

Instructions regarding War Diaries and Intelligence Summaries are contained in F.S. Regs., Part II. and the Staff Manual respectively. Title pages will be prepared in manuscript.

2nd Battalion Devonshire Regiment.

Place	Date	Hour	Summary of Events and Information	Remarks and references to Appendices
	22/12/16.		In Billets. Battalion Training. 2/Lieut. Hughes joined the Battalion on first appointment, attached "C" Coy. 2/Lieut. P. Gay appointed to command "D" Coy.	
	23/12/16.		In Billets. Battalion Training. 1 Offr. (2/Lt. Slater) and 52 other ranks proceeded to Musketry Camp, PONT REMY. 2/Lieut. C.E. Copplestone joined Battalion on 1st appointment and attached to "C" Coy. 2/Lieuts. Thomson and Drake went on leave to U.K. "A" Coy returned from Divisional School. Horse Race in the afternoon, all Officers up. 2/ Lieut. Roberts - CAMEL. First. Major Tillett - RAJAH. Second.	
	24/12/16.		In Billets. Church Parades. Xmas Day functions were observed to-day owing to preparations to move back to the line. All Officers dined at H.Q.	
	25/12/16.		Xmas Day. No parades.	
	26/12/16.		G.O.C., 8th Division, made his first inspection of the 23rd Brigade at ST MAULVIS at 10 a.m.	
	27/12/16.		Left VERGIES at 4.30 a.m. and entrained at OISEMONT at 10 a.m. and arrived at EDGE HILL (ALBERT) at 3.15 p.m. The Battalion then marched to Camp 12 near SAILLY LAURETTE and arrived in a very	

Army Form C. 2118.

WAR DIARY
or
INTELLIGENCE SUMMARY.
(Erase heading not required.)

2nd Battalion Devonshire Regiment.

Place	Date	Hour	Summary of Events and Information	Remarks and references to Appendices
	27/12/16. (Contd).		exhausted condition. 1 Officer and draft of 6 other ranks joined the Battalion. (2/Lieut. Bidgway).	
	28/12/16.		The Battalion fell in at 9.45 a.m. and marched to the forward area. Marching was good, due probably to the air being exceedingly cold and the roads hard. Arrived at Camp 16 near MARICOURT at 12.30 p.m.	
	29/12/16.		Left the Camp at 12 noon and lorries conveyed the Battn. to MAUREPAS en route to the trenches. 2/Lieut. Crang joined the Battalion on first appointment Debussed at 3.30 p.m. and marched by Coys as far as COMBLES, then by platoons to the line. The following Officers accompanied the Battn. into action Temp.Major A.Tillett. Commanding. Capt.H.Archer "B" Coy.&2nd in Command. 2/Lieut. A.Winch. "A" Coy. Commanding. do. L.Pertwee " do. A.C.Bidgway. "B" Coy. do. H.H.Jago. "B" Coy. do. F.R.Brooman. " do. T.R.Johns. "C" Coy. Commanding. do. E.L.Walters. " do. J.F.L.Hughes. "D" Coy. Commanding. do. P.Gay. " do. A.E.Rutledge. " do. L.Vinnicombe. "	

Army Form C. 2118.

WAR DIARY
or
INTELLIGENCE SUMMARY.
(Erase heading not required.)

Instructions regarding War Diaries and Intelligence Summaries are contained in F.S. Regs., Part II. and the Staff Manual respectively. Title pages will be prepared in manuscript.

2nd Battalion Devonshire Regiment.

Place	Date	Hour	Summary of Events and Information	Remarks and references to Appendices
	29/30.12/16.		Took over the line U.26.a.45.85. – U.20.b.2.1. opposite the ST PIERRE VAAST Wood from the 1st Rifle Brigade – "D" Coy in front line, "B" Coy close support and "A" and "C" Coys in Reserve. The trenches are very bad, all full of water. Front line a series of shell holes and held by 10 posts. The night was very quiet and rain fell steadily the whole time. Casualties:- 4 men wounded during the night by shell fire.	
	30/12/16.		Raining all the morning. Enemy guns very active on our front and support line. Brig. Genl Fagan and the Brigade Major came up to look round the line at 11.a.m. Enemy artillery knocked out a Lewis Gun and crew in the front line. Casualties:- 1 Killed and 4 wounded. Slow methodical shelling of our lines continued all the afternoon, during which 1 N.C.O. was wounded. As soon as it was dusk "A" Coy went up and relieved "D" Coy in front line. "D" Coy took over from "B" in support and "B" went back to "A" Coy's old area. At 8 p.m. Capt Archer took 20 men down to the front line to endeavour to improve the trench and assist "A" Coy in pumping water out. "C" Coy supplied a working party carrying pumps up to "A" Coy. On "D" Coy coming into the support trench 2/Lieut L. Vinnicombe went sick, chiefly due to exhaustion. Capt Blencowe (Chaplain) came into the line this evening at about 7 p.m. Total Casualties for the day:- 1 killed and 9 wounded.	

Army Form C. 2118.

WAR DIARY
or
INTELLIGENCE SUMMARY.
(Erase heading not required.)

2nd Battalion Devonshire Regiment.

Place	Date	Hour	Summary of Events and Information	Remarks and references to Appendices
	31/12/16.		Everything quite normal till about 10 a.m. when enemy's guns became active. Coy Commanders of West Yorks came to look round. About 3 p.m, a 5.9 knocked out a Lewis Gun, wounded two and of one man no trace could be found. "C" Coy went up from support and relieved "A" Coy. "D" went into reserve and "A" went into support. Evening very quiet. Enemy shelling during the day was above normal and appeared to be concentrated rather on the left of front line, the road (BAPAUME-PERONNE) was heavily shelled during this period – from 7 p.m. to midnight very quiet – artillery unusually quiet.	

Major.
Commanding 2nd Battalion Devonshire Regiment.

23rd Brigade.

8th Division.

2nd BATTALION

DEVONSHIRE REGIMENT

JANUARY 1917.

Army Form C.2118.

WAR DIARY
or
INTELLIGENCE SUMMARY.
(Erase heading not required.)

2nd Battalion Devonshire Regiment.

Place	Date	Hour	Summary of Events and Information	Remarks and references to Appendices
	1/1/17.		Battalion in the line. The day fairly quiet. At midnight. "B" Coy. went up from Reserve and relieved "C" Coy in front line. At "stand to" in the morning 2 men were observed approaching No.1 Post. It was thought that they were our own men when about ten yards from the Post it was observed they were Germans. When challenged they failed to put up their hands and ran away. Fire was opened on them and both men fell. One was recovered wounded in about six places. The second man totally disappeared and it is thought he was hit and fell into a shell hole of liquid mud. The man brought in eventually died of wounds. He belonged to the 106th Bavarian R.I.R. (normal). Both men were, it seems, on a ration party and had lost their way and had passed through own line (i.e. the 2nd Lincolns area). Shelling throughout the rest of the day was normal. At 4.30 p.m. the 2nd West Yorks relieved the reserve line - by 7 p.m. the relief was completed. The Battalion went back individually to Camp "Y" MAUREPAS. Two men were reported missing from the march from the line.	
	2/1/17.		2/Lieut. A.M. Taylor joined the Battalion on 1st Appointment on the 1st instant and posted to "A" Coy. 2/Lieut. L.N.L. Tindal went to 4th Army School and in the afternoon 2/Lieut. G.F. Thuillier went to Lewis Gun Course at BOUCHON. 2/Lieut. A.E. Slater left for England for M.G. Course. Draft of 28 other ranks joined the Battalion today.	

Army Form C. 2118.

WAR DIARY
or
INTELLIGENCE SUMMARY.
(Erase heading not required.)

Instructions regarding War Diaries and Intelligence Summaries are contained in F.S. Regs., Part II. and the Staff Manual respectively. Title pages will be prepared in manuscript.

Place	Date	Hour	Summary of Events and Information	Remarks and references to Appendices
			2nd Battalion Devonshire Regiment.	
	3/1/17.		Battalion in Camp. Details furnished a Working Party of 20 men in the morning and another at midnight. In the evening "D" Coy supplied a Working Party for the C.R.E. and Draft of 5 O.R. joined the Battalion this day. The following Officers were appointed Temp. Captains from the dates shown :- 2/Lieut. A.Winch apptd. Temp. Capt. 14/10/16. " B.D.Hill. do. 28/10/16. " J.H.Vincent. do. 25/11/16. Lieut. Mackinnon.R.A.M.C. reported sick and Capt. D.Whyte R.A.M.C. reported for duty. 2/Lieut. H.H.Jago took over Temporary Command of "A" Coy vice Capt. Winch on Leave.	
	4/1/17.		"D" Coy supplied two parties of 20 at 8 a.m. for the C.R.E Two Coys "A" and "C" (200 strong) working under the C.R.E. on Camp construction. Draft of 4 other ranks joined the Battalion. Working Party furnished by "A" and "C" Coys under the C.R.E.	
	5/1/17.		Battalion in Camp. 2/Lieut. A.C.Bidgway "A" Coy and 2/Lieut. F.R.Brooman proceeded to 8th Divnl. School, AVESNE. Working Party of 200 O.R. furnished by "A" and "B" Coys. Enemy Artillery very busy all day, also German Aeroplanes very busy.	

WAR DIARY
or
INTELLIGENCE SUMMARY.
(Erase heading not required.)

Army Form C. 2118.

2nd Battalion Devonshire Regiment.

Place	Date	Hour	Summary of Events and Information	Remarks and references to Appendices
	6/1/17.		Battalion left Y Camp at 3 p.m. and marched by Coys as far as COMBLES, then by platoons to the lines. Ankle boots were changed for gum boots just beyond COMBLES. The following Officers accompanied the Battalion into action	
			Major A. Tillett. Commanding.	
			Capt. H.Archer. "B" Coy. Second in-Command.	
			2/Lieut. H.H.Jago. "B" Coy. Commanding.	
			" J.L.H.Richards. "A" Coy. do.	
			" A.M.Taylor. do.	
			Capt. H.Archer. "B" Coy. Commanding.	
			2/Lieut. A.B.Kitson. "B" Coy.	
			" A.C.Faulkner. L.G.O. attached "B" Coy.	
			" T.R.Johns "C" Coy. Commanding.	
			" B.L.Walters. "C" Coy.	
			" P.Gay. "D" Coy. Commanding.	
			" A.E.Rutledge. "D" Coy.	
			" H.B.Brooman. do.	
			Took over line opposite ST PIERRE VAAST WOOD. POLLUX SECTOR, from the 2nd West Yorkshire Regiment. The front line is almost the same as that taken over on 29/30th ultimo, with the exception of 9 and 10 posts being given up by us and four extra posts on the left added to our Sector.	
			During the night the enemy artillery was exceptionally quiet.	

Army Form C. 2118.

WAR DIARY
or
INTELLIGENCE SUMMARY.
(Erase heading not required.)

Instructions regarding War Diaries and Intelligence Summaries are contained in F. S. Regs., Part II. and the Staff Manual respectively. Title pages will be prepared in manuscript.

Place	Date	Hour	Summary of Events and Information	Remarks and references to Appendices
			2nd Battalion Devonshire Regiment.	
	7/1/17.		Hostile aircraft very active during the morning. Enemy shelled the BAPAUME–PERONNE ROAD on both sides of B.H.Q. with 5.9 from 2.15 p.m. to 10 p.m.	
			2nd Scottish Rifles furnished a working party during the night to place wire in front of the Support line.	
			"B" Coy were employed in carrying material to the front and support lines.	
			No casualties during the day.	
			Two new posts were begun in the Support line under R.E. supervision.	
			A patrol of 1 Officer, 2 N.C.O's and 5 men went out from No 8 Post and discovered that the enemy's wire immediately in front was from 3' to 3' 6" high and fairly deep.	
	8/1/17.		Hostile artillery fire was much below normal during the day, 2 salvoes of 4 shells of the 5.9 calibre fell near the Reserve line at 4.15 p.m.	
			"D" Coy from the Support line and half of "C" Coy relieved the front line between 11.30 p.m. and 12.30 a.m. on the night of 8/9th inst. "A" Coy coming back to the Support line and half Coy of "C" to the Reserve line.	
			No casualties occurred during the day.	
			2/Lieut. W.M.Thomson and 2/Lieut W.W.Drake returned from leave and joined the Details.	
	9/1/17.		Draft of 105 other ranks joined the Battalion this day and taken on strength.	

Army Form C. 2118.

WAR DIARY
or
INTELLIGENCE SUMMARY.
(Erase heading not required.)

Instructions regarding War Diaries and Intelligence Summaries are contained in F.S. Regs., Part II. and the Staff Manual respectively. Title pages will be prepared in manuscript.

Place	Date	Hour	Summary of Events and Information	Remarks and references to Appendices
			2nd Battalion Devonshire Regiment.	
	9/1/17.		At 1 a.m. a German came across "No Man's Land" and gave himself up at No 7 Post. He was marched to B.H.Q. and searched. The prisoner spoke English fluently and remarked that he saw our relief distinctly which took place an hour earlier. The captured man looked very fit and none the worse for his experience in the trenches. He was sent to Brigade H.Q. under escort. Capt. R.J.Andrews joined the Battalion from a Course at ALDERSHOT. 2/Lieut. George Archer and 2/Lieut. Maurice Gilbert Beck reported for duty this day. A Working Party of 50 men from the Reserve Coy were improving the front line posts during the night. A Forward Post, bomb store or ammunition dump was blown up by our artillery at U.20.d.3.6½. at 11.25 a.m. Hostile artillery fire was below normal.	
	10/1/17.		The Battalion was relieved by the 2nd Bn. Irish Guards on the night of 10/11th instant. The Support and Reserve Coys were relieved between 4 and 5 p.m. and the front line later, having to proceed under cover of darkness. During the four days in the POLLUX SECTOR one man was killed (attached T.M.Bty) and 1 wounded by shrapnel. The Battalion marched to CRUCIFIX CORNER, MAUREPAS, independently by Coys and thence by lorry to No 14 Camp, leaving CRUCIFIX CORNER at 9.30 p.m. and arriving at the Camp about 12 midnight.	

A5834 Wt.W4973/M687 750,000 8/16 D.D.&L. Ltd. Forms/C.2118/13.

Army Form C. 2118.

WAR DIARY
or
INTELLIGENCE SUMMARY.
(Erase heading not required.)

Instructions regarding War Diaries and Intelligence Summaries are contained in F.S. Regs., Part II. and the Staff Manual respectively. Title pages will be prepared in manuscript.

Place	Date	Hour	Summary of Events and Information	Remarks and references to Appendices
			2nd Battalion n Devonshire Regiment.	
	11/1/17.		The Battalion fell in at 11.30 a.m. Order of March - A, B, C and D Coy. and proceeded to billets. "A" Coy and 2 platoons of "B" Coy were billetted by the BRAY-CAPPY ROAD, about 1½ miles from BRAY. The Detachment being under the Command of Capt. R.J.Andrews. 2/Lieut. H.H.Jago being responsible for the two platoons of "B" Coy. The remaining 2 platoons of "B" Coy and "C" and "D" Coys being billeted in BRAY, arriving about 2.p.m. The u/m Officers who joined the Battalion on the 9th instant were posted to Coys as follows:- 2/Lieut. G.Archer "D" Coy 2/Lieut. M.G.Beck "B" Coy. 2/Lieut. C.E.Copleston rejoined the Battalion from Brigade H.Q. Capt. R.J.Andrews takes over Command of "A" Coy this day.	
	12/1/17.		In Billets. "A" Coy and 2 platoons of "B" Coy are working under 217th Coy R.E. at B.T.Dump. 1 Officer and 40 men from "B" Coy (BRAY) are employed daily loading wagons at the BRAY-ALBERT ROAD. 1 Officer and 40 men from "C" Coy are employed under the 239th Coy.R.E. "D" Coy are at the dosposal of XVth Corps. 2/Lieut. L. Vinnicombe "D" Coy embarked for England "sick" on the 3rd instant and is struck off strength accordingly. The draft of 105 other ranks taken on strength on the 9th instant were posted to Coys this day. 2/Lieut. G.F.Thuillier "A" Coy rejoined from L.G. Course at G.H.Q. School, Le Touquet.	

A.5834 Wt.W4973/M687 750,000 8/16 D.D.&L.Ltd. Forms/C.2118/13.

Army Form C. 2118.

WAR DIARY
or
INTELLIGENCE SUMMARY.
(Erase heading not required.)

Instructions regarding War Diaries and Intelligence Summaries are contained in F. S. Regs., Part II. and the Staff Manual respectively. Title pages will be prepared in manuscript.

Place	Date	Hour	Summary of Events and Information	Remarks and references to Appendices
			2nd Battalion Devonshire Regiment.	
	13/1/17.		In Billets, usual working parties. 2/Lieut. M.G.Beck and 32 other ranks proceeded to the Brigade Bomb School on a Course of Instruction in Bombing. Between 1.30 and 2.30 p.m. the enemy dropped about 20 shells of 8" calibre in different parts of BRAY. Several falling in the square near the Church, causing considerable damage. No 17900 Pte C.Huxter "D" Coy was killed No 33206 Pte F. Radford "D" Coy wounded. About fifty casualties were caused to other troops in the Town, one shell falling in a billet occupied by the D.C.L.I.	
	14/1/17.		In Billets. Usual working parties. 2/Lieut. T.R.Johns "C" Coy proceeded on a Lewis Gun Course at XV Corps School, BOUCHON. Divine Service was held at 11 a.m. (Parade). Holy Communion " " 11.30 a.m. (Voluntary). Hostile shells were heard passing over BRAY between 8.30 and 9.30 a.m. in the direction of ETINEHEM. The C.O., Lieut. Col. A.J.E. Sunderland rejoined the Battalion, having been absent owing to illness since 17/12/16. The u/m Officers and N.C.O. have been mentioned in Dispatches by Field Marshall Sir Douglas Haig, C-in-C. 13/11/16. Lieut. Col. A.J.E. Sunderland. Capt. F.R.Cobb, M.C. Hon. Lieut. & Qr. Mr. G. Palmer. 2/Lieut. C.O.R. Jacob. No 10832 Sgt M. Reilly. Major A. Tillett has been awarded the M.C. 1/1/17.	

WAR DIARY or INTELLIGENCE SUMMARY.

Army Form C. 2118.

(Erase heading not required.)

Place: 2nd Battalion Devonshire Regiment.

Date	Hour	Summary of Events and Information	Remarks and references to Appendices
14/1/17.	(Contd).	Capt. A. Tillett to be Acting Major, 25/11/16.	
15/1/17.		In Billets. Working Parties as usual. Lieut. Col. A.J.E. Sunderland proceeded to Brigade H.Q. and is Acting Brigadier during Brig.-Genl. Fagan's absence. 2/Lieut. A.C.C.Pendrigh reported for duty this day. 2/Lieut. P.J.Crang "D" Coy rejoined from 8th Divisional School, AVESNE, this day.	
16/1/17.		In Billets. Working Parties as usual. 2/Lieut. A.C.C.Pendrigh having joined the Battalion yesterday the 15th inst., is taken on strength and posted to "B" Coy.	
17/1/17.		In Billets. Working Parties as usual. The following Officers proceeded on Leave to the U.K. from 18th to 28th instant. 2/Lieut. A.E.Rutledge "D" Coy. 2/Lieut. E.L.Walters "C" Coy.	
18/1/17.		In Billets. Working Parties as usual. A Battle Platoon has been formed and composed of the following Officers. 2/Lieut. G.Archer "D" Coy. 2/Lieut. R.Yandle "B" Coy. 6 N.C.O's and 52 men.	
20/1/17.		In Billets. Working Parties as usual.	

Army Form C. 2118.

WAR DIARY
or
INTELLIGENCE SUMMARY.
(Erase heading not required.)

Instructions regarding War Diaries and Intelligence Summaries are contained in F. S. Regs., Part II. and the Staff Manual respectively. Title pages will be prepared in manuscript.

Place	Date	Hour	Summary of Events and Information	Remarks and references to Appendices
			2nd Battalion Devonshire Regiment.	
	20/1/17. (Contd).		The Battle Platoon move to B.T.Dump to do R.E.Fatigues. Capt. A.Winch has returned from leave and takes over Tempy. Command of "D" Coy from this day. 2/Lieut. L.Pertwee "A" Coy returned from Leave.	
	21/1/17.		In Billets, usual working parties. Major A. Tillett, M.C. proceeded to FLIXECOURT to attend a Senior Officers' Conference. Capt. R.J.Andrews, M.C. will temporarily Command the Battalion from this date. 2/Lieut. T.R.Johns "C" Coy rejoined from XV Corps L.G.School Bouchon, and will temporarily Command "A" Coy from this date. 2/Lieut. P.Gay "D" Coy and 25 other ranks proceeded this day to form part of the Divnl. Composite Coy. 2/Lieut. W.M.Thomson "D" Coy and 3 O.R. proceeded to XV Corps School, BOUCHON, on a Course of Instruction in Stokes Mortar.	
	22/1/17.		In Billets. Usual Working Parties. 2/Lieut. G.Parker having rejoined the Battalion on the 21st is taken on strength and posted to "B" Coy. 2/Lieut. A.B.Kitson "B" Coy will be a Member of a F.G.C.M. on the 23rd inst. assembling at H.Q. 1st Home Counties Field Coy.R.E. 2/Lieut. J.D.Harcombe "B" Coy rejoined from Baggage Store, 8th Div. BELLOY ST LEONARD on the 21st instant.	
	23/1/17.		In Billets. Usual Working Parties. 2/Lieuts. J.D.Harcombe "B" Coy and H.B.Brooman "D" Coy. and 2/Lieut. A.S. Gover proceeded on leave to the U.K.	

Army Form C. 2118.

WAR DIARY
or
INTELLIGENCE SUMMARY.
(Erase heading not required.)

2nd Battalion Devonshire Regiment.

Place	Date	Hour	Summary of Events and Information	Remarks and references to Appendices
	24/1/17.		In Billets. Usual Working Parties. The u/m Officers having joined the Battalion this day are taken on strength and posted to Coys as under :- 2/Lieut. J.L.Hiley "G" Coy. 2/Lieut. D.V.M.Mansel-Carey "D" Coy. 2/Lieut. J.H.Willman "D" Coy. 2/Lieut. J.M.Haswell "A" Coy. 2/Lieut. J.L.Bowden "B" Coy. Capt. E.D.Hill and 2/Lieut. H.H.Goodman were granted Leave of Absence to proceed to PARIS from the 22nd to 24th instant inclusive. On the night of 23/24th instant the enemy dropped bombs in and around BRAY causing some damage to property and killing 16 mules. They were driven off by our machines and gun fire.	
	25/1/17.		In Billets. Usual Working Parties. On the night of 25/26th instant three bombs were dropped from an hostile aeroplane on BRAY at about 8.15 p.m. killing one horse and wounding 7 others belonging to the Battalion Transport. The enemy machine was driven off by gun fire.	
	26/1/17.		In Billets. Usual Working Parties. 2/Lieut. R.S.Holmes "C" Coy rejoined from 1st Corps H.Q. this day. Capt. H.Archer "B" Coy took over the duties of Senior Major from the 21st instant.	

Army Form C. 2118.

WAR DIARY
or
INTELLIGENCE SUMMARY.
(Erase heading not required.)

2nd Battalion Devonshire Regiment.

Place	Date	Hour	Summary of Events and Information	Remarks and references to Appendices
	27/1/17.		Usual Working Parties during the morning. The Battalion proceeded to No 21 Camp at A.27.d.5.l. arriving about 4 p.m. Enemy shells of 8" calibre were falling about 400 yards from B.T. Dump between 1 and 2.30 p.m. The Battalion is now in Divisional Reserve.	
	28/1/17.		In Camp. Battalion Training. Enemy aeroplanes very busy both day and night. 2/Lieut. T.R.Johns "C" Coy took over the duties of Areas Commandant, MARICOURT AREA, this day. 2/Lieut. G.Parker "B" Coy took over Temporary Command of "A" Coy from this date.	
	29/1/17.		In Camp. Battalion Training. The BATTLE PLATOON were inspected by Brig. Genl. FAGAN and complimented on their smart appearance and general turnout. 2/Lieut. M.G.Beck and 23 other ranks returned from a Course at the Brigade Bomb School.	
	30/1/17.		In Camp. Battalion Training. 2/Lieut. C.W.White "A" Coy reported to the A.P.M. Camp 17, this day for Traffic Control Duties.	

Army Form C. 2118.

WAR DIARY
or
INTELLIGENCE SUMMARY.
(Erase heading not required.)

Place	Date	Hour	Summary of Events and Information	Remarks and references to Appendices
			2nd Battalion Devonshire Regiment.	
	31/1/17		In Camp. Battalion Training. Major A. Tillett rejoined the Battalion from the Senior Officers' Conference at FLIXECOURT.	

Commanding 2nd Battalion Devonshire Regiment.

23rd Brigade.
8th Division.

2nd BATTALION

DEVONSHIRE REGIMENT

FEBRUARY 1917.

WAR DIARY
or
INTELLIGENCE SUMMARY.

Army Form C. 2118.

2 Devon Regt

(Erase heading not required.)

Place	Date	Hour	Summary of Events and Information	Remarks and references to Appendices
	1/2/17.		2nd Battalion Devonshire Regiment. In Camp. Battalion Training. 2/Lieut.W.M.Thomson, "D" Coy, rejoined the Battalion from a Stokes Mortar Course at XV. Corps School, BOUCHON. 2/Lieut.F.R.Brooman, "B" Coy, and 2/Lieut.A.C.Bidgway, "A" Coy, rejoined the Battalion from 8th Divisional School.	
	2/2/17.		In Camp. C. of E. Parade Service in the Church Hut at 10 a.m.	
	3/2/17.		In Camp. Battalion Training.	
	4/2/17.		In Camp. Battalion Training. 2/Lieut.V.C.Emery to the 8th Divisional School.	
	5/2/17.		In Camp. Battalion Training.	
	6/2/17.		In Camp. Battalion Training.	
	7/2/17.		In Camp. Battalion Training. Lieut.Col. A.J.E.Sunderland rejoined the Battalion from Hospital and resumes Command of the Battalion.	
	8/2/17.		In Camp. Battalion Training. Captain Archer proceeded on a Course of Instruction at the G.H.Q. School, LE TOUQUET.	
	9/2/17.		In Camp. Battalion Training. Lieut.A.C.G.Roberts and 2/Lieut.F.R.Brooman, "B" Coy, proceeded on leave to the U/K.	
	10/2/17.		The Battalion left Camp 21 and marched to Camp 112 being inspected	

Army Form C. 2118.

WAR DIARY
or
INTELLIGENCE SUMMARY.
(Erase heading not required.)

Place	Date	Hour	Summary of Events and Information	Remarks and references to Appendices
			2nd Battalion Devonshire Regiment.	
	11/2/17.		The Battalion left 112 Camp and marched to CORBIE arriving about 2 p.m.	
	12/2/17.		In Billets. Battalion training. No.8834 Sgt.J.H.Barrett to be 2/Lieut. and posted to 9th Battalion 23/1/17. No.6588 Sgt.Major E.H.Littlewood to be 2/Lieut. and posted to 8th Battalion 20/1/17. Lt.Col.A.J.E.Sunderland proceeded on leave of absence to the U/K.	
	13/2/17.		In Billets. Battalion Training. Lieut.U.B.Burke joined the Battalion and posted to "D" Coy. 2/Lieut.H.H.Jago, "B" Coy, rejoined from Musketry Course at CAMIERS.	
	14/2/17.		In Billets. Battalion on digging fatigue by SAILLY-LAURETTE MORLANCOURT Road - practice trenches. 2/Lieut.E.L.Walters "C" Coy proceeded to R.F.C. Hd.Qrs. on probation as Observer.	
	15/2/17.		In Billets. Battalion training. Capt.H.Archer "B" Coy rejoined from G.H.Q.Lewis Gun School, LE TOUQUET. 2/Lieut.A.C.C.Pendrigh, "B" Coy, returned from a Course of Musketry at PONT REMY.	
	16/2/17.		In Billets. Battalion Training.	
	17/2/17.		In Billets. Battalion Training.	

Instructions regarding War Diaries and Intelligence Summaries are contained in F.S. Regs., Part II. and the Staff Manual respectively. Title pages will be prepared in manuscript.

Army Form C. 2118.

WAR DIARY
or
INTELLIGENCE SUMMARY.
(Erase heading not required.)

Place	Date	Hour	Summary of Events and Information	Remarks and references to Appendices
	18/2/17.		**2nd Battalion Devonshire Regiment.** In Billets. Battalion Training. Divine Service C.of E.Parade for 23rd Infantry Brigade in the Square, CORBIE, at 10.30 a.m. Divisional Band was present Holy Communion at 11 a.m. in the Tivoli. Evening Service (Voluntary) in the Tivoli at 6 p.m.	
	19/2/17.		Battalion left CORBIE at 8.40 a.m. and marched to Camp 112 arriving about 1.15 p.m. Capt.R.J.Andrews, M.C. proceeded for Duty at 8th Divl.Hd.Qrs.	
	20/2/17.		Battalion left Camp 112 at 10 a.m.and marched to Camp 17. SUZANNE, arriving about 12 o&c midday. Battalion was filmed en route. 200 yards interval was observed between Companies. Capt.H.Archer, "B" Coy, is granted special Leave to the U/K from 20/2/17 to 1/3/17.	
	21/2/17.		Battalion left Camp 17 at 3 p.m. and were conveyed from the Camp to MAUREPAS (Crucifix Corner).in motor lorries and marched from there to CRANIERES, arriving about 6 p.m. The Battalion was in support and supplied a working party of all available men carrying ammunition, etc. to the dumps immediately behind the front line. Gum Boots were drawn at ANDOVER en route. 2/Lieut.J.H.Vincent relinquishes the Rank of Temporary Captain on ceasing to Command a Company.	
	22/2/17.		Battalion in support. Supplied a working party of 300 other ranks carrying ammunition,etc. from ANDOVER to front line. 2/Lieut.H.H.Goodman took over the duties of Camp Commandant at ANDOVER.	

Army Form C. 2118.

WAR DIARY
or
INTELLIGENCE SUMMARY.
(Erase heading not required.)

2nd Battalion Devonshire Regiment.

Date	Summary of Events and Information
22/2/17.	2/Lieut.E.L.Walters and 2/Lieut.W.L.Sparkes are both struck off strength of the Battalion.
23/2/17.	Battalion in support. Supplied a working party of Officers and 263 other ranks carrying ammunition,etc. from ANDOVER to front line. Major A.Tillett, M.C. proceeded on leave to U/K being granted leave of absence from 24/2/17 to 23/3/17. Capt. R.J.Andrews, M.C. rejoined from Divnl.Hd.Qrs and took over Command of the Battalion. 2/Lieut.C.E.Copleston rejoined from Hospital.
24/2/17.	Battalion in support. Supplied a working party of 9 Officers and 249 other ranks carrying ammunition,etc. from ANDOVER to front line. The u/m Officers rejoined from Leave. Lieut.Col.A.J.E.Sunderland. Lieut.A.C.G.Roberts. Lieut.& Qr.Mr. G.Palmer. 2/Lieut.F.R.Brooman.
25/2/17.	Battalion relieved 2/Scottish Rifles "A" and "D" Coys - AISNE DUMP. "B" Coy - Front line. BOUCHAVESNES. N.Sector. "C" Coy - Support line. LANGTON BARRACKS. Battalion Hd.Qrs (advanced) Langton Barracks. Capt.R.J.Andrews, M.O. and I.G.Officer. Battalion H.Q., C.O., Adjutant, O.C.Battle Platoon, Signalling Officer, Intelligence Officer.
26/2/17.	Disposition as 25th. Situation Normal. 3 Casualties.

Army Form C. 2118.

WAR DIARY
or
INTELLIGENCE SUMMARY.
(Erase heading not required.)

Instructions regarding War Diaries and Intelligence Summaries are contained in F. S. Regs., Part II. and the Staff Manual respectively. Title pages will be prepared in manuscript.

Place	Date	Hour	Summary of Events and Information	Remarks and references to Appendices
			2nd Battalion Devonshire Regiment.	
	26/2/17.		2/Lieut.J.L.Bowden, "B" Coy, having been invalided "sick" to England is struck off strength from 16/2/17.	
	27/2/17.		Disposition as 26th. Situation normal. One casualty. "C" Coy relieved "B" Coy on the night of the 27/28th inst.	
	28/2/17.		"C" Coy in front line. "B" in support. "A" and "D" Coys relieved "C" and "B" on the night of the 28/1st inst.	

Lieut.Col.
Commanding 2nd Battalion Devonshire Regiment.

23rd Brigade.

8th Division.

2nd BATTALION

DEVONSHIRE REGIMENT

MARCH 1917.

Army Form C. 2118.

WAR DIARY
or
INTELLIGENCE SUMMARY.
(Erase heading not required.)

2ND BATTALION DEVONSHIRE REGIMENT.

Date	Hour	Summary of Events and Information	Remarks and references to Appendices
1917. 1st March		Front Line. "A" Coy. Support Line. "B" and "C" Coys, AISNE DUMP. Hd. Qrs. YELLOW CAMP. "B" and "C" Coys, and Battn Platoon supplied a Working Party carrying ammunition to the Front Line. 2/Lieut. P.J.Crang "D" Coy having been invalided "sick" to England is struck off the strength from 21/2/17. 2/Lieut. V.G.Emery "C" Coy took over the duties of Bde. Transport Officer on the 23rd ultimo.	
2nd March		Hd. Qrs., "B" and "C" Coys left YELLOW CAMP and AISNE DUMP at 10 a.m. and marched to Camp 17 SUZANNE. "A" and "D" Coys were relieved on the night of 2/3rd inst by 1st Worcestershire Regt. 2/Lieut. H.H.Goodman having rejoined the Battalion this day resumes the duties of Bombing Officer. "A" and "D" Coys when relieved marched to 23 CAMP.	
3rd March	about 3 p.m.	"A" and "D" Coys joined the Battalion at CAMP 17 arriving about 3 p.m. 2/Lieut. J'H'Willman "D" Coy having been invalided "sick" to England is struck off strength 23/2/17. 2/Lieut. M.G.Beck "B" Coy proceeded to the 15th Corps Sniping School, BOUCHON.	
4th March		2/Lieut. J.L.F.Hughes "C" Coy proceeded to the 4th Army Telescopic Sight School, Pont NOYELLES. The Battalion moved from Camp 17 at 4 a.m. on the morning of the 4th inst and marched to GRANIERES. Captain R.J.Andrews M.C. remained at Camp 17 in charge of details. The Battalion was at the disposal of the 24th Brigade, and received orders about 4 p.m. to proceed to the line to relieve the 2nd Battalion Northampton Regt in the Sector newly captured east of BOUCHAVESNES.	

WAR DIARY
or
INTELLIGENCE SUMMARY.

(Erase heading not required.)

Army Form C. 2118.

Place	Date	Hour	Summary of Events and Information	Remarks and references to Appendices
	1917. 4th March cont.		(2) 2nd BATTALION DEVONSHIRE REGIMENT: The following Officers accompanied the Battalion in action. Lt. Col. A.J.E.Sunderland, Commanding - Capt E.D.Hill, Adjutant - 2/Lieut. G.F.Thiller, Commanding "A" Coy - 2/Lieut. H.H.Jego, Commanding "B" Coy - 2/Lieut. W.W.Drake, Commanding "C" Coy - 2/Lieut U.E.Burke, Commanding "D" Coy - 2/Lieut. G.Archer, O.C. Battle Platoon. 2/Lieut. J.D.Harcombe, 2/Lieut. J.L.N.Richards, 2/Lieut. A.C.C.Pendrigh, 2/Lieut. A.Bidgway, 2/Lieut. W.K.Thomson, 2/Lieut. V.G. Emery, 2/Lieut. L.Pertwee, 2/Lieut. R.S.Holmes, 2/Lieut. A.B.Kitson, 2/Lieut. F.R.Brooman, 2/Lieut. D.V.M.Mansel-Garey, 2/Lieut. A.E.Rutledge. Extra Other Ranks- 326. During the relief enemy artillery opened a heavy barrage on our support line. Orders were received that FRITZ TRENCH (still in enemy hands) must be raided during the early morning of the 5th and the position captured during the day, consolidated. "A" Coy was allotted the triangle to consolidate where heavy fighting had taken place all the day; "B" Coy had the task of digging a new trench approximately about 150 yards long to connect "A" to "C" Coy. "D" Coy held the left of the Battalion Front. "A" Coy of the 2nd East Lancashire Regt attached to this Battalion, held the newly line dug across "NO MAN'S LAND" connecting our old line with the newly captured trench on the extreme left. Great difficulty was experienced during consolidation owing to intense barrages every half hour and little or no material to consolidate with. "B" Coy in consequence dug a new line almost entirely with entrenching tools, this trench in the morning was about 3 feet deep, which, under the circumstances, was a remarkable feat to the credit of the Coy.	
	5th March		FRITZ TRENCH Relief reported complete about 4.30 a.m. The raid on FRITZ TRENCH took place about 3 a.m. by a small party of the Battle Platoon under 2/Lieut. G.Archer. 3 dugouts were bombed but this order to destroy the dugouts was not carried out owing to the fact that the Mobile Charges were not obtainable.	

Army Form C. 2118.

WAR DIARY
or
INTELLIGENCE SUMMARY.
(Erase heading not required.)

Instructions regarding War Diaries and Intelligence Summaries are contained in F.S. Regs., Part II. and the Staff Manual respectively. Title pages will be prepared in manuscript.

Place	Date	Hour	Summary of Events and Information	Remarks and references to Appendices
	1917. 5th March cont.	(3)	2ND BATTALION DEVONSHIRE REGIMENT. During the early morning "A" Coy did good work consolidating the triangle under very adverse conditions. They also put in a double Bombing Block in FRITZ TRENCH and wired round it. Other Coys also put in Bombing Blocks where necessary but were unable to fire them. About 5.30 a.m. the enemy delivered two feeble attacks against "D" Coy which were easily driven off. Consolidation was carried out during the day and parties sent from Coys to find wiring material to further consolidate during the night. 2/Lieut. J.D. Harcombe made an effort to get "A" Coy in communication with Battalion Hd. Qrs. The first line laid was cut in places, no sooner it was out. After persistent work communication was eventually obtained but was cut several times during the night and following day. In the evening the enemy opened several barrages at half hour intervals and bombarded with intensity about 11 o'clock. The "S.O.S." Signal was sent up by the Battalion on our right. Our artillery opened up an exceedingly intense barrage on the enemy's trenches. Orders were received late in the evening that MObile Charges being obtainable, FRITZ TRENCH would be raided again in the early hours of the 6th. Dugouts were to be destroyed and the trench wrecked. A party of 20 men including 5 sappers under 2/Lieut. G. Archer carried out the raid. They proceeded along FRITZ TRENCH about 200 yards and saw none of the enemy. On the return journey the 3 dugouts bombed the previous evening were blown up, the explosion wrecking the trench in that vicinity. Prisoners captured Casualties during the 4/5th. 17. wounded 2, unwounded 8.	

Army Form C. 2118.

WAR DIARY
or
INTELLIGENCE SUMMARY.
(Erase heading not required.)

Place	Date	Hour	Summary of Events and Information	Remarks and references to Appendices
	1917.		(A) 2ND BATTALION DEVONSHIRE REGIMENT:	
	6th March		Enemy artillery was active throughout the day. Coys were engaged wiring during the night. "D" Coy's Covering Party had one man killed by an enemy sniper. Our artillery bombarded our own trenches doing considerable damage to our FRONT and SUPPORT Lines and buried a few men. Patrols went out from each Coy. "D" Coy reported that the enemy were working a Bombing Block about 70 yards from our own block. Coy patrolled as far as the Northern end of FRITZ Trench and reported that men were talking in the trench. The patrol was fired upon. The Coy of Sherwoods attached to the Battalion were withdrawn from the line on the night of the 6/7th inst. Casualties.	
	7th March		2/Lieut. Holmes and a party of 50 men were engaged clearing the battlefield. Enemy artillery was less active during the day. During the afternoon enemy Trench Mortars and Rifle Grenades were active for the first time during these operations. Light Mortars in the region opposite the triangle fired about 20 rounds and registered our wire. An enemy aeroplane flew over our trench and fired on "D" Coy but did no damage. "A" Coy were relieved from the triangle by the 2/Lincoln Regt. After relief they withdrew to the Support Line, PALLAS TRENCH. During the night wiring continued. The Coy of 2nd East Lancs (attached) had one man killed whilst wiring. Casualties 2.	
	8th March		In the morning the Brigadier General 24th Bde. visited the captured trenches and complimented the C.O. on the good work done by the Battalion in consolidating. In the evening the Battalion and the Coy of E.Lancs attached were relieved by the 2nd Worcester Regt. Relief was reported complete about 9 p.m. The Battalion proceeded to Camp 163. Casualties 2.	

Army Form C. 2118.

WAR DIARY
or
INTELLIGENCE SUMMARY.
(Erase heading not required.)

Instructions regarding War Diaries and Intelligence Summaries are contained in F. S. Regs., Part II. and the Staff Manual respectively. Title pages will be prepared in manuscript.

Place	Date	Hour	Summary of Events and Information	Remarks and references to Appendices
	1917.		(5) 2ND BATTALION DEVONSHIRE REGIMENT.	
	9th March		In Camp 163. Routine. The C.O. complimented Coy Commanders upon the good work done in the trenches from the 4th to the 8th inst.	
MAUREPAS - CURLU ROAD.	10th March		In Camp. Furnished working parties repairing screen on	
	11th March		In Camp. Furnished Working Parties repairing RANCOURT Road. 2/Lieut W.H. Thomson joined with the Grenade School	
	12th March		RANCOURT Sector. The Battalion relieved the 2/Scottish Rifles in the Sector on the night of 12/13th inst. The line extended from C.9.b.8.4. to C.3.b.4.3. Disposition:- "C" and "D" Coys FRONT LINE, "A" Coy SUPPORT "B" Coy and Battle Platoon RESERVE in dugouts. Battalion H.Q. ARTHURS SEAT C.8.a.0.7. Guides met the Battalion at end of duck boards at ABODE LANE at 7.45 p.m. The following Officers joined the Battalion: 2/Lts A.M.Taylor, J.L. Farquharson, H.D. Grahwill, A.R. Newton. W.D.R. joined	
	13th March		Relief reported complete at 4 a.m. Situation Normal during the day until 2 p.m. when about 50 5.9 and 77. mm. shells fell near the Right Coy Hd. Qrs. Retaliation was asked for and our heavies replied about 4.30 p.m. Our patrols were active throughout the night. 2/Lieut J.H. Hughes M.C. rejoined from the Anthony Bleuenjoined nightfall.	
	14th March		Enemy Artillery was active during the day. In the evening arrangements had been made for "A" and "B" Coys to relieve "C" and "D" Coys. Meanwhile, orders were received to cancel the relief and vigourous patrolling to take place throughout the night owing to the Division on our left reporting the enemy trenches in front of them had been vacated. The W. Yorks on our left reported having occupied the enemy line. Consequently the C.O. issued orders about 10 p.m. to enter the enemy trench. Strong patrols were out all the night and reported the enemy holding the line.	

WAR DIARY
or
INTELLIGENCE SUMMARY.

(Erase heading not required.)

Army Form C. 2118.

Place	Date	Hour	Summary of Events and Information	Remarks and references to Appendices
	1917.		(6) 2ND BATTALION DEVONSHIRE REGIMENT.	
	15th March		At 4.15 a.m. 2 Platoons of "C" Coy entered the enemy trench without opposition, 2 platoons of "D" Coy following at 5.45 a.m. and took up their position on the right of "C" Coy. At 12 noon patrols went out from both front line Coys to the far end of ST PIETER VAAST, the line reached was later taken up by the outposts. At 5 p.m. we extended out line 500 yards to the right. The Battalion was relieved by the 2nd Scottish Rifles. Disposition being :- Outpost Line. C.4.o.8.4. to C.10.d.5½.5. Picquet Line. C.3.c.8.5½. to C.10.a.2.2. Line of Resistance. C.3.c.2.6. to C.9.b.8.4. After Relief, Hd. Qrs and "A" and "B" Coys proceeded to ANDOVER. "C" and "D" Coys to LANGTON BARRACKS.	
	16th March.		ROUTINE. 2/Lieut. H.H. Jago rejoined from the 2nd Field Coy R.E. 2/Lieut. A.M. Taylor "A" Coy proceeded to PONT REMY on a Musketry Course. Captain A. Winn "A" Coy rejoined from hospital.	
	17th March		ROUTINE. 2/Lieut. A.R. Newton "D" Coy proceeded to LE TOUQUET on a Lewis Gun Course. 2/Lieut. G. Parker "B" Coy rejoined from a Course of General Instruction at the 4th Army School. 2/Lieut. R.M. Haswell and 2/Lieut F.S. Holmes proceeded to the 8th Divisional School AVESNE.	
	18th March		ROUTINE. 2/Lieut. M.C. Beck "B" Coy rejoined from 15th Corps School, BOUCHON.	
	19th March		ROUTINE. On the night of the 19th the Battalion was warned to hold itself in readiness to attack NURLU the following morn- at 10 a.m. the 20th inst.	

Army Form C. 2118.

WAR DIARY
or
INTELLIGENCE SUMMARY.
(Erase heading not required.)

Place	Date	Hour	Summary of Events and Information	Remarks and references to Appendices
	1917.		(6) 2ND BATTALION DEVONSHIRE REGIMENT.	
	20th Mar.		The Battalion left Camp and marched to Canal Bank, MOISLAINS from where the attack was going to start. "A" and "B" Coys had been allotted VILLEWOOD and the factory respectively. About 9.15 a.m. the O.C. Outposts reported to the Brigadier that NURLU had been vacated by the enemy. The attack was therefore not necessary and the Battalion was detailed to take over the Outpost Line from the 2/West Yorks on the Divisional Front. In the afternoon this was again altered and the Outpost Line on the Divisional Front was held by 2/West Yorks and 2/Devons, Lt.Colonel A.J.E. Sunderland being O.C.Outposts.	
	21st March		Day and Night - Quiet. Snow fell at intervals covering the ground.	
	22 March		Situation quiet, except for occasional shelling on the NURIN ROAD. 2/Lieut. Pertwee and 12 men from the Battalion men were sent to occupy AIZECOURT as an advanced post. "C" Coy were relieved by "D" Coy.	
	23 March		About 4.55 a.m. on the 23rd the advanced post in AIZECOURT was attacked by enemy Cavalry. 2 parties of about 50 approached the Village from Right and Left Flanks. After some shooting the enemy were dispersed. Casualties. 5 killed, 1 Officer and 6 O.R. wounded. The Battalion were relieved by the 2 Scottish Rifles at 4 p.m. After relief the Battalion marched to Billets in MOYSLAINS.	
	24 March		In Billets. A Working party of 200 were engaged on the New Line under R.E. Supervision.	

Army Form C. 2118.

WAR DIARY
or
INTELLIGENCE SUMMARY.
(Erase heading not required.)

Instructions regarding War Diaries and Intelligence Summaries are contained in F. S. Regs., Part II. and the Staff Manual respectively. Title pages will be prepared in manuscript.

Place	Date	Hour	Summary of Events and Information	Remarks and references to Appendices
	1917.		(v). 2ND BATTALION DEVONSHIRE REGIMENT	
	25 March		In Billets. A working party of 200 proceeded to the Few Line. Meanwhile instructions were received that no work would be carried but the relief with the 2/Scottish Rifles would take place and the battalion would attack LIERAMONT that night. "D" Coy "B" and "C" Coys were detailed to do the attack. "D" Coy to act as Carrying Party and "A" Coy to hold the present Outpost Line with 1 Company of Scottish Rifles attached. Owing to extreme darkness the attacking Coys lost touch and were unable to carry out the operation.	The 4th Officers were the Battle to-day Major G.W. WATTS, 2/Lieut. S.CLARKE. 2/Lieut. A.E. TURLEY, 2/Lieut. W.E.H. PERRY 2/Lieut. R.E. HART. Received Orders 9th M.R.
	26th Mar.		Day and Night Quiet. Our Front Posts were pushed forward nearer LIERAMONT.	
	27 March		It was reported by the R.C.D. that LIERAMONT had been vacated consequently the C.O. immediately gave orders for "A" Coy to enter the village. Our troops occupied LIERAMONT at 11 a.m. and dug themselves in beyond the village. Enemy artillery was active during the day. The Battalion were relieved in the afternoon by the 2/Scottish Rifles and after relief proceeded to MOISLAINS.	
	28th March		In Billets. Routine.	
	29 Mar.		Paraded for Trenches at 12 noon and completed relief of Scottish Rifles by 8 p.m. H.Q. were at AIZECOURT. At 6 p.m. orders were received to hold ourselves in readiness to attack HEUDECOURT the following afternoon if the village had not fallen before then. Disposition of Battalion :- "C" Coy and half the Battalion Platoon, Outpost Line, "B" and "D" in Support with "A" in reserve.	
	30 Mar		The Brigadier arrived at H.Q. about 8 a.m. and discussed plans for the attack. A Coy/Officers Conference was held at "C" Coy Hd. Qrs at GUYENCOURT at 11 a.m. "A" Coy was told off to attack the Right, "D" Coy to attack the Left, the Battle Platoon to "Mop Up" and "B" Coy of the village of HEUDECOURT	

Army Form C. 2118.

WAR DIARY
or
INTELLIGENCE SUMMARY.
(Erase heading not required.)

Instructions regarding War Diaries and Intelligence Summaries are contained in F. S. Regs., Part II. and the Staff Manual respectively. Title pages will be prepared in manuscript.

Place	Date	Hour	Summary of Events and Information	Remarks and references to Appendices
	1917.		(8) 2ND BATTALION DEVONSHIRE REGIMENT.	
	(30th Mar contd)		to attack to the flank the village of REVELON on right flank. The attack was launched at 4.15 p.m. "D" Coy went through without much resistance capturing only five prisoners. "A" Coy however, came under M.G. fire from the right flank and were temporarily held up. A platoon was thrown back to deal with the trouble, which it did very effectively, enabling the advance to go on. At 6.40 p.m. our troops were through the Village and on the way to the high ground, East and North of the Village. On reaching the far side of HEUDECOURT the Companys reorganised and pushed up the hill and dug themselves in clear of the captured village. Casualties - 3 Killed and 22 Wounded. "A" Coy captured a Machine Gun. "D" Coy captured 5 prisoners, 3 of whom were wounded.	

	31st March.		Dispositions much the same as that of the 30th inst. "D" Coy withdrew from the Outpost line to trench rear of GUYENCOURT together with "C" Coy and the Battle Platoon.
			2/Lieut. A.M. Taylor, "A" Coy, rejoined from a Course of Instruction in Musketry at PONT REMY.
			2/Lieut. J.L. FARQUHARSON, "C" Coy proceeded on a Course of Instruction in Signalling at the 4th Army School, LE QUESNOY.
			
			The following is an extract from the 8th Divisional Commander's letter written on the 31st March 1917.
			"To take, during the 24 hours, in face of strong opposition, 1 large town, 2 villages, 1 hamlet, 1 railway station, 1 wood, and 3 copses, and to advance the line in places 6,000 yards, is a fine achievement.
			Special credit is due to the 2/Devon Regt and 2/Middx Regt. of 23r. Inf.Bde. and to the 1/R.Irish Rifles and 2/Rifle Brigade of the 25th Inf.Bde."
			
			                                   Lt.Col.
			         Commanding 2nd Battalion Devonshire Regiment
			2/4/17	

23rd Brigade.

8th Division.

2nd BATTALION

DEVONSHIRE REGIMENT

APRIL 1917.

Army Form. C. 2118

WAR DIARY
or
INTELLIGENCE SUMMARY
(Erase heading not required.)

Vol 29

16V
sheet

Place	Date	Hour	Summary of Events and Information	Remarks and references to Appendices
	1917. March April 1st.		(1). 2nd BATTALION DEVONSHIRE REGIMENT. "A" and "B" Coys still holding the Outpost Line. GUYENCOURT shelled heavily by the enemy artillery but without damage. 2 German aeroplanes flew over our lines but were driven off by M.G. Fire. "A" Coy captured 1 German M.G. in REVELON during attack on HEUDECOURT. 2/Worcester Regt relieved the Battalion at GUYENCOURT. "A" Coy taking over the outpost line from "B" Coy. "A" Coy of the 2nd Northampton Regt relieving "A" Coy. 2/Lieut. H.D.Grattrick having been wounded in action on the 30th ultimo is at ruck off at length. 2/Lieut. A.E.Rutledge "D" Coy rejoined from a Course of Instruction in Bayonet Fighting at the Divisional School. AVESNE. 2/Lieut. A.WINCH "B" Coy relinquishes the Acting Rank of Captain on ceasing to Command a Coy. "A" and "B" Coys arrived from the line at 5.30 a.m. ceased bath. In billets. In billets. Battalion supplied Working Parties during the day. The Brigadier General inspected dumps of 75 other ranks at Bde. H.Q. and expressed his opinion that they should all go before the A.D.M.S. Board. In billets. Battalion supplied Working Parties during the morning. The Battalion stood to from 2 to 7 p.m. owing to an attack being carried out by the 25th Inf. Bde. In billets. Battalion supplied Working Parties at MOISLAINS. The C.O. inspected the Battalion. No. 15270 Pte. W.STEPHENS "D" Coy was awarded the Military Medal for gallantry in action at BOUCHAR BOUCHAVESNES on the 6th March 1917. In billets. Brigadier inspected "A" Coy and expressed	
	2nd.			
	3rd.			
	4th.			
	5th.			
	6th			

Army Form. C. 2118

WAR DIARY
or
INTELLIGENCE SUMMARY
(Erase heading not required.)

Instructions regarding War Diaries and Intelligence Summaries are contained in F. S. Regs., Part II. and the Staff Manual respectively. Title Pages will be prepared in manuscript.

Place	Date	Hour	Summary of Events and Information	Remarks and references to Appendices
			(2). 2ND BATTALION DEVONSHIRE REGIMENT	
	6th contd.		his entire satisfaction with the turnout of all a men. After the inspection the Coy formed up on the road and marched past. The Battalion supplied Working Parties during the day. Capt E.D.Hill granted leave and then had over duties of Adjt to Major Tillett M.C.	
	7th		The Battalion moved from MOISLAINS to AIZECOURT LE BAS.	
	8th		In billets. Working Parties supplied during the day. The C.O. saw all Platoon Officers at 2 p.m. The Brigadier, 23rd I.B. interviewed all Officers and Section Commanders at AIZECOURT and spoke on the present situation and generally on the war. (6 p.m.). Captain R.J.Andrews M.G. proceeded to the 8th Divisional School for Cmdg. Lieut. S.V.C. who was proceeded to the 23rd Bde. Bomb School. 2/Lieut. R.E.Burr "G" Coy has admitted to Hospital from the 23rd Bde. Bomb School.	
	9th		In billets. Working Parties supplied during the day. Capt. H. Archer was a Member of a Field General Court Martial at the Headquarters 2nd Middx. Regt. at NURLU. Lt. Col A.J.E.SUNDERLAND was President of a F.G.C.M. at the 2/W.Yorks. Regt H.Q. at NURLU. Lt. and Qr.Mr. G.Palmer proceeded on an Army Gas Course at the 4th Army School. 2/Lieut. H.B.Brennan "D" Coy took over the duties of O.C. Bombing Platoon.	
	10th		In billets. The Battalion marched from AIZECOURT to NURLU and was inspected by the Divisional Commander at Bde. I-------- On completion of Inspection he presented the M.M. Ribbon to No. 15370 Pte. W.Stephens "D" Coy for Gallantry in Action at BOUCHAVESNES.	

Army Form. C. 2118

WAR DIARY
or
INTELLIGENCE SUMMARY
(Erase heading not required.)

Instructions regarding War Diaries and Intelligence Summaries are contained in F.S. Regs., Part II. and the Staff Manual respectively. Title Pages will be prepared in manuscript.

Place	Date	Hour	Summary of Events and Information	Remarks and references to Appendices
			(3). 2ND BATTALION NITCHELL CHESIRE	
	10th contd.		Battalion on their recent good work also the above for his gallantry and devotion to duty. The B'n. then marched past the B.val. Company in Column of Route. Working Parties were found by the Battalion in the afternoon. 2/Lieuts. H.D. Garwick and L. Pardoe proceeded for England (Leave).	
	11th		The Batt. have moved into reserve position and billeted at GUYENCOURT billets over from the R.F.A.Bde. "C" & "D" Coys. Two sections on L.M.G. Gun Course at 158th Corps School.	
	12th		The Battalion arranged to place 2 C.S.M. in Villers. The Battalion also did so in addition D once Lemo Mc 2/Lt. 2.W/O. Yorks Regt to be in addition Y evening. Coys to take over 2/Lieut. Yorks H.Q. by 6 p.m. "C" and "D" Coys were relieved. 2/Lieut. A.D.Wilson proceeded to 23rd I.B. as Liaison Officer. 2/Lieut. L.M.L.Thore 23/4/17.	
	13/4/17 to 25/4/17		"C" and "D" Coys still in quiet defence line. Hostile Artillery actively shelled the Sunken Road and its vicinity from K.25.c.2.10 to K.19.c.6.5. From 6 a.m. to 8 a.m. and at intervals throughout the night 12/13th with 77 mm. shells and 4.2 shells. Our own "D" Coys who were not shelled, to 2/W.Yorks Regt. main force attack on VILLERS GUISLAINS on the morning of the 14th. "C" and "D" Coys to get in position on the S.W. and S.E. of the Village which on the 14.5 "E" H by the 14th. 2/Lieut. A.B. Wilson rejoined from cable as Liaison Officer at 23rd I.B. H.Q. 2/Lieut. C.E.Collesson "C" Coy proceeded for duty with prisoners of War. C.C. 33rd Division.	

WAR DIARY
or
INTELLIGENCE SUMMARY
(Erase heading not required.)

Army Form. C. 2118

Place	Date	Hour	Summary of Events and Information	Remarks and references to Appendices
	14th		(4) 2ND BATTALION DEVONSHIRE REGIMENT	

"A" and "B" Coys in Bizerte.
"C" and "D" Coys and Battle Platoon 1 Front L--- around Villers Guislains.

The attack on VILLERS GUISLAINS was unopposed owing to Strong M--- D Gun--- on H--- vt M.G. F---.

Casualties sustained by 2 Coys and "B.P." 2/Lieut. J.H. Vincent Wounded, 2/Lieut. W.E.H.Perry Reported "Missing" under 17 O.R. Killed, 26 O.R. Wounded.

The following is a copy of the report of the action /taken by "C" "D" Coys and Battle Platoon on the attack on VILLERS GUISLAINS,. This report was rendered to 23rd I.B. Hd. Qrs. by the 2/W.Yorks. Regt.

"I have the honour to report that in accordance with 23rd Infantry Brigade Operation Order No. 38 I ordered "D" and "C" Coys and Battle Platoon, 2/Devon.R. to be in position ready to move forward at 4 a.m. behind posts of 2/W.York. R. "D" Coy and ½ Battle Platoon on the right of and including PEZIERE - VILLERS GUISLAIN road; "C" Coy on left of same road. There was some delay in getting into position and after giving Officers information gained by patrols of 2/W.York. R. I ordered them to move forward at 5 a.m. "C" Coy is finding difficulty on right and front was to push forward a strong patrol to get round to northern face of village and then work inwards. Coys were to work in patrols of six after getting through the wire and Battle Platoon was to be used to form chain of posts around villages as Coys advanced through and around it.

2. The sky was just getting a bit light behind the villages as Coys advanced thus showing up objective.

3. About 5.10 a.m. considerable M.G. fire and heavy sniping opened from the S.E. of village, probably from M.Guns near X.9.C.9.4. Most of M.G.s fire from this face and one from about X.9.C.5.3 ---

Army Form C. 2118.

WAR DIARY
or
INTELLIGENCE SUMMARY.
(Erase heading not required.)

Instructions regarding War Diaries and Intelligence Summaries are contained in F. S. Regs., Part II. and the Staff Manual respectively. Title pages will be prepared in manuscript.

Place	Date	Hour	Summary of Events and Information	Remarks and references to Appendices
	1/2nd contd.		(5) 2ND BATTALION DEVONSHIRE REGIMENT.	

was directed on to "D" Coy but one of these M.G. shot "C" Coy as well. The Rifle regiment "C" Coy was not so heavy. Machine Guns reported to be firing from about X.8.b.9.5. and X.2.b.6.3. The considerable shelling. "D" Coy cut through the wire and got inside but was held up by heavy M.G. fire from a house heavily wired. Rifle Grenade fire was opened on to this but without effect, and the Company C8th order withdrew most of his Company outside the wire and dug in. "C" Coy advanced about 100 yards beyond posts of 2/A Nor. R. and then came under M.G. fire and heavy shelling, and owing to this and the formidable nature of the wire and to casualties was unable to reach its objective, and this Coy commenced to dig in. In this position by M.G. with him by the W. Yorks fire, about 40 yards from the wire, the O.C. "C" Coy directed the Stokes Gun attached to him to open fire on the M.G. in the southern face of the village, but before the gun could come into action all the team but one were casualties. 2/Lieut. A. Ritchie, who was in command of this gun was himself wounded as No. 1. Owing to the Gun owing to casualties, and so crowded with great craters to get its No. 1 position, but was shot through the thigh and chin just before he could open fire. The enemy sent up a light brilliance into the green lights soon after the advance began and this resulted in Artillery fire on the S.E, S, and S.W. faces of the wire round the village. A considerable number of Very Lights were put up as the Coys were advancing.

It is of the opinion on that the attack failed owing to the strong defences of the village (v) Machine Guns - 5 in the village and one to the right flank, and one to the left.
(b) The heavy and continuous shelling, estimate 60 to 100 rifles.
(c) The wire.
(d) The enemy's Artillery fire.
(e) Assembling troops being seen by the use of Very Lights.

Army Form C. 2118.

WAR DIARY
or
INTELLIGENCE SUMMARY.
(Erase heading not required.)

Place	Date	Hour	Summary of Events and Information	Remarks and references to Appendices
			(6) 2ND BATTALION DEVONSHIRE REGIMENT.	
	14th contd.		The troops acted well under trying conditions. Capt. J.H.Vincent led his Company well only failing at the last to gain the objective on account of the carefully protected M.G. This Officer was shot through the arm and another bullet through his Field Glasses, and another through his Gas H—t.	
			(Sd) R.J. McLAREN, Major. 2/W.Yorks Regt.	
			"A" and "B" Coys and H.Q. moved off from GUYENCOURT at 6.50 p.m. to relieve 2/Sco. Rifs. Relief completed at 9 p.m. "A" Coy held east of GAUCHE WOOD, with posts. "B" Coy held line of hedges—ditch with 3 posts had 2 Lewis Guns, one other Platoon of "B" Coy relieving 2 Platoons of 2/Sco. Rifs. at X.8.b.2.7. Night fairly quiet, only occasional shelling. Our own artillery very active.	
	15th.		2/Lieut. V.G.EASBY rejoined from Hospital. "A" and "B" Coys remained in same positions as 14th. "C" and "D" Coys and Battn Platoon at GUYENCOURT in billets. Military Medals awarded to No.9336 L/Cpl. E.G. Redwood and No. 17292 as follows:— No.9336 L/Cpl. E.Redwood. Whilst working through the village of HEUDECOURT he spotted a hostile M.Gun and engaged it in a duel with his Lewis Gun Team, and directed his fire, with the effect that the Hostile Gun was knocked out and captured. No. 17292 Pte H.Rogers. For coolness during a duel with a Hostile M.Gun which he knocked out, causing the enemy to abandon it after several attempts had been made to get it away. A new Brigade boundary was decided on and "A" Coy moved their posts North of GAUCHE WOOD. "B" Coy moving further to their right in main line of Resistance. Details of new boundary received us during	
	16th			

Army Form C. 2118.

WAR DIARY
or
INTELLIGENCE SUMMARY.
(Erase heading not required.)

Instructions regarding War Diaries and Intelligence Summaries are contained in F.S. Regs., Part II. and the Staff Manual respectively. Title pages will be prepared in manuscript.

Place	Date	Hour	Summary of Events and Information	Remarks and references to Appendices
			(7) 2ND BATTALION DEVONSHIRE REGIMENT.	
	16th contd.		The afternoon. "C" "D" and "B" Battle Platoon at GUYENCOURT in billets. Orders sent to these Coys to hold themselves in readiness to move at a moments notice.	
	17th.		"A" and "B" Coys position unchanged. "C" "D" and Battle Platoon at GUYENCOURT. Operation Orders sent to these Coys to move up today and take over line held by "B" Coy. "B" Coy to move and dig themselves in to the N.W. end of the village at VILLERS GUISLAINS at a point X.2.c.4.5. approx. and act as inlying picquet, and is instructed despatch "A" Coy to form a strong defensive flank to assist attack by 2/W.York R. on VILLERS GUISLAINS on the morning of the 18th.	
	18th.		"A" Coy then in position were ordered to advance and establish themselves East of VILLERS GUISLAINS as soon as 2/W.YORK.Regt had taken the village. "B" Coy dug themselves in west of VILLERS GUISLAINS and formed inlying picquet. 2/Sco.Rifs relieved the Battalion in positions held by A. and B. Coys - relief completed at 3 a.m. "C" "D" and Battle Platoon remained in brown line. Were received from Division that one Coy of the Battalion to occupy permanently and construct line W. of VILLERS GUISLAINS, which would be support line to main defence line. "B" Coy detailed to do this and start work by 10 a.m. on the 19th. Capt. R.J. ANDREWS, M.C. appointed to Major on Headquarters, 17th Bn.Welsh Regt. 40th Division. Capt. E.D.HILL rejoined from leave and resumed duties of Adjutant.	
	19th.		"A" "C" "D" and Battle Platoon in main Defence line (Reserve) "B" Coy working a new line west of Villers Guislains in accordance with wire.	

T2134. Wt. W708-776. 500000. 4/16. Sir J. C. & S.

Army Form C. 2118.

WAR DIARY
or
INTELLIGENCE SUMMARY.
(Erase heading not required.)

Instructions regarding War Diaries and Intelligence Summaries are contained in F. S. Regs., Part II. and the Staff Manual respectively. Title pages will be prepared in manuscript.

(8) 2ND BATTALION DEVONSHIRE REGIMENT.

Place	Date	Hour	Summary of Events and Information	Remarks and references to Appendices
	19th contd.		Usual working parties supplied by "C" "D" and "B.P." "C" Coy relieved "B" Coy at 8 p.m.	
	20th.		Usual working parties supplied. Day passed quiet. Disposition of Battalion same as on 19th. only "D" Coy relieved "C" Coy in the line. rest of VILLERS GUISLAINS.	
	21st.		Disposition of Battalion unchanged. Usual working parties supplied. Our artillery very active shelling GONNELIEU preparatory to attack on the village by the 25th Brigade. "A" Coy relieved "D" Coy in the line west of VILLERS GUISLAINS.	
	22nd.		Lieut. S.V. Clarke rejoined from a Course at Brigade BOMB School. Disposition of Battalion unchanged. Operation Orders received that the Battalion would relieve the 2/Sco. Rifs. in the left sub-sector in the evening, "C" "D" and Battle Platoon holding Front line which "B" Coy in support. "A" Coy in reserve. Orders received from Brigade that Coy on the right ("C" Coy) should push forward and occupy high ground. X.4.b.9.5, X.4.b.9.5, X.5.a.4.4. X.5.c.4.0. Sheet 57.c.S.E. The night passed quiet.	
	23rd.		The Battalion was relieved by 2/Northampton Regt. and Royal Berkshire Regt. Relief completed by 3 a.m. on 24th. Battalion withdrew to SOREL.	
	24th.		Major G.I. Watts proceeded to England for duty. "A" and "B" Coys. arrived in Billets at SOREL at 12.30 a.m. "C" Coy "D" Coy and Battle Platoon about 3 a.m. Baths were clothed the Battalion during the afternoon. Battalion in Billets at SOREL.	
	25th.		Working parties found by all Coys to work on roads at SOREL LIERAMONT and HEUDECOURT.	

Army Form C. 2118.

WAR DIARY
or
INTELLIGENCE SUMMARY.
(Erase heading not required.)

(9) 2ND BATTALION DEVONSHIRE REGIMENT.

Place	Date	Hour	Summary of Events and Information	Remarks and references to Appendices
	26th.		In Billets. Usual working parties on roads. 2/Lieut.W.M.Thomson "D" Coy proceeded to XV.Corps School for duty as Instructor in Bombing.	
	27th.		Capt.R.Yandle granted leave of absence to U.K. 26/4/17 to 6/5/17. Baths allotted the Battalion at SOREL. Battalion in Billets at SOREL-LE-GRAND. Working parties of all Coys employed in the BRUGGLISEN to work on BROWN LINE running behind the village of VILLERS GUISLAINS. 2/Lieut.V.G.Emery "C" Coy proceeded to Royal Flying Corps for duty and struck off strength.	
	28th.		In Billets. Working parties by all Coys to work on BROWN LINE. Capt.P.Gay rejoined from a Course of Instruction in Lewis Guns. 2/Lieut.J.F.L.Hughes "C" Coy admitted to Hospital - sick.	
	29th.		In Billets. Working parties found by all Coys for work under R.E. on BROWN LINE. 2/Lieut.W.H.Ivory and 2/other ranks joined the Battalion.	
	30th.		In Billets. Working parties found by all Coys and Battle Platoon for work under R.E. on BROWN LINE. 2/Lieut.P.Gay took over the duties of Intelligence Officer. 2/Lieut.W.W.Drake "C" Coy appointed Temp. Capt. whilst Commanding Coy - dated 26/1/17. 2/Lieut.G.F.Thwaites "A" Coy appointed Temp. Capt. whilst Commanding Coy - dated 27/2/17. 2/Lieut.E.D.Hill and 2/Lieut.P.Gay relinquish their rank of Acting Captain on ceasing to Command Coys.	

Lieut.Col.
Commanding 2nd Battalion Devonshire Regiment.

23rd Brigade.
8th Division.

2nd BATTALION

DEVONSHIRE REGIMENT

MAY 1917

WAR DIARY or INTELLIGENCE SUMMARY

2nd Battalion Devonshire Regiment.

Date	Hour	Summary of Events and Information	Remarks
1/5/17.		Battalion in Billets. 2/Lts. A.M.Taylor, A.C.C.Pendrigh and A.C.Bidgway leave for Courses of Instruction. The Battalion left SOREL-LE-GRANDE for the line and relieved the 2/Royal Berks, 25th Bde. Battalion occupied outpost line, disposition as follows:- Battn. H.Q. X.2.b.5.2. Ref. Map. 57C. S.E. "A" Coy in Right Sector of Front Line, "B" Coy – Left. (R.33.b.5.8. to R.34.d.5.9.). "C" Coy in Support, near Cemetery of VILLERS-GUISLAINS. "D" Coy in Reserve with H.Q. on road X.2.a.1.55. The relief was commenced at 9 p.m. and completed by 11.15 p.m. The enemy shelled GONNELIEU very heavily during the night.	
2/5/17.		Disposition the same. Our Artillery active bombarding the enemy line, cutting wire, principally in preparation for attack on LA VACQUERIE, SONNET FARM and Strong Post R.28.d.2.5. One man slightly wounded by shrapnel.	
3/5/17.		Disposition the same. The night was quiet and patrols were sent out at 12 m.n. by "A" and "B" Coys to examine the enemy wire. Both patrols returned at 1.30 p.m. One casualty in the afternoon (B Coy) through a trench mortar exploding. Capt.J.H.Vincent "D" Coy embarked for England (Wounded) 22/4/17. 2/Lt.F.R.Brooman "B" Coy is transferred to "D" Coy from 2/5/17. 2/Lt.J.L.H.Richards proceeds to England on leave.	

Army Form C. 2118.

WAR DIARY
or
INTELLIGENCE SUMMARY.

(Erase heading not required.)

Instructions regarding War Diaries and Intelligence
Summaries are contained in F. S. Regs., Part II.
and the Staff Manual respectively. Title pages
will be prepared in manuscript.

2nd Battalion Devonshire Regiment.

Place	Date	Hour	Summary of Events and Information	Remarks and references to Appendices
	3/5/17. (Contd)		Inter Coy relief took place at 9 p.m. "C" and "D" Coys proceeded to the front line - "A" and "B" Coys occupy Support and Reserve Trenches. "C" and "D" Coys sent out patrols. "D" Coy patrol sustained 2 casualties from enemy rifle fire.	
	4/5/17.		Practice bombardment carried out by our Artillery at 4.5 a.m. Enemy replied, but did no damage. 2/Lt. F. R. Brooman was slightly wounded in the hand. C.O. held a Conference at Battn. H.Q. for Coy Commanders on preparations for the forthcoming raid. The M.O. proceeded on leave, being relieved by Capt. J. Hill. Capt. M. R. Mostyn Reed of the 3rd Battn. was attached to the Bn. for 3 days from the 4th Army School of Instruction. 2/Lt. A. R. Newton "D" Coy granted permission to wear the badges of rank of Captain pending his appointment in the London Gazette. At 9 p.m. the Battle Platoon took over 7 posts on our left and relieved the 2/Middx. Regt. Platoon held a frontage of 500 yards East of GONNELIEU R.27.d.4.4. to R.27.a.9.1.	
	5/5/17.		Practice barrage by our Artillery at 4.45 a.m., practically no reply by the enemy. Disposition the same. Preparations were made to carry out a large raid on enemy trenches including SONNET FARM, the BARRACKS, LA VACQUERIE by the 23rd Bde. (2/Sco. Rifs. 2/Middx) and the 40th Division on our left flank. "B" Coy supplied a carrying party to carry T.M. Bombs. 16 H.Q. Stretcher Bearers attached to the 2/Sco. Rifs. The attack commenced at 11 p.m. and ended at 1 p.m. At midnight extra stretcher bearers were asked for by the 2/Sco. Rifs. Parties from "A" and "B" were sent. "C" and "D" Coys in the line also assisted. The enemy offered great resistance and inflicted many casualties by M.G. fire and shelling.	

WAR DIARY
or
INTELLIGENCE SUMMARY

(Erase heading not required.)

Army Form C. 2118

2nd Battalion Devonshire Regiment.

Place	Date	Hour	Summary of Events and Information	Remarks and references to Appendices
	6/5/17.		Attack ended at 1 a.m. and the bombardment ended at 2 a.m. Our bearers were busy with the wounded. Lieut. S.V.Clarke and 8 O.R. reported missing. Letter received from the O.C. 2/Sco. Rifs. expressing his appreciation of the way in which our Stretcher Bearers and helpers worked to evacuate the wounded and dead from the raid area. Capt. M.R.McCleod returned to the 4th Army School of Instruction. Battn. remained in the line in order to give another day's rest to the 2/Sco. Rifs. The Battle Platoon was relieved by the 2/West Yorks and returned to its former position at Battn. H.Q. "A" and "B" Coys relieved "C" and "D" Coys in front line. "C" Coy came back to Support and "D" to reserve. 2/Lieut. F.R.Brooman "B" Coy rejoined Battn. from Hospital.	
	7/5/17.		Disposition the same. Line very quiet. Lieut. S.V. Clarke previously reported missing was now reported killed and 5 of his party wounded and one killed. The Brig. Genl. and Bde. Major (23rd Bde) called at H.Q. and visited the line. We were relieved by the 2/Sco. Rifs., relief was complete by 11.30 a.m. The Battn. moved into Bde. Reserve and lived in Dug-outs and shelters in SUNKEN ROAD, W.6.d.6.0. to W.6.d.5.55. "C" and "D" Coys and Battle Platoon worked on GREEN LINE (Intermediate) from 9 a.m. to 2 a.m. Capt. R.J. Andrews M.C. was appointed 2nd in Command, 17th Battn. Welsh Regt on this date and struck off strength.	

WAR DIARY
or
INTELLIGENCE SUMMARY

(Erase heading not required.)

Army Form C. 2118

Place	Date	Hour	Summary of Events and Information	Remarks and references to Appendices
			2nd Battn. Devonshire Regiment.	
	7/5/17. (contd)		2/Lieut. A.B.Kitson "B" Coy proceeded on a course of Instruction at 23rd Bde. Bomb School.	
	8/5/17.		The Battn. was engaged in cleaning SUNKEN ROAD and building new shelters. Except for occasional shelling, which did no damage, the day was quiet. Lieut. and Qr.Mr. G.Palmer proceeded on leave to England. 2/Lieut. W.W.Drake proceeded to take over duties of Qr. Mr. 2/Lieut. H.H.Goodman takes over Temp. Command of "C" Coy. "A" and "B" Coys formed a Working Party to dig trenches in Front Line R.27. a.5.10. to R.34.d.5.9. "C" and "D" Coys and Battle Platoon formed a Working Party to work on Green Line (Intermediate) from R. 26.c.10.10. to R. 31.c. 5.0.	
	9/5/17.		Dispositions same. Battn. constructed more shelters. Area very quiet. At 9 p.m. "A" and "B" Coys supplied Working Parties for GREEN LINE, "C" and "D" Coys and Battle platoon for BLUE LINE. 2/Lieut. H.H.Jago "B" Coy proceeded to the 4th Army School for a Course of Instruction.	
	10/5/17.		Disposition the same. Area Quiet. The Battalion supplied Working Parties for GREEN AND BLUE LINES. 2/Lieut. G.L.Hiley proceeded to LIERAMONT to take up the duties of Town Major. No 8202 Pte. V.Harvey "C" Coy (Stretcher Bearer) was awarded the MILITARY MEDAL for Gallantry and Devotion to Duty when in action. Captain R.Yandle "C" Coy rejoined from Leave to U.K.	
	11/5/17.		Disposition the same. Area quiet. (contd.)	

Army Form C. 2118.

WAR DIARY
or
INTELLIGENCE SUMMARY.
(Erase heading not required.)

2nd Battalion Devonshire Regiment.

Place	Date	Hour	Summary of Events and Information	Remarks and references to Appendices
	11/5/17 (cont)		Lieut. U.B.Burke and 20 men from "A" Coy proceeded to LIERAMONT as Working Party to erect tents there. The Battalion relieved the 2/Sco. Rifs. in the line at dusk. Relief commenced at 9 p.m. and finished 11.30 p.m. Front fairly quiet. Dispositions. GONNELIEU SECTOR (Map Reference 57c. S.E. Edition 3.). Battn H.Q. X.2.b.7.4. VILLERS GUISLAINS "C" and "D" Coys in Front Line viz:- R.27.d.5.0. to R.34.d.6.8. "A" Coy in support X.2.b.75.15. "B" Coy in Reserve X.2.a.5.55. "A" and "B" Coys found Working Parties for the GREEN LINE (Intermediate).	
	12/5/17		Dispositions the same. Night fairly quiet except for a little shelling on Front. 1 O.R. slightly wounded. VILLERS GUISLAINS was heavily shelled, otherwise a quiet day. The Battalion supplied Working Parties for the BLUE LINE. The Front Line Posts were connected and continuous trench made.	
	13/5/17		Disposition the same. Lieut. Col. A.J.E.Sunderland proceeded on leave to the U.K. from 14th to 24th May. Major A.Tillett M.C. took over the Command of the Battalion. The Battalion was to be relieved by the 14th H.L.I. 120th Bde., 40th Divn. At 10.50 p.m. the enemy opened a heavy barrage of 5 T.M's and Shrapnel Fire on our Right Coy Frontage. At 1 a.m. a party of the enemy, about 40 strong, were seen moving towards No. 2 Post, situated at R.34.b.3.1. from the direction of the Ravine. The garrison withheld their fire until the enemy were upon the wire. Rapid Rifle and Lewis Gun Fire was then opened upon them and several of the enemy were seen to fall and groans and cries were heard. The enemy replied with Rifle Fire but hastily retreated in disorder. A patrol was at once sent out to obtain any identification, meanwhile the	

WAR DIARY
or
INTELLIGENCE SUMMARY.
(Erase heading not required.)

Army Form C. 2118.

Place	Date	Hour	Summary of Events and Information	Remarks and references to Appendices
			2nd Battalion Devonshire Regiment.	
	13/5/17 (contd).		14th H.L.I. had arrived and relieved the Post, they too, sending out a Patrol. 2 enemy wounded were brought in. We suffered no Casualties. The relief commenced at 10.30 p.m. and was completed by 12.30 a.m. The 8th Division was relieved and went back for rest and training.	
	14/5/17.		The Battalion proceeded to Camp at AIZECOURT LE BAS. (Map Reference FRANCE 62c.N.E. D.23.a.75.6.). The first party arrived at 2.30 a.m. The rest of the Battalion were caught in a storm and arrived in Camp drenched to the skin, but cheerful, about 5 a.m. The men were busy all day cleaning kit, equipment etc. The C.O. and Adjutant attended a Bde. Conference at Hd. Qrs. NURLU.	
	15/5/17.		Disposition the same. The Battalion commenced training according to Bde. Programme. 2/Lieut. G.L.Hiley "C" Coy. rejoined from duty as Town Major of LIERAMONT.	
	16/5/17.		Battalion Training. Bad weather prevented work in the Afternoon. The G.O.C. 8th Division, Major General W.C.G.Heneker D.S.O. A.D.C. visited the Battalion.	
	17/5/17.		Battalion training. 2/Lieut. P.Gay proceeded on Leave to the U.K. Lieut. U.B.Burke took over duties, temporarily, of Intelligence Officer during absence of 2/Lieut. P.Gay on Leave. The u/m Officers joined the Battalion and were posted to Coys as shown :- 2/Lieut. C.A.L.Briggs "A" Coy. 2/Lieut. E.C.Luxon "D" Coy. 2/Lieut. H.C.Squire "B" Coy. 2/Lieut. J.L.H.Richards rejoined from Leave to U.K. (contd.)	

WAR DIARY or INTELLIGENCE SUMMARY.

(Erase heading not required.)

2nd Battalion Devonshire Regiment.

Place	Date	Hour	Summary of Events and Information	Remarks and references to Appendices
	18/5/17.		Battalion Training. The Officers attended a Lecture on Barracks by General Lloyd G.O.C., R.A. at LIERAMONT during the afternoon.	
	19/5/17.		Battalion Training. Captain Duncan M.C., 23rd T.M.Battery Lectured the Officers and N.C.Os of the Battalion on uses of Stokes Guns in attack. The following Officers proceeded to join the 1st Devonshire Regt:- 2/Lieut. A.Winch "B" Coy. 2/Lieut. J.L.H.Richards "A" Coy. 2/Lieut. C.A.L.Briggs "A" Coy. 2/Lieut. H.C.Squire "B" Coy. The Battalion played the 2/Sco. Rifs. at Cricket in the afternoon and beat them by 22 runs.	
	20/5/17.		Church Parade at 11.30 a.m. with the 2/Sco. Rifs. and 2nd Field Coy R.E. The Battle Platoon, played the R.G.A. at Football and won.	
	21/5/17.		In Camp. Battalion under training.	
	22/5/17.		Battalion training. Major W.C.G.Henneker D.S.O., A.D.C., visited the Camp.	
	23/5/17.		Battalion Training.	
	24/5/17.		Battalion Training. A cricket match between Officers and N.C.Os. resulted in favour of the N.C.Os. Lieut. G.A.W.Monk joined the Battalion and was posted to "A" Coy.	
	25/5/17.		Battalion Training. Lieut. Colonel A.J.E.Sunderland rejoined from Leave to the U.K.	

(contd.).

Army Form C. 2118.

WAR DIARY
or
INTELLIGENCE SUMMARY.
(Erase heading not required.)

Instructions regarding War Diaries and Intelligence Summaries are contained in F. S. Regs., Part II. and the Staff Manual respectively. Title pages will be prepared in manuscript.

Place	Date	Hour	Summary of Events and Information	Remarks and references to Appendices
			2nd Battalion Devonshire Regiment.	
	26/5/17.		The Regiment held Athletic Sports at AIZECOURT LE BAS. The Brigadier and his Staff attended. Also many Officers and Other Ranks of the Division.	
	27/5/17.		Church Parade. Captain H. Archer proceeded on 1 month's leave to the U.K.	
	28/5/17.		Battalion Training. 2/Lieut. W.H.Radcliffe joined Battalion and was posted to "B" Coy.	
	29/5/17.		The Battalion struck Camp at AIZECOURT LE BAS at 7.15 a.m. and paraded at 8.45 a.m. and marched to Camp 162 at CURLU, arriving at 1.30 p.m.	
	30/5/17.		Battalion Training. 2/Lieut. J.F.L. Hughes rejoined from hospital.	
	31/5/17.		Battalion Training. In the morning the Battalion practised the attack before the Divisional Commander and Brigadier General. During training in afternoon 1 Other Rank was badly wounded by stepping on an old bomb. The following Officers rejoined the Battalion from Courses :- 2/Lieut. A.M.Taylor "A" Coy. 2/Lieut. A.&.Bidgway "A" Coy. 2/Lieut. A.C.C.Pendrigh "B" Coy.	

Lieut. Colonel.

Commanding, 2nd Battalion Devonshire Regiment.

23rd Brigade.

8th Division.

2nd BATTALION

DEVONSHIRE REGIMENT

JUNE 1917.

Army Form C. 2118.

WAR DIARY
or
INTELLIGENCE SUMMARY.
(Erase heading not required.)

Instructions regarding War Diaries and Intelligence Summaries are contained in F.S. Regs., Part II. and the Staff Manual respectively. Title pages will be prepared in manuscript.

Place	Date	Hour	Summary of Events and Information	Remarks and references to Appendices
			2nd Battalion DEVONSHIRE REGIMENT.	
	1/6/17.		Battalion left CURLU at 6.30 a.m. and marched to VILLE, arriving about 10.45 a.m.	
	2/6/17.		Battalion paraded at 10.50 p.m. and marched to EDGEHILL Station where the Battalion entrained. 2/Lieut.T.R.Johns "C" Coy embarked to England "sick".	
	3/6/17.		Arrived at BAILLEUL at 1 p.m. and marched to MERRIS about 6 kilos. Battalion billetted on outskirts of Village of OUTTERSTEENE. Captain G.F.Thuillier "A" Coy proceeded on leave to U.K.	
	4/6/17.		General clean up in Billets. 2/Lieut.P.Gay "D" Coy returned from leave.	
	5/6/17.		Battalion in training. 2/Lieut.J.H.Vincent to be temporary Captain whilst Commanding a Company from 12/4/17 to 14/4/17. 2/Lieut.A.R.Newton to be temporary Captain whilst Commanding a Company from 29/4/17.	
	6/6/17.		Battalion in training. C.O. inspected the Battalion. Draft of 15 other ranks joined from Base. Cross Country run of 3 miles in the evening, won by Pte Gaylard "C" Coy time - 18¼ minutes.	
	7/6/17.		Battalion in training. Cricket Match between Battalion and Hd.Qrs of 1st Worcesters won by the latter by 6 wickets.	

Army Form C. 2118.

WAR DIARY
or
INTELLIGENCE SUMMARY.
(Erase heading not required.)

Place	Date	Hour	Summary of Events and Information	Remarks and references to Appendices
			2nd. Battalion DEVONSHIRE REGIMENT.	
	8/6/17.		Battalion in training. Draft of 15 other ranks joined from Base.	
	9/6/17.		Battalion in training. C.M.G. D.S.O. Brigadier-General G.W.St.G.Grogan/inspected the new Draft. Cricket Match between the Battalion and 1st Bn Worcester Regt. resulted in a win for the Battn. as follows – 100 runs to 59 runs. The Divisional Band played during the afternoon. Draft of 32 other ranks joined from Base.	
	10/6/17.		Battalion in training. Church Parade held at OUTERSTEENE at 11.30 a.m. Lt.Col. A.J.E.Sunderland was President of a F.G.C.M. at 2/W.York Regt Hd.Qrs. Orders received from 23rd Inf.Bde to prepare to move early the following morning.	
	11/6/17.		Battalion moved at 6.50 a.m. to BORRE area. Warning Order received to prepare to move to area of Square G.11 Sheet 28 N.W.	
	12/6/17.		Battalion in training. Draft of 126 other ranks joined from Base. Captain R.Yandle "C" Coy rejoined from Course of Instruction. Battle Platoon abolished by Divisional Order. 2/Lieut.H.B.Brooman "D" Coy is attached to and takes over temporary command of "A" Coy.	
	13/6/17.		Battalion moved at 2 a.m. to H.19 a. Sheet 28 N.W. arriving at 9 a.m. Marched to Dominion Camp at 7 p.m.	
	14/6/17.		Preparations made to move to the line. All Officers of the Brigade paraded on the Square at Dominion Camp to meet G.O.C. II.Corps to which the 8th Division is now attached. Lt.Gen.Sir Claude Jacob, K.C.B. addressed those present and in a short speech welcomed the 8th Division to the Corps.	

Army Form C. 2118.

WAR DIARY
or
INTELLIGENCE SUMMARY.
(Erase heading not required.)

Place	Date	Hour	Summary of Events and Information	Remarks and references to Appendices
			2nd Battalion Devonshire Regiment.	
	30/6/17.		The Battalion embussed at 6.30 a.m. at HALIFAX CAMP and journeyed to BLANC PIGNON and billets around. See HAZEBROUCK Map. (Near AUDRUICQ.), arriving at 2.30 p.m. 2/Lieut. H.H.Jago took over Temp. Command of "A" Coy.	

M.........
Lieut. Colonel.
Commanding, 2nd Battalion Devonshire Regiment.

Army Form C. 2118.

WAR DIARY
or
INTELLIGENCE SUMMARY.
(Erase heading not required.)

Place	Date	Hour	Summary of Events and Information	Remarks and references to Appendices
			<u>2nd Battalion Devonshire Regiment.</u>	
	14th contd.		Battalion moved at 10 p.m. and marched to the ECOLE at YPRES I.9.c. and billetted for the night in Cellars. Enemy shelling caused five casualties amongst our Lewis Gunners who were unloading a Lewis Gun Limber. Major General L.J.Bols, C.B. (of the Devon Regt) Commanding 24th Division, visited the C.O. 2/Lieut.A.C.Bidgway proceeded to U.K. on leave. 2/Lieut.H.H.Jago "B" Coy rejoined Battalion from Course at 4th Army School.	
	15/6/17.		The C.O. and Coy. Commanders went round the line in the morning. The Battalion moved up at 10 p.m. and relieved the 2/Northampton Regt. The Battn held the line from the Railway I.11.b.6.8. to BELLEWARRDE BEEK I.12.c.3.15. Reference Sheet 28 N.W. 1/20,000. Ed. 5a. A and D Coys in the Front Line, B Coy in Support (Beck Trench) C Coy in Reserve at the ECOLE-YPRES. I.9.6. Hd. Qrs. at I.11.b.55.20. Line fairly quiet, No casualties.	
	16/6/17.		Dispositions the same, night quiet. Enemy artillery very active on back area. Batt. employed on cleaning up the trenches which were badly hit about. The 1/N.Lancashire Regt on out left carried out a small raid on an enemy sap at 11.45 p.m. covered by T.M.Barrage, otherwise the night was quiet.	
	17/6/17.		Disposition the same. The Brigadier, Genl. G.W.St.G.Grogan C.M.G, D.S.O. visited the line in the evening. Capt Thuillier rejoined from leave. A large party were sent out to dig a new trench from No. 1 Crater to BELLEWARRDE BEEK (out right flank). Enemy were very active with Rifle Grenades and Snipers. 5 casualties were sustained 1 killed and 4 wounded. The trench was half dug and two (contd)	

WAR DIARY
or
INTELLIGENCE SUMMARY.
(Erase heading not required.)

Army Form C. 2118.

2nd Battalion Devonshire Regiment.

Place	Date	Hour	Summary of Events and Information	Remarks and references to Appendices
	17/6/17 (contd)		Communication Trenches begun and wired.	
	18/6/17.		Night Quiet. Disposition the same. Enemy artillery/active. The work was continued on the new Front Trench and more wiring finished. 2/Lieut. (A/Major) R.J. Andrews M.C., attached 17th Bn. Welsh Regt was awarded the D.S.O. for Gallantry and Devotion to duty in action.	
	19/6/17.		Dispositions the same. At 2 a.m. the enemy opened a Barrage on our Front Line (right flank). We retaliated with rapid T.M. Fire. The Reserve Coy moved from ECOLE to ESPLANADE - I.7.d.40.15. Work on new Front Trench continued. Revetting was commenced. Enemy Artillery still very active. The C.O. attended a Conference held at Bde. H.Q. at YPRES.	
	20/6/17.		Disposition the same. The Coy Commanders attended a Conference held at H.Q. by C.O. The General Outline of Operations for the new future was brought forward. The Battalion was relieved by the 2/W.Yorks Regt and moved to ESPLANADE-YPRES. Relief commenced at 11 p.m. and was completed by 1 a.m. 21st June, the enemy shelling YPRES during the move. "A" Coy had Casualties passing through the town, 2/Lieut. H.B.Brooman being wounded, 5 O.R. Killed, 2 Died of Wounds and 9 wounded. Captain R.Yandle proceeded on a Course at the 2nd Army School.	
	21/6/17.		The Battalion arrived at ESPLANADE at 4 a.m. The enemy shelled the vicinity of billets and all troops had to remain in dugouts. The men were billetted in Long Tunnell under the Ramparts. Officers and Hd.Qrs. in shelters against Ramparts. The men rested and cleaned up. The Brigadier General 23rd Bde visited the Battalion. The enemy shelling was quieter during the evening. Lieut. U.B.Burke proceeded to Bde. as Bde Observer.	

Army Form C. 2118.

WAR DIARY
or
INTELLIGENCE SUMMARY.
(Erase heading not required.)

2nd Battalion Devonshire Regiment.

Date	Hour	Summary of Events and Information	Remarks and references to Appendices
21/6/17. (contd).		2/Lieut. A.E.Rutledge and 12 O.R. proceeded to Second Army Summer Rest Camp, AMBLETEUSE.	
22/6/17.		Disposition the same. The enemy shelling continued but with less violence as previously. Battalion supplied Working Parties.	
23/6/17.		Disposition the same. Enemy Artillery was still active, increasing towards evening. Orders were received that the Battalion would relieve the 2/Sco. Rifs. on the night of 24/25th inst in the Right Battalion Sector. The Bombardment of the Ramparts and vicinity was widdent violent. All Officers of H.Q. retired to Mined Passage under Ramparts, for the night. Battalion supplied Working Parties. 2/Lieut. J.F.L. Hughes and 3 N.C.Os proceeded to BUSSEBOOM for Course of Instruction in Anti-Gas Duties.	
24/6/17.		The C.O. and Second in Command proceeded to the Front Line in the early morning to prepare for relief. One Coy to be left out of the line this tour and retruned to Details Camp at HALIFAX CAMP. "A" Coy were detailed for this. Coy Commanders and Intelligence Officer moved to the Front Line in Advance at 4 p.m. The Battalion relieved the 2/Sco. Rifs. at 10 p.m. Relief completed at 2 a.m.	
25/6/17.		Battalion in the line - Right Sector. Dispositions. Reference ZILLEBEKE 1/10,000. "C" Coy Left Front-Line Coy, H.Q. BIER CROSS ROADS - I.17.b.5.8.; "B" Coy Right-Front Coy, H.Q. ZOUAVE WOOD I.18.c.4.5. "D" Coy, Support Coy, H.Q. RITZ TRENCH I.23.a.6.5.; Battalion Hd.Qrs. I.17.c.25.55. "A" Coy with Details at HALIFAX CAMP. Night was fairly quiet. The Enemy Heavy Artiller shelled YPRES. (cont).	

WAR DIARY
or
INTELLIGENCE SUMMARY.
(Erase heading not required.)

Army Form C. 2118.

Place	Date	Hour	Summary of Events and Information	Remarks and references to Appendices
			2nd Battalion Devonshire Regiment.	
	25/6/17. (Contd).		2/Lieut. J.D.Harbombe was granted Leave to the U.K. from 25/6/17 to 25/7/17.	
	26/6/17.		Disposition the same. Enemy artillery was still active. The Battalion set out to dig a new trench in front of outpost line. About 60 yards of trench was dug about 3' 6" deep and 2' 6" wide. Battalion also repaired communication trenches.	
	27/6/17.		Disposition the same. Enemy artillery was still busy, especially during the night. The enemy aeroplanes was also very active. Work continued at night on the new front trench. 30 yards were dug by "C" Coy, making their trench 60 yards. "B" Coy lengthened theirs to 130 yards. More work was also carried out in communication trenches	
	28/6/17.		Disposition the same. The enemy artillery was very active during the night, especially against our communication trenches. The Brigade Major, Capt. F.C.Roberts, D.S.O. visited the line.	
	29/6/17.		The morning was fairly quiet. The enemy opened a heavy barrage at 9 a.m. to 9.15 a.m. No casualties. The Battalion prepared for relief by the 2/East Lancs. Regt. Coy Commanders of the East Lancs. arrived in advance of the troops and took over. Relief commenced at 10 p.m. and was completed by 2.30 a.m. (30th). The enemy it appears had planned a raid on the frontage of the Battalion on our right, a heavy barrage being put by them at 11 p.m. Some of which reached our right flank, causing 5 casualties in "B" Coy. The barrage finished at midnight, though no infantry attack materialised. 2/Lieut. J.F.L.Hughes "C" Coy rejoined from Anti-Gas Course. Lieut. W.B.Burke "D" Coy rejoined from duty with Brigade.	

23rd Brigade.
8th Division.

2nd BATTALION

DEVONSHIRE REGIMENT

JULY 1917.

Army Form C. 2118.

WAR DIARY
or
INTELLIGENCE SUMMARY.
(Erase heading not required.)

Instructions regarding War Diaries and Intelligence Summaries are contained in F. S. Regs, Part II. and the Staff Manual respectively. Title pages will be prepared in manuscript.

Place	Date	Hour	Summary of Events and Information	Remarks and references to Appendices
			2nd Battalion DEVONSHIRE REGIMENT.	
	July 1st 1917.		Dispositions the same. Voluntary Church Parade – Army Chaplain visits and speaks to men. Captain H. Archer rejoined from leave to U.K.	
	2/7/17.		Battalion in training. 2/Lieut.A.M.Taylor granted 10 days leave to U.K. 2/Lieut.F.R.Brooman proceeded for attachment to 24th Infantry Brigade. 2/Lieut.H.H.Goodman took over temporary Command of "C" Coy from 20/6/17.	
	3/7/17.		Dispositions the same. Battalion in training. Captain J.R.Cartwright has been awarded the D.S.O. (Extract London Gazette No.30111 dated 4/6/17). 2/Lieut.H.B.Brooman embarked to England "wounded" on 24/6/17. No.4761 Sgt.A.Wheaton "B" Coy and No.4812 L/Cpl.J.G.Dymond "B" Coy have been awarded medal for "Long Service and Good Conduct". Temp.2/Lieut.A.B.Kitson to be Temporary Lieut. from 24th July 1916 (but not to carry pay or allowances prior to 16th August 1916). Temp.2/Lieut.J.H. Vincent and Temp.2/Lieut.R.S.Holmes to be Temp.Lieuts from 22nd Novr 1916. Concert given by the Detonators at Scottish Churches Hut AUDRUICK to the Battalion at 6.30 p.m.	
	4/7/17.		Dispositions the same. Battalion paraded at 8 a.m. and marched to new Training ground at TOURNEHEM. Orders received to prepare to move tomorrow. 2/Lieut.A.E.Rutledge rejoined the Battn from Summer Rest Camp. 2/Lieut.H. Edwards joined the Battn and is posted to "C" Coy.	
	5/7/17.		Battalion paraded at 9 a.m. and proceeded to training ground at TOURNEHEM. After morning training Battn moved to new Billets at BONNINGUES, with the exception of "B" Coy who were Billetted at 8148/45 HARICAT.	
	6/7/17.		Dispositions the same. Battn in training. Capt.T.Lawder, R.A.M.C. 24th Field Ambulance joined the Battn for duty as Medical Officer, vice Capt.D.	

Army Form C. 2118.

WAR DIARY
or
INTELLIGENCE SUMMARY.
(Erase heading not required.)

2nd Battalion DEVONSHIRE REGIMENT.

(2)

Date	Hour	Summary of Events and Information	Remarks and references to Appendices
6/8/17 (contd)		Whyte who proceeded to England.	
7/8/17		Dispositions the same. Battalion in training. 2/Lieut.J.L.Gregory joined the Battn and is attached to "D" Coy. 2/Lieut.W.W.Drake "C" Coy who proceeded to 23rd T.M.Bty for duty on 18/5/17 is struck off strength. C.O. and 2nd in Command attended a Conference held at 23rd Inf.Bde Hd.Qrs. at 4.30 p.m. The Revd.C.F.Bateman joined the Battn for duty as Chaplain.	
8/7/17		Church Parade held in field at Village at 11 a.m.	
9/7/17		Dispositions the same. Battn in training. Lieut.A.B.Kitson proceeded to II. Corps Reinforcement Camp for duty as Platoon Commander. Lieut.R.S.Holmes proceeded to G.H.Q.Lewis Gun School, LE TOUQUET, for a Course of Instruction.	
10/7/17		Dispositions the same. Battn paraded for demonstration in the "Tanks inthe attack". 2/Lieut.H.V.I.Watts joined the Battn and posted to "B" Coy. 2/Lieut.M.G.Beck "B" Coy proceeded for attachment to 24th Inf.Bde.	
11/7/17		Battn left BONNINGUES in Busses at 10.30 a.m. for DELETTE, and arrived 3.30 p.m	
12/7/17		Battn paraded at 9.15 a.m. and marched to Training ground to do the attack in conjunction with the other Battns of the Brigade and returned to Billets at 10.30 a.m.	
13/7/17		Dispositions the same. Battn paraded at 9 a.m. and marched to training ground where an attack was made by the Brigade. Col.Campbell gave a Lecture on Physical Training. 2/Lieut.J.F.L.Hughes "C" Coy proceeded on leave to U.K.	

WAR DIARY
or
INTELLIGENCE SUMMARY.
(Erase heading not required.)

2nd Battalion DEVONSHIRE REGIMENT.

(3)

13/7/17 (contd)
The Divisional Commander awarded Parchment Certificates to the u/m N.C.O. and men for gallantry and devotion to duty in action near YPRES between 10/6/17 and 21/6/17.
No.8595 L/Cpl.H.R.COLLINS "A" Coy. No.18108 Pte F.D.LLOYD "A" Coy.
No.8561 Pte E.W.FLEMING "A" Coy.
2/Lieut.F.R.Brooman "D" Coy rejoined from duty with 24th Inf. Bde.

14/7/17. The Battn again practised the attack with the Brigade.

15/7/17. 2/Lieut.V.T.J.Rainey joined the Battn on the 11th inst and was posted to "B" Coy The Battn went out for the day and practised an attack with the Division. Afterwards all Officers of the Division assembled at COYECQUE and the Corps Commander gave a Lecture on the forthcoming operations.

16/7/17. Battn had a rest, and general clean up. In the afternoon a Concert was held. At 5 p.m. all Officers attended a Lecture at COYECQUE. 2/Lieut.A.C.Faulkner "B" Coy proceeded on leave to U.K.

17/7/17. Lieut.A.B.Kitson proceeded on leave to U.K. The Battn practised the attack on the training ground with the Brigade. At 5.30 p.m. a Lecture was given by General HENEKER to all Officers at COYECQUE.

18/7/17 The Battn practised the attack in conjunction with the Division. Sir DOUGLAS HAIG was present. At 5.30 p.m. a Lecture was given to Officers at COYECQUE.

19/7/17. Battn had a general clean up. A Concert was held in the afternoon.

Army Form C. 2118.

WAR DIARY
or
INTELLIGENCE SUMMARY.
(Erase heading not required.)

(4)

2nd Battalion DEVONSHIRE REGIMENT.

Date	Summary of Events and Information
20/7/17.	The Battn embussed at 9.30 a.m. and left DELETTE for BOESEGHEM, arriving at 12.30 p.m.
21/7/17.	Battn in training. Embussed at 2.30 p.m. and proceeded to STEENVOORDE, where a halt was made. Moved on at 9 p.m. and arrived at destination at 11 p.m which was a Camp about 3 kilos behind POPERINGHE.
22/7/17.	The Battn rested, and paraded at 9.20 p.m. and marched to VANCOUVER CAMP.
23/7/17.	The Battn moved from Camp at 9.30 a.m. and took up its position in the RAMPARTS at YPRES. Details moved back to DOMINION CAMP.
24/7/17.	Dispositions the same.
25/7/17.	The Battn was shelled all day. Proceeded to take over from 2/W.York.R. in the RAILWAY WOOD Sector. "A" and "D" Coys in the front line. "B" Coy and Hd.Qrs in dugouts at Railway Wood. "C" Coy at MONTREAL CAMP. Casualties during the day were slight.
26/7/17.	Dispositions the same. At 5 p.m. 12 men of "A" Coy under 2/Lieut.A.E.Tilley raided the enemy lines successfully. Our casualties were 2 men killed.
27/7/17.	Dispositions the same.
28/7/17.	"C" Coy came up from MONTREAL CAMP and in the evening relieved "D" Coy. "B" Coy relieved "A" Coy. "A" and "D" Coys returned to Dugouts at RAILWAY WOOD.

WAR DIARY
or
INTELLIGENCE SUMMARY.

(Erase heading not required.)

Army Form C. 2118.

2nd Battalion DEVONSHIRE REGIMENT.

(5)

Date	Hour	Summary of Events and Information
29/7/17.		Dispositions the same.
30/7/17.		The day was rather wet. In the evening (10.30 p.m.) "A" and "D" Coys moved from RAILWAY WOOD dugouts to take up their assembly positions for the attack.
31/7/17.		At ZERO hour 3.50 a.m. the attack was launched and the Battalion moved forward according to the Programme. The 1st 3 lines of trenches were taken and the Battalion then moved forward to the BLUE LINE which was the final objective. Battalion H.Q. were established at LAKE FARM by 8 a.m. The Coys then re-organised and at 10.50 moved forward to take up positions in support of the 25th Inf. Bde. It was during this advance that our troops came under a heavy hostile shelling and Machine gun fire from the right. Many Casualties were sustained including Lieut. Colonel. A.J.E.SUNDERLAND who was killed by Rifle Fire whilst leading the Battalion. The advance to the GREEN LINE had been held up owing to the troops on our right not gaining their objective. This brought enfilade fire upon our troops whilst in this vicinity. The Battn. finally took up a position approximately 200 yards East of South Station Buildings. The last part of the advance being by short rushes. About 2 p.m. a message was received from the O.C. 2/Rifle Bde. who were on our immediate front asking for reinforcements for his right flank as a hostile Counter Attack was expected. A platoon of "B" Coy was immediately sent forward. Defensive Flanks were then formed by the remainder of the Battalion. At 10 p.m. the Battalion commenced to relieve the 2/Rifle Bde., our dispositions then being 2 Coys in the Front Line and 2 in support with Bn. H.Q. at SEXTON HOUSE. All night and early the next morning the Battalion was subjected to very heavy hostile shelling and Machine Gun fire. The following Officers accompanied the Battalion into action :- Lt. Col. A.J.E. Sunderland, Captain H.Archer, 2nd in Command, Lieut. U.B.Burke, Intelligence Officer, Capt. T.Lawder R.A.M.C., Medical Officer. (Contd)

Army Form C. 2118.

WAR DIARY
or
INTELLIGENCE SUMMARY.
(Erase heading not required.)

Instructions regarding War Diaries and Intelligence Summaries are contained in F. S. Regs., Part II. and the Staff Manual respectively. Title pages will be prepared in manuscript.

Place	Date	Hour	Summary of Events and Information	Remarks and references to Appendices
	31/7/17.		(6)	
			2/Lieut. P.Gay A/Adjutant.	
			2/Lieut. H.H.Jago.(Comdg Coy.). "A" Coy. 2/Lieut. A.M.Taylor.	
			2/Lieut. A.E.Titley. 2/Lieut. R.M.Haswell.	
			2/Lieut. G.Parker (Comdg Coy). "B" Coy. 2/Lieut. A.C.C.Pendrigh.	
			2/Lieut. W.H.Radcliffe. 2/Lieut. H.V.I.Watts.	
			2/Lieut. H.H.Goodman (Comdg Coy). "C" Coy. 2/Lieut. L.N.L.Tindal.	
			2/Lieut. G.E.Hiley. 2/Lieut. J.F.L.Hughes.	
			Capt. A.R.Newton (Comdg Coy). "D" Coy. 2/Lieut. F.R.Brooman.	
			2/Lieut. E.C.Luxon. 2/Lieut. W.H.Ivory.	
			2/Lieut. A.E.Rutledge Liaison Officer to Left Battalion.	
			2/Lieut. A.C×Bidgway Liaison Officer to Right Battalion.	
			(signature) Major.	
	4/8/17.		Commanding 2nd Battalion Devonshire Regiment.	

REPORT ON RAID BY 2nd DEVONSHIRE REGT.
=*=*=*=*=*=*=*=*=*=*=*=*=*=*=*

26/7/1917.

The raiding party left our lines about MOMBER CRATER, proceeded to IDENTITY TRENCH, which was found to be empty.

The trench was entered from about I.12.a.0.4. - I.12.a.30.26.

The enemy was holding IDENTITY SUPPORT and rifle fire estimated at the strength of about 1 platoon was opened on our party.

The front line was found to be only 18" deep and much knocked about. There was an empty concrete M.G. emplacement at about I.12.c.42.92.

A hostile machine gun was in action at about I.12.a.9.4., and 4 or 5 snipers opened fire from some point about I.12. central.

No prisoners were obtained.

---*---

Herewith Report of Officer Commanding 2/Devon.R. on Raid carried out at 5 p.m. the 26th instant.

- - - - - - - - - - - - - - - - -

1. **BARRAGES.** I watched the operation from our Front Line just N. of 2 A Crater.

The R.A. and Stokes Mortar Barrage appeared excellent. I thought the men got up rather too close to the barrage but none were hit by it.

A weak barrage opened on BEEK TRENCH about Zero plus 2.

The following are reported by other observers:-

Zero plus 3. WEST LANE, CRATER TRENCH and RAILWAY.

Zero plus 9. Junction of WEST LANE and Front Line.

Zero plus 17. RAILWAY, WEST LANE and BEEK TRENCH.

Barrage generally weak. Most shells fell in WEST LANE and Front Line. Shells came from N.E. and S.E. chiefly 77mm and 4.2" with a few 5.9's.

Zero plus 2. The enemy sent up rockets which burst into two Green Stars.

2. **ENEMY ACTION.**

The Raid left our lines at Zero and proceeded as ordered. They met with no obstacle. The front line was only knee deep and was reported empty except by one man who stated that he was shot at from a dugout into which he threw six or seven bombs. I do not place much confidence in his statement.

There was an empty Concrete Machine Gun Emplacement at the South end of the trench.

2nd Lieut TITLEY reports enemy's second line held by about 20 men who opened on them with rifle fire.

A machine gun was in action about I.12.a.9.4.

There were 4 or 5 snipers further South.

Our men claim to have hit 4 or 5 Germans.

Hostile Artillery ceased with ours.

3. **CASUALTIES.**

1 other rank killed.
1 other rank missing believed killed.
Lt. V.B.BOURKE (Observing) hit by splinter (At duty).

4. I regret that no prisoner was obtained, but consider that the party behaved very gallantly and did everything possible.

(sd) A.J.ELTON SUNDERLAND, Lt.Col.
26th July 1917. Commanding 2nd Bn. Devonshire Regiment.

--2--

For information.

Captain,
27th July 1917. Brigade Major, 23rd Infantry Brigade.

23rd Brigade.

8th Division.

2nd BATTALION

DEVONSHIRE REGIMENT

AUGUST 1917.

WAR DIARY or INTELLIGENCE SUMMARY

2nd Battalion DEVONSHIRE REGIMENT.

August 1st 1917.
Battalion in the line near SOUTH STATION BUILDINGS, WEST OF BLACK LINE. Enemy counter-attack withstood in the afternoon. Our casualties rather heavy. Battalion relieved at night by the 8th SOUTH LANCASHIRE REGIMENT (25th Division). Troops march to RAILWAY WOOD then to DOMINION CAMP AREA. Officer Casualties:- Killed - Lt.Col. A.J.E.Sunderland, 2/Lieut. A.M.Taylor. Wounded - 2/Lieut. W.H.Radcliffe, 2/Lieut. G.Parker, Capt. A.R.Newton, 2/Lieut. A.C.Bidgway, 2/Lieut. A.C.C.Pendrigh, 2/Lieut. W.H.Ivory, Lieut. U.B.Burke, 2/Lieut. H.V.I.Watts, 2/Lieut. R.M.Haswell, 2/Lieut. J.F.L.Hughes. Casualties to other Ranks - 22 Killed, 170 wounded, 37 Missing, up to August 4th.

2/8/17. Battalion resting at DOMINION CAMP. 2/Lieut. P.GAY ceases to do duty as A/Adjutant. 2/Lieut. J.D.HARCOMBE takes up duties as A/Adjutant.

3/8/17. Battalion still at DOMINION CAMP but move in the evening to DEVONSHIRE CAMP except "A" and "B" Coys. Major General HENEKER, D.S.O. G.O.C. 8th Division calls upon the officers of the Battalion to thank them and all ranks upon the splendid work done by the Battalion during the operations.

4/8/17. Battalion in DOMINION and DEVONSHIRE CAMPS. The Corps Commander, Lieut. Gen. Sir CLAUDE JACOB, K.C.B., visits the Battalion to thank the Officers and men for the work done - especially in withstanding the enemy counter-attacks. 2/Lieut. M.G.BECK "B" Coy proceeded to Fifth Army Summer Rest Camp. Lieut. F.A.F.BONE joined the Battalion and posted to "B" Coy. Draft of 42 other ranks joined the Battalion. Captain A.R.NEWTON "B" Coy relinquishes the Acting rank of Captain on ceasing to Command a Company 1/8/17.

Army Form C. 2118.

WAR DIARY
or
INTELLIGENCE SUMMARY.
(Erase heading not required.)

Instructions regarding War Diaries and Intelligence Summaries are contained in F.S. Regs., Part II. and the Staff Manual respectively. Title pages will be prepared in manuscript.

Place	Date	Hour	Summary of Events and Information	Remarks and references to Appendices
			2nd Battalion DEVONSHIRE REGIMENT.	
	5/8/17.		Battalion in DEVONSHIRE CAMP re-organizing, refitting and training. Lieut. G.A.W.MONK and 2/Lieut.V.T.J.RAINEY rejoined from II.Corps Reinforcement Camp.	
	6/8/17.		Battalion in training. Divisional Band visits the Battalion. Captain R.YANDLE "C" Coy rejoined Battalion from II.Corps Reinforcement Camp. 2/Lieut.H.H.JAGO "A" Coy proceeded on leave to U.K. Captain H. ARCHER took over duties of 2nd in Command from 31/7/17. 2/Lieut.H.H. GOODMAN took over command of "C" Coy from 1/8/17. Captain R.YANDLE took over Command of "D" Coy from 1/8/17. 2/Lieut.A.C.FAULKNER "B" Coy took over command of that Coy from 31/7/17. Draft of 10 Signallers joined the Battalion.	
	7/8/17.		Battalion in same Camp. Parades under Company arrangements and training for Specialists. 2/Lieut.H.H.JAGO (S.R) to be Acting Captain whilst commanding a Company. 2/Lieut.G.F.THUILLIER "A" Coy relinquishes the Acting Rank of Captain on ceasing to Command a Company, 25/6/17.	
	8/8/17.		Battalion in Training. 2/Lieut.P.GAY proceeded for duty with 23rd Infantry Brigade. 2/Lieut. L.N.L.TINDAL "C" Coy took over duties of Intelligence Officer 7/8/17. 2/Lieut.D.V.M.MANSEL-CAREY "D" Coy rejoined for duty from 490th Field Coy, R.E.	
	9/8/17.		Battalion in same Camp. Moved to RAILWAY WOOD. "A" Coy had about 10 casualties while on the WARRINGTON ROAD.	
	10/8/17.		Battalion returned to DOMINION CAMP. 2/Lieut.A.E.RUTLEDGE "D" Coy proceeded to Second Army School, WISQUES, for a Course of Instruction.	

Army Form C. 2118.

WAR DIARY
or
INTELLIGENCE SUMMARY.
(Erase heading not required.)

2nd Battalion DEVONSHIRE REGIMENT.

Date	Summary of Events and Information
11/8/17.	Battalion moved up to SWAN CHATEAU. Lieut. R.S. HOLMES "C" Coy rejoined from leave to U.K.
12/8/17.	Battalion remained at SWAN CHATEAU until the afternoon when it moved forward to BEELEWARDE RIDGE, with H.Q. in dug-outs in MUD LANE. Dispositions:- "B" and "C" in front line, "A" and "D" in second line with their left on the YPRES-ROULERS Railway.
13/8/17.	Battalion in same dispositions, except that "A" Coy had to move their two platoons on the right about 200 yards to the rear owing to heavy shelling. Casualties 10 other ranks.
14/8/17.	Same dispositions. "A" and "D" Coys found working parties in the evening carrying stores to make Brigade Dump.
15/8/17.	Battalion in same dispositions. At dusk H.Q. moved forward to Battle H.Q. in old German dug-out under the YPRES-ROULERS Railway in WYLDE WOOD. "B" and "C" Coys moved into their assembly positions about midnight on WESTHOEK Ridge. "A" and "D" Coys moved back to the vicinity of Brigade Dump ready to carry.
16/8/17.	2/Lieut.J.L.FARQUHARSON embarked for England "sick" on the 5th inst. 2/Lieut.C.E.COPLESTON "C" Coy struck off strength from this date. Captain A.R.NEWTON and 2/Lieut.G.PARKER embarked for England "wounded" on the 4th inst. The following operations were carried out:- "C" Coy. This Coy was in support of the 2/Middlesex Regt in support of its objective. 3 strong points held up the advance. These were all in the Railway. They were successfully cleared but resulted in the lines being about 600 yards in rear of the barrage. This enabled the hostile machine guns to come into action. Later the 2/Middlesex Regt had to

WAR DIARY
or
INTELLIGENCE SUMMARY.

(Erase heading not required.)

2nd Battalion DEVONSHIRE REGIMENT.

Summary of Events and Information

Date	
16/8/17. (contd)	withdraw. This Coy assisted the withdrawal by hanging on to the position as long as possible and opening a covering fire with rifles and lewis guns. Large numbers of the enemy were killed including the enemy on the north side of the Railway. "B" Coy. This Coy was in support of the 2/W.Yorks Regt and reached its objective with little difficulty, except for Sans Souci which contained 2 machine guns and about 12 men, and the HANNEBEKE WOOD which contained machine guns. These were successfully dealt with. The 2/W.Yorks had later to withdraw when this Coy assisted by opening covering rifle and lewis gun fire "A" Coy and "D" Coy. These Coys were employed as carriers. The first request was received about 2 p.m. Parties had to go to BIRR CROSS ROADS for water and S.O.S. rockets. The following is a list of stores sent forward:- 74 boxes S.A.A., 32 tins of water, 134 boxes Rifle Grenades, 6 boxes rods for R.G's, 88 boxes Very lights, 2 boxes S.O.S. Rockets, 50 Shovels, 2 Lewis Guns, 60 L.G. magazines. All these were carried forward under heavy fire. The following Officers went into the attack, Lt.Col. A.TILLETT, M.C. Commanding, Capt R.YANDLE 2nd in Command, 2/Lieut J.D.HARCOMBE Adjutant, 2/Lieut.L.N.L.TINDAL Intelligence Officer, Capt.LAUDER Medical Officer, 2/Lieut A.E.TITLEY and Lieut G.A.W.MONK "A" Coy, 2/Lieut.A.C.FAULKNER and 2/Lieut.V.T.J.RAINEY "B" Coy, 2/Lieut H.H.GOODMAN and Lieut.R.S.HOLMES "C" Coy. 2/Lieut.E.C.Luxon, 2/Lieut F.R.BROOMAN and 2/Lieut.D.V.M.Mansel-Carey "D" Coy.
17/8/17.	Headquarters in MUD LANE dug-outs. Remainder of Battalion in old trenches just outside with the exception of "A" and "D" Coys who still held their positions on BELLEWARDE RIDGE. After dark "A" and "D" were withdrawn to vicinity of MUD LANE. 2/Lieut A.C. Bidgway embarked for England "wounded" 7/8/17. 2/Lieut. H.V.I.WATTS died of wounds 11/8/17. 2/Lieut. M.G.BECK rejoined from 5th Army Summer Rest Camp. The u/m N.C.O's and men were granted the MILITARY MEDAL for gallantry

WAR DIARY
or
INTELLIGENCE SUMMARY.

(Erase heading not required.)

Army Form C. 2118.

Place	Date	Hour	Summary of Events and Information	Remarks and references to Appendices
			2nd Battalion DEVONSHIRE REGIMENT.	
	17/8/17. (contd)		and devotion to duty 31/7/17 and 1/8/17. No.6851 Pte.W.Fleming, No.9065 Pte.F.Edwards, No.7374 Sgt.W.Cockram, No.33101 Cpl.B.Kidger, No.8260 Pte.W.Hopkins, No.15402 L/Cpl.A.E. Shepherd, No.30443 Pte.S.C.Rundle, No.8595 Cpl.H.R.Collins, No.16709 Pte.J.Lock, No.14864 Pte.C.Rockley, No.8869 Sgt.E.Jordan, No.33233 Pte.W.Sandford. The following were awarded PARCHMENT CERTIFICATES, 2/Lieut C'W.White, No.4812 L/Cpl. J.Dymond.	
	18/8/17.		Battalion remained at MUD LANE until the evening when they moved back to SWAN CHATEAU. 2/Lieut.R.H.IVORY embarked for England "wounded" 8/8/17. Capt H.H.JAGO rejoined from leave to U.K. 17/8/17. Lieut.A.B.KITSON rejoined from II Corps Reinforcement Camp.	
	19/8/17.		Battalion remained at SWAN CHATEAU until about 10.30 p.m. when they were relieved by the 41st Division and moved to HALIFAX AREA. The following were the casualties from 13/8/17 to 19/8/17. Killed:- 2/Lieut.H.H.GOODMAN, 16 Other Ranks; Wounded :- 2/Lieut. A.C.FAULKNER, 67 Other Ranks, Missing :- 7 Other Ranks.	
	20/8/17.		Battalion embussed at 2.30 p.m. and proceeded to billets about 1½ miles N.W. of CAESTRE. 2/Lieut.H.EDWARDS and 2/Lieut.J.L.GREGORY rejoined from II Corps Reinforcement Camp. 2/Lieut.M.G.BECK and 2/Lieut.C.L.HLLEY were granted leave to U.K. from 20/8/17 to 30/8/17. 2/Lieut.A.J.SNOWDEN joined the Battalion and took over the duties of Lewis Gun Officer. A draft of 314 Other Ranks joined the Battalion today. 2/Lieut. A.C.C.Pendrigh died of wounds 19/8/17.	

Army Form C. 2118.

WAR DIARY
or
INTELLIGENCE SUMMARY.
(Erase heading not required.)

2nd Battalion DEVONSHIRE REGIMENT.

Date	Hour	Summary of Events and Information	Remarks and references to Appendices
21/8/17.		Battalion paradeded at 10.15 a.m. and marched to Divisional Parade ground at LE BREARDE where the Division was inspected by Field Marshal SIR DOUGLAS HAIG at 12.30 p.m. who complimented the Division on the excellent work done in the recent attacks. Lieut.W.W.DRAKE, attached T.M.Bty. wounded 11/8/17. Lieut.F.A.F. BONE was admitted to Hospital 12/8/17. Hon. Lieut. & Qr.Mr.G. PALMER to be Hon. Captain and & Qr (Extract London Gazette 3/6/17, 2/Lieut.H.L.R.BAKER joined the Battalion. 2/Lieut.R.M.HASWELL and 2/Lieut.L.N.L.TINDAL were awarded the Military Cross. No.8005 C.S.M. (A/R.S.M) F.H.RADFORD, No.8826 Sgt L.CRISPIN and No 8915 Sgt A.H.PARTRIDGE were awarded the Distinguished Conduct Medal. 2/Lieut (A/Capt) A.R.NEWTON and 2/Lieut. G.PARKER mentioned in Despatches.	
22/8/17.		Battalion in same Billets. A Memorial Service for those killed in the late fighting round YPRES was held in the Field at Battalion H.Q. About 100 men from each Battalion in the Brigade attended. Lieut.W.W.DRAKE died of wounds 16/8/17.	
23/8/17.		Battalion in same Billets. Company training 8.30 a.m. to 12.30 p.m and 2 to 2.45 p.m. 2/Lieut.W.H.RADCLIFFE rejoined the Battalion from the Base. A Draft of 4 other ranks joined this day.	
24/8/17.		Battalion in same Billets and carried on with Company Training. The Divisional Commander visited the Battalion about 3 p.m. The following Officers joined the Battalion this day;- 2/Lieut.L.M. Easterbrook, 2/Lieut.G.D.Ferard, 2/Lieut.L.Lacey Smith, 2/Lieut.T.H Haine, 2/Lieut.H.S.Heard, 2/Lieut.S.T.Mears.	

WAR DIARY
or
INTELLIGENCE SUMMARY.

(Erase heading not required.)

Army Form C. 2118.

2nd Battalion DEVONSHIRE REGIMENT.

Date	Hour	Summary of Events and Information	Remarks and references to Appendices
25/8/17.		Battalion in same billets and carrying on with Coy training. Lieut.(A/Capt) H.ARCHER awarded the D.S.O., and Lieut.H.K.WILLIAMS (attached 8th Divisional Signal Coy) awarded M.C. for gallantry and devotion to duty East of YPRES on 31/7/17 - 1/8/17.	
26/8/17.		Battalion in same billets. There was a service for R.C's in CAESTRE Church at 9 a.m. and for C.of E's in the field at Headquarters at 10 a.m.	
27/8/17.		Battalion paraded at 4 a.m.and marched to camp opposite The Custom House about a mile S. of NEUVE EGLISE. 2/Lieut.A.R.NEWTON relinquishes the acting rank of Capt on ceasing to command a Coy 31/7/17. 2/Lieut.W.W.DRAKE to be Act. Lieut whilst 2nd in Command of 23rd T.M.Battery 1/6/17. 2/Lieut.H.S.HEARD proceeded to 23rd T.M.Battery and is struck off the strength of the Battalion.	
28/8/17.		Battalion in same camp. The weather was bad, high wind and rain all day and training had to be carried out in the huts. The C.O. went up to see the line which the Battalion is to take over. 2/Lieut.J.H.C.WILLY and 2/Lieut B.W.JEFFERY joined the Battalion. 2/Lieut F.R.BROOMAN and 2/Lieut D.V.M.MANSEL-CAREY proceeded on 10 days leave to the U.K. The following are awarded PARCHMENT CERTIFICATES for gallantry and devotion to duty east of YPRES between 31/7/17 and 16/8/17. Lieut A.C.G.ROBERTS, No.8648 Sgt.F.E.Way, No.4761 Sgt.A.Wheaton, No.8990 Pte.J.Prince, No.10829 Pte.S.Gale, No.16442 Pte.D.J.Rees, No.13185 Pte.H.Downey, No.13099 Pte.A.J.Davies, No.11478 Pte.G.Pugsley No.8208 L/Cpl.V.Harvey	

Army Form C. 2118.

WAR DIARY
or
INTELLIGENCE SUMMARY.
(Erase heading not required.)

Instructions regarding War Diaries and Intelligence Summaries are contained in F. S. Regs., Part II. and the Staff Manual respectively. Title pages will be prepared in manuscript.

Place	Date	Hour	Summary of Events and Information	Remarks and references to Appendices
			2nd Battalion DEVONSHIRE REGIMENT:	
	29/8/17.		Dispositions the same. Coy Commanders went up to see the new line. Lieut U.B. Burke rejoined the Battalion from the Base and drafts of 7 Other ranks and 16 Other ranks joined the Battalion	
	30/8/17.		Battalion in same camp. There was a Voluntary Church Service and Holy Communion held in the Y.M.C.A. Hut at 12 noon. 2/Lieut. S.T. MEARS proceeded on a Course of Instruction in Observation and Sniping at the Second Army School, DE SEULE.	
	31/8/17.		Battalion moved up to the trenches in PLOEGSTEERT WOOD sector. Dispositions:- Front Line, Right "C" Company. Front Line, Left "A" " Support Coy. "B" " Reserve Coy. "D" " 2/Lieut G.D.FERARD proceeded to ETAPLES, on a Tour of Duty.	
	2/9/17.			

Aleur

Lieut Colonel,
Commanding 2nd Battalion Devonshire Regiment.

23rd Brigade.
8th Division.

2nd BATTALION

DEVONSHIRE REGIMENT

SEPTEMBER 1917.

Army Form C. 2118.

WAR DIARY
or
INTELLIGENCE SUMMARY.
(Erase heading not required.)

Instructions regarding War Diaries and Intelligence Summaries are contained in F. S. Regs., Part II. and the Staff Manual respectively. Title pages will be prepared in manuscript.

Place	Date	Hour	Summary of Events and Information	Remarks and references to Appendices
			2nd Battalion DEVONSHIRE REGIMENT. ++++++++++++++++++++++++	
	1/9/17.		In trenches. Dispositions unchanged. 2/Lieut.B.W.JEFFERY "B" Coy proceeded to 23rd Brigade Bomb School near NIEPPE. Lieut.A.C.G.ROBERTS and Lieut.U.B.BURKE proceeded to U.K. on 10 days leave.	
	2/9/17.		Dispositions unchanged. 2/Lieut.T.KEILLER joined Battalion on 1st inst. 2/Lieut.M.B.BECK and 2/Lieut. G.L.HILEY returned from Leave to U.K.	
	3/9/17.		Dispositions unchanged. Casualties - 2 Killed, 3 Wounded. Draft of 17 other ranks joined Battn yesterday.	
	4/9/17.		Dispositions unchanged. Casualties - 2 Killed, 3 wounded. Lieut.Col.H.St.J.JEFFERIES, 2/W.York R. (Acting Brigadier) visited the line.	
	5/9/17.		Dispositions the same. Casualties - 3 Killed, 2 wounded.	
	6/9/17.		Dispositions the same. The Corps Commander, Major Gen. (temp.Lt.Gen) SIR.A.G. HUNTER-WESTON, K.C.B., D.S.O. visited the Battalion. About 10 p.m. Battn was relieved by 2/W.York R. and moved back to Billets in LE ROSSIGNOL area with the exception of "B" Coy who stayed in SUPPORT FARM, C.1.b.7.4. S.E. of PLOEGSTEERT. The following Officers joined the Battn. They were taken on strength and posted to Coys as shewn :- 2/Lieut.J.GEDDES "A" Coy. 2/Lieut.G.E.BAXTER "B" Coy. 2/Lieut.E.T.SANDFORD "D" Coy. 4 Other Ranks joined Battn.	
	7/9/17.		Coys proceeded to Divnl.Baths at PAPOT. The remainder of the day was spent in cleaning up.	

Army Form C. 2118.

WAR DIARY
or
INTELLIGENCE SUMMARY.
(Erase heading not required.)

Instructions regarding War Diaries and Intelligence Summaries are contained in F. S. Regs., Part II. and the Staff Manual respectively. Title pages will be prepared in manuscript.

Place	Date	Hour	Summary of Events and Information	Remarks and references to Appendices
			2nd Battalion DEVONSHIRE REGIMENT.	
	7/9/17		(contd). 2/Lieut. L. CORRY joined Battn. and posted to "C" Coy. 2/Lieut (A/Capt) G.F. THUILLIER took over Command of "C" Coy. Capt.T.A.LAWDER, M.O., R.A.M.C. returned from leave to U.K. The Rev. G. BATEMAN, Chaplain, proceeded on leave to U.K. A Draft of 17 other ranks joined Battn.	
	8/9/17.		In Billets at LE ROSSIGNOL. The following Officers proceeded on leave to U.K.:- Lieut.Col.A.TILLETT, M.C., 2/Lieut.L.N.L.TINDAL, M.C., 2/Lieut.A.E.TITLEY "A" Coy.	
	9/9/17.		There was a Voluntary C.of E.Service at Battn.H.Q. at 11.30 a.m. A Football match between the Officers and Sergts of the Battn resulted in a win for the latter by 3 goals to 2.	
	10/9/17.		2/Lieut.D.V.M.MANSEL-CAREY "D" Coy returned from leave to U.K. and proceeded for duty as Right Brigade Tramways Officer. A Football Match between the Battn. and 249th M.G.Coy resulted in a win for the latter by 5 Goals to Nil.	
	11/9/17.		2/Lieut.F.R.BROOMAN "C" Coy returned from leave to U.K. A Football match between Hd.Qrs and "A" Coy resulted in a draw of 1 Goal each.	
	12/9/17.		2/Lieut.G.L.HILEY "C" Coy proceeded for duty with 15th Field Coy, R.E. The Battalion relieved the 2/W.York R. in the PLOEGSTEERT Sector. Dispositions as follows:- Front line, right - "B" Coy. Front line, left - "D" Coy. Support Coy - "C" Coy. Reserve Coy - "A" Coy. Battn.H.Q. at the CONVENT.	

Army Form C. 2118.

WAR DIARY
or
INTELLIGENCE SUMMARY.
(Erase heading not required.)

2nd Battalion DEVONSHIRE REGIMENT.

++++++++++++++++

Date	Summary of Events and Information
13/9/17.	Dispositions the same. The u/m Officer and N.C.O. were awarded decorations as follows for gallantry and devotion to duty East of YPRES between 15th – 17th August 1917 :– The Military Cross – 2/Lieut. A.C. FAULKNER "B" Coy. The Distinguished Conduct Medal – No.8595 Corpl. H.R. COLLINS "A" Coy. The following Officers returned from leave to U.K. :– Lieut. U.B. BURKE and Lieut. A.C.G. ROBERTS.
14/9/17.	Dispositions the same. Lieut. F.A.F. BONE "B" Coy having embarked for England "sick", was struck off strength.
15/9/17.	Dispositions the same. Lieut. G.A.W. MONK "A" Coy and 2/Lieut. H. PARKER "B" Coy proceeded on leave to U.K.
16/9/17.	Dispositions the same. 2/Lieut. A.E. RUTLEDGE "D" Coy rejoined from Course of Instrn at 2nd Army School.
17/9/17.	Dispositions the same.
18/9/17.	Dispositions the same. The Battn was relieved by 2/W.York R. in the evening and returned to the Billets they had vacated.
19/9/17.	In Billets. Interior economy. In the evening there was a Football match between "A" and "B" Coys. The latter Coy won by 2 Goals to 1. A Draft of 10 Other ranks joined the Battalion.

Army Form C. 2118.

WAR DIARY
or
INTELLIGENCE SUMMARY.
(Erase heading not required.)

2nd Battalion DEVONSHIRE REGIMENT.

Date	Hour	Summary of Events and Information	Remarks and references to Appendices
20/9/17.		Company training. A practice Rugby match was played in the evening.	
21/9/17.		Company training. In the afternoon all available officers witnessed an exhibition in Bayonet Fighting by a party of men under the Brigade P.T. Staff Sgt.Major. At 9 p.m. all Officers and Senior N.C.Os practised marching on a Compass. The final of the Inter-Platoon Football /Competition was played at 5 p.m. between H.Q. and "B" Coy, resulting in a win for H.Q. by 3 Goals to Nil. A Concert was held at H.Q. at 6 p.m. Lieut (A/Major) A.TILLETT, M.C., to be Acting Lieut.Col. whilst commanding a Battalion, 15th August 1917. Lieut (A/Capt) H.ARCHER, D.S.O., to be Acting Major whilst employed as Major on H.Q. 15/8/17. 2/Lieut.A.C.FAULKNER, M.C. and 2/Lieut.H.H.GOODMAN to be Acting Capts.from 15/8/17 and 16/8/17. whilst Commanding Coys. The following N.C.Os and men were awarded the MILITARY MEDAL for gallantry and devotion to duty East of YPRES between 15th - 17th August 1917 :- No.9040 Sgt.E.S.AYRE "B" Coy. No.20540 L/Sgt.H.UNSWORTH "B" Coy. No.11333 L/Cpl.J.K.HOSKINGS "A" Coy. No.6710 Sgt.A.F.R.SUTTON "C" Coy. No.8953 Sgt.P.H.COX "C" Coy. No.9522 Sgt W.T.PILE "C" Coy. No.204881 Pte A.WEARY "C" Coy. No.30813 Pte J.SMALE "C" Coy. 2/Lieut.A.E. Captain R.YANDLE "D" Coy proceeded to U.K. on 10 days leave. TITLEY "A" Coy and 2/Lieut.L.N.L.TINDAL, M.C. returned from leave 20/9/17.	
22/9/17.		Dispositions the same. At 5 p.m. a Football Match between the Lewis Gunners and 2/W.York R.drummers was won by the latter. At 6 p.m. there was a Battalion run - Course 2 miles. Won by Sgt. GILL "A" Coy. 2nd - 2/Lieut.E.T.SANDFORD "D" Coy. 3rd - 2/Lieut. J.P.TUCKER "D" Coy. 4th - L/Cpl.JOUSIFFE "D" Coy. Lieut.Col.A.TILLETT, M+C., rejoined from leave to U.K. 2/Lieut.A.E.RUTLEDGE "D" Coy proceeded on leave to U.K.	

Army Form C. 2118.

WAR DIARY
or
INTELLIGENCE SUMMARY.
(Erase heading not required.)

2nd Battalion DEVONSHIRE REGIMENT.

Date	Summary of Events and Information
23/9/17.	Dispositions the same. Voluntary Church Parade at 11 a.m. at H.Q. R.C's and Nonconformists had a Service at NIEPPE. Battalion played 25th Field Ambulance at Rugby at 5 p.m. resulting in a win for the latter by 8 points to 6. 2/Lieut. H.S. HEARD "C" Coy (attached 23rd M.G.Coy) was wounded on 21st inst. No.8876 Pte M.BOND (attached 23rd M.G.Coy) awarded the M.M. for gallantry and devotion to duty East of YPRES between 15th and 17th August 1917.
24/9/17.	There was a Lecture by the Brigadier to all Officers at NIEPPE at 11 a.m. on Defence Scheme. The Battalion moved up to take over the line from 2/W.York R. at 8.30 p.m. "A" left front Coy; "C" right front Coy; "B" in support; "D" in reserve. Casualties - 8 wounded, 1 Missing believed killed.
25/9/17.	In the trenches. The Brigadier visited H.Q. about 12.30 p.m. A quiet day. Our patrols were busy all night. Casualties - 1 wounded. Capt. & Qr.Mr. G.PALMER proceeded on leave to U.K.
26/9/17.	In the trenches. The Brigadier visited LAURA and LILLIAN Posts at about 10.30 p.m. The Brigade Major and an R.E.Officer went out and patrolled bridges over River LYS. Special Coy, R.E, fired Gas Bombs on enemy trenches. Casualties - 2 killed and 4 wounded. A Draft of 10 other ranks joined the Battalion.
27/9/17.	In Trenches. No casualties. 2/Lieut.H.PARKER "B" Coy rejoined from leave to U.K.
28/9/17.	In Trenches. Casualties - 1 other rank gassed.

Army Form C. 2118.

WAR DIARY
or
INTELLIGENCE SUMMARY.
(Erase heading not required.)

Place	Date	Hour	Summary of Events and Information	Remarks and references to Appendices
			2nd Battalion DEVONSHIRE REGIMENT. ++++++++++++	
	29/9/17.		In Trenches. Casualties - 1 wounded, 2 shell shock. 5 Other ranks joined the Battn from Base. 2/Lieut.L.M.EASTERBROOK "A" Coy proceeded to 4th Army School of Instrn. 2/Lieut.S.P.TOZER and 15 other ranks joined the Battalion. 2/Lieut (A/Capt) G.F.THUILLIER "C" Coy was admitted to Hospital "sick".	
	30/9/17.		The Battalion was relieved by 2/W.York R. at 9.30 p.m. and moved back to LE ROSSIGNOL area in Billets. "A" Coy to PONT DE NIEPPE. Casualties - 1 wounded. 2/Lieut.V.T.J.RAINEY "B" Coy killed.	

R. Vivian
Lieut.Col.
Commanding 2nd Battalion Devonshire Regiment.

23rd Brigade.

8th Division.

2nd BATTALION

DEVONSHIRE REGIMENT

OCTOBER 1917.

Army Form C. 2118.

WAR DIARY
or
INTELLIGENCE SUMMARY.
(Erase heading not required.)

Instructions regarding War Diaries and Intelligence Summaries are contained in F. S. Regs., Part II. and the Staff Manual respectively. Title pages will be prepared in manuscript.

2ND BATTALION DEVONSHIRE REGIMENT. (1).

Place	Date	Hour	Summary of Events and Information	Remarks and references to Appendices
	1917. October 1st.		Battalion resting. Draft of 10 other ranks joined. 2/Lieut. G.D. FERARD rejoined from tour of duty at STAPLES. 2/Lieut. G.D. A Rugby Match between the Officers and the remainder of the Battalion was won by the latter by 21 points to Nil.	
	2nd.		Battalion training. The Divisional Commander presented Medal Ribbons at 11.30 a.m. 2/Lieut. A.E. TITLEY "A" Coy and 4 other ranks proceeded to Summer Rest Camp at VILLEREAUX. A Football Match between the Battalion and 26th Field Ambulance resulted in a win for the Ambulance by 2 goals to 1.	
	3rd.		Battalion training. Draft of 44 other ranks joined. Captain R. YANDLE "D" Coy rejoined from leave to U.K. A Soccer Match between H.Q. and 3/W.Yorks Drummers resulted in a win for H.Q. by 5 goals to 2.	
	4th.		Battalion training. 2/Lieut. J.L. GREGORY "D" Coy proceeded to Bde. Bomb School for Course of Instruction. 2/Lieut. M.G. BECK proceeded for duty with 23rd Bde. Bomb School. 2/Lieut. T. KETTLER "B" Coy reported to 3rd T.M. Battery for duty. Lieut. G.A.W. MONK "A" Coy granted extension of leave until 6th October. A Rugby Match PROBABLES versus POSSIBLES resulted in a draw of 6 points each.	
	5th.		Battalion training. 2/Lieut. S.H. HEARD "C" Coy attached 23rd T.M. Battery embarked for England wounded. 2/Lieut. A.E. RUTLEDGE "D" Coy rejoining from leave to U.K. Capt. T. LANDER, M.C. proceeded to 24th F.A. for duty. Lieut. K.P. KANE, U.S.A.M.C. joined for duty. Battalion training. 2/Lieut. E.G. LUXOM "D" Coy proceeded on leave to U.K. 2/Lieut. J.J. HUNTINGFORD joined the Battalion and posted to "C" Coy.	
	6th.		Battalion Run resulted as follows :- 1st 2/Lieut. BAXTER "B" Coy, 2nd Pte. PITTS "A" Coy, 3rd Sgt. SEERY "C" Coy.	

WAR DIARY or INTELLIGENCE SUMMARY

Army Form C. 2118.

Place	Date	Hour	Summary of Events and Information	Remarks and references to Appendices
	October		**2nd BATTALION DEVONSHIRE REGIMENT (2).**	
	7th.		Battalion training. Lieut. L.N.L.TINDAL, M.C. proceeded for duty with 23rd Inf. Bde.	
	8th.		2/Lieut. D.V.M.MANSEL-CAREY "D" Coy rejoined from duty as Tramway Control Officer. Battalion relieved the 2/W.Yorks. Regt in the line.	
	9th.		In the trenches. Captain G.A.V.MONK "A" Coy rejoined from leave.	
	10th.		In the trenches. Lieut. W.H.RADCLIFFE "B" Coy proceeded on leave to the U.K. 2/Lieut. B.W.JEFFERY "B" Coy proceeded to Corps Reinforcement Camp for duty as Bombing Instructor.	
	11th.		In the trenches. Lieut. A.B.KITSON "B" Coy appointed Actg.Capt. whilst Commanding a Company.	
	12th.		In the trenches.	
	13th.		In the trenches. 2/Lieut. L.CORRY "C" Coy admitted to hospital "sick".	
	14th.		In the trenches. 2/Lieut. A.E.TITLEY "A" Coy rejoined from Sunnex Rest Camp, MILLEREAUX.	
	15th.		In the trenches.	
	16th.		Battalion was relieved by 2/W.Yorks. Regt.	
	17th.		Interior Economy. 2/Lieut. L.CORRY "C" Coy proceeded on leave to the U.K. Major H.ARCHER D.S.O. granted leave to the U.K. Lieut. R.S.HOLMES appointed Actg. Capt. whilst Comdg. a Coy from 31/8/17 to 7/9/17.	
	18th.			

Army Form C. 2118.

WAR DIARY
or
INTELLIGENCE SUMMARY.

(Erase heading not required.)

2ND BATTALION DEVONSHIRE REGIMENT. (3).

Place	Date	Hour	Summary of Events and Information	Remarks and references to Appendices
	October.			
	18th.		Battalion training. 2/Lieut. A.G.FAULKNER M.C. embarked for England wounded. 2/Lieut. M.G.BECK rejoined from duty at 23rd Bde. Bomb School. 2/Lieut. E.C.LUXON "D" Coy rejoined from leave. A Rugby Match between "B" and "D" Coy resulted in a win for "D" Coy by 21 points to Nil.	
	19th.		Battalion training. 2/Lieut. S.P.TOZER to be T/Lieut. from 4/7/17. A Soccer Match between Battalion and 5th Black Watch Labour Battalion resulted as follows :- Battn 3 goals Black Watch Nil.	
	20th.		Battalion in training. 2/Lieut. E.E.BEANE joined the Battalion and posted to "C" Coy. A Rugby Match played between the Battalion and Rifle Bde. resulted as follows, Battalion 23 points, Rifle Bde. Nil. A very successful concert was held in the evening.	
	21st.		Divine Service. Battalion.	
	22nd.		Battalion training. A Football Match between H.Q. and 2/W.Yorks Drummers resulted in a win by 2 goals to Nil. A Soccer Match between "D" Coy and 3rd Canadian Light Railway was won by the former by 3 goals to 1.	
	23rd.		Battalion training. Lieut. W.H.RADCLIFFE "B" Coy rejoined from leave to U.K. A Bde. Boxing Tournament was held in the afternoon.	
	24th.		Battalion training. 2/Lieut. S.T.MEARS "D" Coy proceeded on a Course of Instruction at the II Corps Infantry School, MILLAM. In the evening the Battalion the Battalion relieved 2/W.Yorks. R.	
	25th.		In the trenches. Lieut. R.S.Holmes "C" Coy and 2/Lieut. G.E.BAXTER of Instruction at X Corps Inf. School, (BOESCHEPE.	

Army Form C. 2118.

WAR DIARY
or
INTELLIGENCE SUMMARY.
(Erase heading not required.)

Place	Date	Hour	Summary of Events and Information	Remarks and references to Appendices
	October.		2ND BATTALION DEVONSHIRE REGIMENT. (4).	
	26th.		In the trenches.	
	27th.		In the trenches. 2/Lieut. W.H.EDWARDS "C" Coy proceeded on leave to U.K. from 28/10/17 to 7/11/17.	
	28th.		In the trenches. Casualties 3 other ranks killed 4 other rank wounded.	
	29th.		In the trenches. Casualties 3 other ranks wounded.	
	30th.		In the trenches. The G.O.C. 23rd Infantry Brigade visited the Battalion. Casualties 1 other rank killed.	
	31st.		In the trenches.	

A. Witt Lieut. Colonel,
Commanding 2nd Battalion Devonshire Regiment.

23rd Brigade.
8th Division.

2nd BATTALION

DEVONSHIRE REGIMENT

NOVEMBER 1917.

1st Divisional Artillery.

1ST DIVISIONAL AMMUNITION COLUMN WAR DIARY JANUARY 1916

WAR DIARY
or
INTELLIGENCE SUMMARY.
(Erase heading not required.)

Army Form C. 2118.

2ND BATTALION DEVONSHIRE REGIMENT.

Place	Date	Hour	Summary of Events and Information	Remarks and references to Appendices
	1917. Novr. 1st.		In the Trenches. On the night 1/2nd the Battalion was relieved in the line by the 2/West Yorks. Regt., and proceeded to billets - H.Q. "A" and "D" Coys at LE ROSSIGNOL, "C" Coy at PONT de NIEPPE "B" Coy in HUNTERS AVENUE, PLOEGSTEERT WOOD at disposal of O.C. 2/W.Yorks Regt.	
	2nd.		Coy Training was carried out. 2/Lieut. G.L.HILEY rejoined from duty with 15th Field Coy R.E.	
	3rd.		Battalion in Training. Major H. ARCHER D.S.O. rejoined from leave. 2/Lieut. J.L.GREGORY proceeded to U.K. on leave. A Rugby Football Match between the Regimental Team and 24th Field Ambulance resulted in a win for the latter by 12 points to 3.	
	4th.		Divine Service. 2/Lieut. A.J.SNOWDEN proceeded for duty at 23rd Brigade School. "B" Coy moved from HUNTERS AVENUE to billets in NIEPPE.	
	5th.		Battalion in Training. 2/Lieut. E.E.BEARE proceeded to U.K. on leave. A Rugby Football Match was played between "A" and "D" Coys and resulted in a win for the former by 14 points to 3.	
	6th.		Battalion in Training. 2/Lieut. M.G.BECK proceeded to VIII Corps School, TERDEGHEM for duty as Bombing Instructor. 2/Lieut. L.Mc.I.EASTERBROOK rejoined from a Course at 4th Army Infantry School. At 6 p.m. the Battalion relieved the 2/W.Yorks. Regt in Support in PONT de NIEPPE, 1 Coy in RESERVE AVENUE, 1 Coy FUSILIER TERRACE, 1 Coy in HUNTERS AVENUE, 1 Coy PONT de NIEPPE.	
	7th.		Same dispositions.	

Army Form C. 2118.

WAR DIARY
or
INTELLIGENCE SUMMARY.
(Erase heading not required.)

Instructions regarding War Diaries and Intelligence Summaries are contained in F.S. Regs., Part II. and the Staff Manual respectively. Title pages will be prepared in manuscript.

Place	Date	Hour	Summary of Events and Information	Remarks and references to Appendices
	1917. Novr.		**2ND BATTALION DEVONSHIRE REGIMENT.**	
	8th.		Captain J.MOYLE joined the Battalion. In the evening the battalion took over the left sector of the line H.Q. the Convent, "C" and "D" Coys in Front Line, "B" Coy in Support and "A" in Reserve. Casualties 3 wounded.	
	9th.		Same dispositions. During the night of 8/9th our Standing Patrol at MOAT FARM was attacked at 1 a.m. and 4.20 a.m. In the first case they were driven off with rifle and L.G. fire. The second time the enemy returned about 60 strong and attacked from all sides but were eventually driven off. Our casualties were 17 wounded and 5 missing. The Brigadier visited the battalion during the morning and again at night when he went round our Standing Patrols himself. Lieut. L.N.L. TINDAL M.O. rejoined from duty with 23rd Inf. Bde. 2/Lieut. E.C.LUXON wounded.	
	10th.		Same dispositions. A quiet day, no casualties. Captain J.D. HARCOMBE proceeded on 14 days leave to U.K.	
	11th.		The Battalion was visited by G.O.C. 4th Australian Inf. Bde. The battalion was relieved at about 7 p.m. by 2/W.Yorks. R. and moved back to LE ROSSIGNOL Camp. Casualties 1 Killed, 1 wounded.	
	12th		The Battalion marched to billets in the BERQUIN Area and temporarily under the orders of 25th Inf. Bde.	
	13th		Same dispositions. Day of rest and Interior Economy. Lieut. S.P.TOZER, 2/Lieut. J.GEDDES, 2/Lieut. L.Mc.I. EASTERBROOK and 2/Lieut. .H.HAINE proceeded to the 9th Battalion Devonshire Regt. Lieut. A.J.SNOWDEN rejoined from duty with 23rd Bde. School. 2/Lieut. H.L.R.BAKER rejoined from hospital on 11th inst.	

Army Form C. 2118.

WAR DIARY
or
INTELLIGENCE SUMMARY.
(Erase heading not required.)

2ND BATTALION DEVONSHIRE REGIMENT

Place	Date	Hour	Summary of Events and Information	Remarks and references to Appendices
	1917 Novr. 14th		Coy Training. Draft of 9 other ranks joined the Battalion.	
	15th		Training continued. Battalion again under the Command of 23rd Inf. Bde.	
	16th		Training continued. A battalion Run in the afternoon resulted as follows :- 1st, Pte. SELLEY, 2nd Pte. STEPHENS, 3rd Pte. BARROW.	
	17th.		Battalion paraded at 12.30 p.m. and marched to new billets in the MERRIS AREA.	
	18th		Battalion paraded at 1.30 p.m. and marched to CAESTRE where they entrained at 4.30 p.m. for BRANDHOEK, detraining at 6 p.m. and moved into Camp "B".	
	19th		Battalion paraded at 1 p.m. and marched to "A" Camp at WIELTJE. Lieut L.L.SMITH was admitted to hospital.	
	20th		Same disposition. Battalion furnished Working Parties. Casualties 4 wounded.	
	21st		Same disposition. Working Parties as usual. 2/Lieut. P.GAY struck off the strength having been ordered a Medical Board whilst on leave to the U.K. 2/Lieut. J.L.GREGORY rejoined from leave to U.K. on the 19th inst Captain G.PALMER admitted to hospital "sick".	
	22nd		Same disposition. The C.O. Second in Command and Coy Commanders visited the line. 2/Lieuts. L.CORRY and E.T.SANDFORD proceeded to VIII Corps School for a Course of Instruction. 2/Lieut. E.F.BEARE rejoined from leave to U.K.	

Army Form C. 2118.

WAR DIARY
or
INTELLIGENCE SUMMARY.
(Erase heading not required.)

Instructions regarding War Diaries and Intelligence Summaries are contained in F.S. Regs., Part II. and the Staff Manual respectively. Title pages will be prepared in manuscript.

Place	Date	Hour	Summary of Events and Information	Remarks and references to Appendices
	1917.		2nd Battalion Devonshire Regiment.	
	Novr 23rd.		The Battalion moved up to the line N. of PASSCHENDAELE by Platoons the leading Platoon starting at 3 p.m. Battalion H.Q. at METCHEELE. Casualties - 1 killed, 10 wounded. 2/Lieut.E.E.BEARE admitted to Hospital on 22nd inst. 2/Lieut.H.Parker rejoined from a P.T. Course at Second Army School.	
	24th.		"A" and "B" Coys in the front line, "C" and "D" Coys in support. Casualties - 2 killed, 13 wounded.	
	25th.		At 12.20 a.m. the front line was advanced about 150 yards. The following is a report of the operations -
On the night of the 23/24th extensive patrolling was carried out with a view to locating exact positions of enemys outpost line and how far the advancement of our line would be interfered with by enemy activity. Patrols reported that many Germans were occupying shell holes and retired on patrols approaching. The supposed strong point at W.25.c.35.40 and M.G. at W.25.c.4.3 were confirmed. Arrangements were made with the O.C. "B" Coy. 2/W.York R. who were advancing on our right. Particular attention was paid to visual reconnaissance by day on the 24th and favourable landmarks etc were pointed out to the men. By 12.20 a.m. the 25th platoons were ready to advance in columns of sections under their section commanders at 28 yards interval.
At 12.30 a.m. the platoons on the left advanced to their new position and dug in, at the same time a platoon under 2/Lieut. Titley advanced against the strong point. This was taken with very little difficulty and the platoon dug in on their new position.
The right platoon was not so fortunate at first although they ultimately gained their position. Delay in starting was due to the fact that both the Officer and N.C.O. detailed to advance on the Machine gun were killed just previous to the advance. On hearing of this Captain H.H.Jago M.C. took charge of this party under orders from	

Army Form C. 2118.

WAR DIARY
or
INTELLIGENCE SUMMARY.

(Erase heading not required.)

Place	Date	Hour	Summary of Events and Information	Remarks and references to Appendices
	1917 Novr 25th.		2nd Battalion Devonshire Regiment. Major H. Archer D.S.O. Owing to the bright moonlight the M.G. crew easily spotted our right post and within 10 minutes another four men were killed or wounded. This made a direct advance on the gun out of the question. Arrangements were then made with the 2/West Yorks Regt for them to detail some men especially to work round the back of the gun while the party covered their advance by occupying the enemy Machine guns attention from the front. This was successful and by an advance from two directions at once the enemy machine gun was forced to retire and evacuate the post. The right platoon were then able to make good their ground and dig in on the new line. Owing to not being able to gain touch with the West Yorks our right flank was thrown back as a defensive flank. The following night patrols were out and succeeded in locating the West Yorks. Information was passed on to the relieving Unit as to how to establish connection and maintain the line. The morning of the 25th saw us in our correct position on the crest with an uninterrupted view for about 400 yards with no dead ground between. Many Germans were killed and wounded as several Stretcher parties were out next morning and picked up their casualties. 5 prisoners were taken for identification purposes and passed on. The enemy was obviously very disorganised as next day a lot of running about between shell holes was observed. Our men made good use of their rifles. No resistance of any strength was encountered. The enemy retired, in some cases leaving rations, etc. behind. The enemy sent out patrols during the night subsequent to our advance but they showed no inclination to fight. Our positions were very alert and any hostile movement was at once checked by accurate rifle and M.G. fire. Our men showed great determination, and their use of the rifle and bayonet showed that they are realising its possibilities. The Battalion was relieved by 2/Sco.Rifs about 8 p.m. and moved back into dugouts and sheltered at CAPRICORN close to SPREE FARM (Sheet 28.N.E. 1/20,000). Casualties - 3 killed, 14 wounded.	

WAR DIARY
or
INTELLIGENCE SUMMARY.
(Erase heading not required.)

Army Form C. 2118.

2nd Battalion Devonshire Regiment.

Date	Summary of Events and Information	Remarks
1917. Novr 25th (contd)	Major H.ARCHER, D.S.O. killed. 2/Lieut.J.H.O.WILLY killed. 2/Lieut.J.L.GREGORY missing.	
26th.	Day spent in clearing up and reorganising. One carrying party furnished for front line. Casualties – 3 wounded. 2/Lieut.D.V.M.MANSEL CAREY, and 2/Lieut.T.KELLER embarked for England on the 18th "sick".	
27th.	Still at CAPRICORN supplying working parties to carry to front line. Captain H.H.JAGO, M.C. assumed duties of Second in Command.	
28th.	Battalion moved off by Coys to relieve the 2/Sco.Rfs in the front line N. of PASSCHENDAELE at 5 p.m. Dispositions – "A" Coy – Right Support. "B" Coy – Left front. "C" Coy – Left Support. "D" Coy – right front. Casualties – 1 killed, 16 wounded. Captain J.D.HARCOMBE rejoined from leave to U.K.	
29th.	Still in line. Casualties – 3 killed, 8 wounded. Captain R.YANDLE, wounded (..t duty). Lt.Col.A.TILLETT, M.C. wounded. Captain H.H.JAGO took over Command of the Battalion. Lieut.R.S.HOLMES and 2/Lieut.G.E.BAXTER rejoined from X.Corps Scl 2/Lieut.S.T.MEARS rejoined from II.Corps School.	
30th.	Still in the line. About 8 a.m. the enemy attempted an attack against out positions but was repulsed by rifle and L.G.fire with heavy losses. Our S-O-S.Barrage came down just as he was getting back to his trenches ard did great damage. After dark the Battm was relieved by the 2/R.I.R. and moved back to "E" Camp, St.JEAN. Casualties – 7 killed, 12 wounded. Captain A.B.KITSON wounded. Captain G.A.W.MONK wounded. 2/Lieut.A.E.RUTLEDGE wounded.	

H.H.Jago
Commanding 2nd Battalion Devonshire Regt, Captain,

T.C.

G.97/2

Very good. D

Congratulate those
concerned on their
excellent work.

Is the M.G. position
& the strong point
both in our line
now?

JHSnickers
27.11.17

Report on Minor Operation carried out by this Battalion
on night of 24th/25th November.
-o-o-o-o-o-o-o-o-o-o-o-o-o-o-o-o-o-o-o-o-o-o-o-

On the night of 23rd/24th extensive patrolling was carried out with a view to locating exact positions of enemy outpost line and how far the advancement of our line would be interfered with by enemy activity.

Patrols reported that many Germans were occupying shell holes and retired on patrols approaching.

The supposed Strong Point at W.25.c.35.40. and M.G. at W.25.c. 4.3. were confirmed. Arrangements were made for dealing with these two points and also final arrangements with the O.C. "B" Company 2/W.York.R. who were advancing on our Right.

Particular attention was paid to visual reconnaissance by day on the 24th and favourable landmarks, etc., were pointed out to the men.

By 12.20 a.m. the 25th Platoons were ready to advance in Columns of Sections under their Section Commanders at 20 yards intervals.

At 12.20 a.m. the Platoons on the Left advanced to their new positions and dug in, at the same time a Platoon under 2/Lt. TITLEY advanced against the Strong Point. This was taken with very little difficulty and the Platoon dug in on their new position.

The Right Platoon was not so fortunate at first although they ultimately gained their position.

Delay in starting was due to the fact that the both the Officer and N.C.O. detailed to advance on the M.G. were killed just previous to the advance.

On hearing of this Capt. H.H.JAGO, M.C. took charge of this party under orders from Major H.ARCHER.D.S.O. Owing to the bright moonlight the M.G. crew easily spotted our right post and within 10 minutes another four men were killed or wounded. This made a direct advance on the gun out of the question.

Arrangements were then made with 2/W.York.R. for them to detail some men especially to work round the back of the gun while the party covered their advance by occupying the enemy M.G's. attention from the front.

This was successful and by an advance from two directions at once the enemy M.G. was forced to retire and evacuate the Post.

The Right Platoon were then able to make good their ground and dig in on the new line.

Owing to not being able to gain touch with the 2/W.York.R. our Right Flank was thrown back as a defensive flank.

The following night patrols were out and succeeded in locating the 2/W.York.R. Information was passed on to the relieving Units as to how to establish connection and maintain the line.

The morning of the 25th saw us in our correct position on the crest with an uninterrupted view for about 400 yards with no dead ground between.

Many Germans were killed and wounded, several German stretcher parties were out next morning and picked up their casualties.

Five prisoners were taken for identification purposes and passed on.

The enemy was obviously very disorganised, as next day a lot of running about between shell holes was observed. Our men made good use of their rifles.

No resistance of any strength was encountered, the enemy retired in some cases leaving rations, etc., behind them.

The enemy sent out patrols during the night sunsequent to our advance, but they shewed no inclination to fight. Our positions were very alert and any hostile movement was at once checked by accurate rifle and L.G.fire.

Our men shewed great determination and their use of the rifle and bayonets shewed that they are realising its possibilities.

27.11.1917.

(sd) A.TILLETT, Lt.-Col.,
Commanding, 2nd Bn. Devonshire Regt.

Received 2 pm 26.11.17

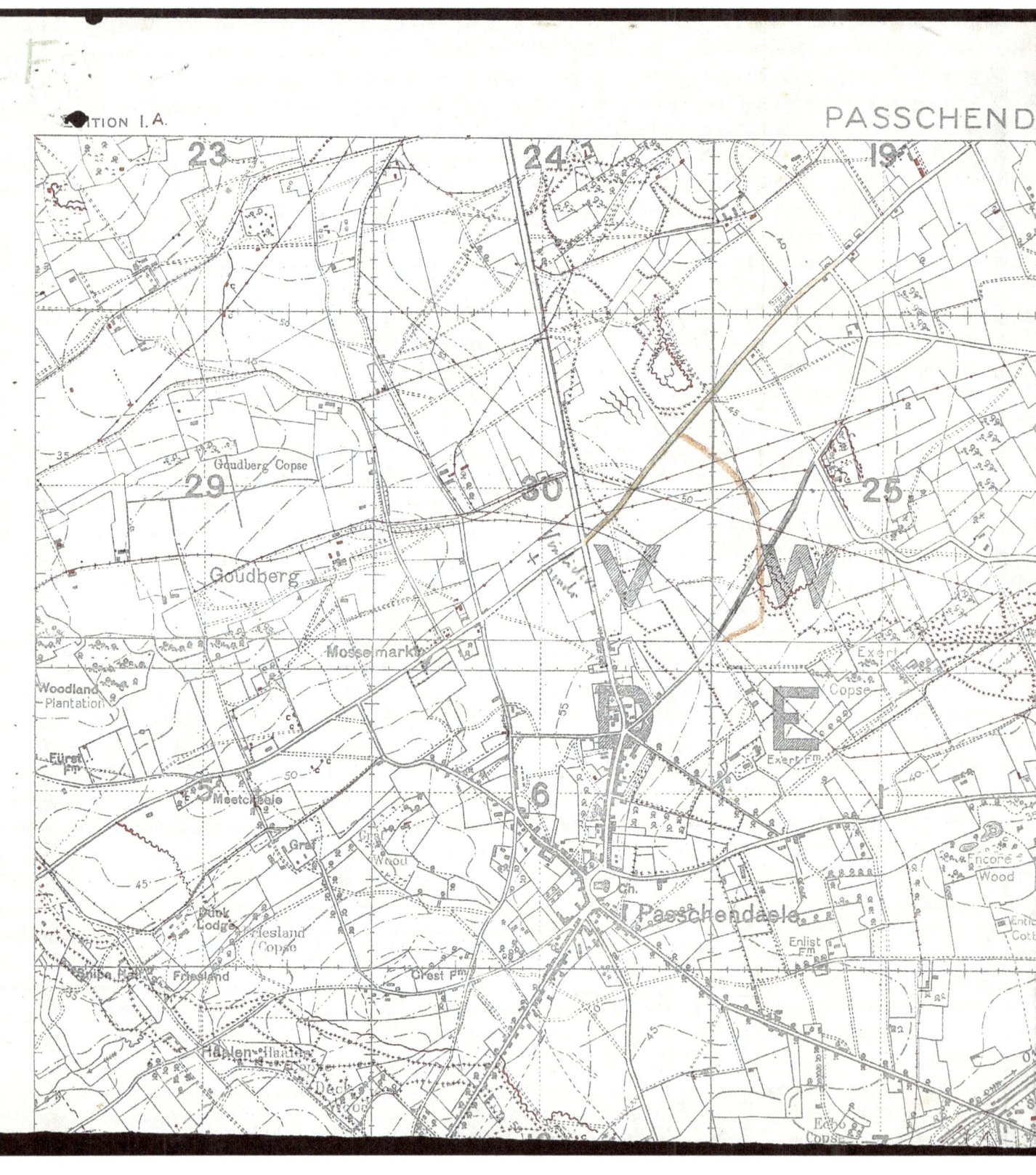

23rd Brigade.

8th Division.

2nd BATTALION

DEVONSHIRE REGIMENT

DECEMBER 1917.

Army Form C. 2118.

WAR DIARY
or
INTELLIGENCE SUMMARY.
(Erase heading not required.)

2nd Battalion Devonshire Regiment.

Place	Date	Hour	Summary of Events and Information	Remarks and references to Appendices
	1917.			
	1/12/17.		Battalion remained in "E" Camp clearing up.	
	2/12/17.		Entrained at St.JEAN Station at 8 a.m. Detrained at WIZERNES and marched into Billets at SETQUES.	
	3/12/17.		Interior Economy and general clean up. Lieut.Col.C.H.M.Imbert-Terry, -D.S.O. took over Command of the Battalion. A congratulatory message was received from the Army Commander, Lieut-General Sir H.RAWLINSON, K.C.B. on the behaviour of the Battalion in recent operations. Lieut.Col.A.TILLETT, M.C. died of wounds.	
	4/12/17.		Continued Interior Economy.	
	5/12/17.		The Divisional General inspected the Officers and N.C.Os of the Battn at 10.35 a.m. and congratulated the Battalion on the good work done by them on the PASSCHENDAELE front. The Lord Lieutenant of Devon, EARL FORTESQUE, K.C.B. lunched with the Battalion and afterwards inspected the men on parade. Captain H.H.JAGO M.C. temporarily took over the duties of Second in Command on 28/11/17. 2/Lieut.A.E.TITLEY temporarily took over Command of "A" Coy, 28/11/17 2/Lieut.F.R.BROOMAN temporarily took over Command of "B" Coy, 30/11/17 Lieut.A.J.SNOWDEN temporarily took over the duties of Quartermaster on 28/11/17. Captain J.MOYLE proceeded on leave to U.K. Rest of Battn beat Officers, W.O's and Sgts in a Football Match by 3 Goals to 2.	
	6/12/17.		Training continued. 2/Lieut.E.T.SANDFORD rejoined from Course at VIII.Corps School 5/12/17 Lieut.A.J.SNOWDEN resumed the duties of L.G.O. No.8565 R.Q.M.Sgt.W.MOYSER took over the duties of Quartermaster.	

WAR DIARY or INTELLIGENCE SUMMARY.

2nd Battalion Devonshire Regiment.

- 2 -

Date	Summary of Events and Information
7/12/17.	Lieut.U.B.BURKE granted permission to wear the Badges of Rank of Captain pending the announcement of promotion in "London Gazette". 2/Lieut.J.J.HUNTINGFORD "C" Coy rejoined from Hospital on 4th inst. Lieut.G.D.FERARD "B" Coy rejoined from duty with 23rd Infantry Bde. "C" Coy defeated "B" Coy in a Rugby Football Match by 10 points to nil.
8/12/17.	Training continued.
9/12/17.	The Chaplain held services at the following times - 8.30 a.m., 10 a.m., and 5 p.m. Captain & Qr.Mr.G.PALMER struck off strength from 28/11/17. 1/Lieut.H.F.KANE, Medical Officer, proceeded on leave to U.K. Parchment Certificate awarded by G.O.C. Division to No.30560 Pte J.E. HAMLEY "A" Coy for gallantry and devotion to duty near PASSCHENDAELE on 24-25/12/17. 2/Lieut.G.F.THUILLIER relinquished the acting rank of Captain on 29/9/17.
10/12/17.	No.8140 C.Q.M.S., S.W.J.COX appointed R.Q.M.Sgt from 6/12/17. 1/Lieut.L.B.FAULK, M.O.R.C, U.S.A. attached to the Battalion as M.O.
11/12/17.	2/Lieut.A.E.RUTLEDGE "D" Coy rejoined the Battalion and taken on strength. Lieut.L.N.L.TINDAL, M.C. proceeded on Intelligence Courseat VIII.Corps School, TERDEGHEM. The following were awarded the Military Medal for gallantry and devotion to duty near PASSCHENDAELE between 25th and 30th Novr 1917 - No.8648 Sgt.F.WAY "D" Coy, No.15596 Pte W.J.PIKE "A" Coy, No.16709 Pte W.LOCK "C" Coy, No.15320 Cpl.T.G.UPSHALL "C" Coy, No.11319 Pte J.G. BROWNING "A" Coy, No.9835 Pte T.CASEY "A" Coy, No.12753 Pte D.WILLIAMS "C" Coy. "D" Coy defeated "C" Coy in an Inter-Coy Rugby Match by 3 pts to nil.

WAR DIARY
or
INTELLIGENCE SUMMARY.

(Erase heading not required.)

Army Form C. 2118.

- 3 -

2nd Battalion Devonshire Regiment

Date	Hour	Summary of Events and Information
12/12/17.		Training continued. A Rugby Football Match between "Possibles" and "Probables" resulted in a win for the former by 3 points to nil.
13/12/17.		Training continued. A Rugby Football Match (Soccer) played between the Battalion and 12th Divnl. Signals was won by the latter by 4 Goals to nil.
14/12/17.		Training continued. Result of Inter-Coy Soccer Knock-out - Left half "A" Coy, 8 goals, "C" Coy, Nil.
15/12/17.		Training continued. Inter-Coy Soccer Knock-out resulted in a win for Right half "D" versus Left half "B" by 2 goals to 1.
16/12/17.		Chaplain held Divine Services at 8.30 a.m., 10 a.m. and 5.30 p.m. Captain A.B.KITSON embarked for England "wounded" on 6/12/17.
17/12/17.		Captain H H.JAGO, M.C. proceeded on leave to U.K. from 17/12/17 to 2/1/18. 1/Lieut.L.B.FAULK, M.O. proceeded on leave to PARIS. 1/Lieut.C.W.MAXSON, M.O.R.C, U.S.A. temporarily attached to Battn as Medical Officer.
18/12/17.		Lieut.K.GATEY, M.C. and Lieut.A.L.NOON joined the Battalion and posted to "A" Coy.
19/12/17.		2/Lieut.B.W.JEFFERY "B" Coy rejoined from duty at Corps Reinft.Camp. 2/Lieut.H.L.R.BAKER "A" Coy proceeded to U.K. on leave from 19/12/17 to 2/1/18. Training continued.

Army Form C. 2118.

WAR DIARY
or
INTELLIGENCE SUMMARY.
(Erase heading not required.)

Summary of Events and Information

- 4 -

2nd Battalion Devonshire Regiment.

Date	Hour	Summary of Events and Information
20/12/17.		Training continued.
21/12/17.		Training continued. Captain J.MOYLE "D" Coy rejoined from leave to U.K. The following decorations were awarded for gallantry and devotion to duty near PASSCHENDAELE between 18th Novr and 2nd Decr 1917. Captain H.H.JAGO, M.C. - Bar to M.C. 2/Lieut.A.E.TITLEY - M.C. The u/m were mentioned in Sir Douglas Haig's Dispatch of Nov 7th. Temp.2/Lt (Act.Major) R.J.ANDREWS, D.S.O.,M.C. Lieut (Act.Captain) H.ARCHER, D.S.O., 2/Lieut (Act.Capt) A.R.NEWTON, 2/Lieut.G.PARKER, 2/Lieut.H.PARKER, Major (Temp.Lt.Col) A J.E.SUNDERLAND, Lieut (Act Lt.Col) A.TILLETT, M.C. No.7673 C.S.M.,J.H.BAUER, No.7296 C.Q.M.S. S.G.CARTHEW, No.8140 C.Q.M.S., S.W.J.COX. R.S.M.RADFORD won semi-final of the Divisional Boxing Competition held at QUELMES.
22/12/17.		Training continued. 2/Lieut.M.G.BECK seconded for duty as Instructor at VIII.Corps Sch 6th November 1917. Lieut.U.B.BURKE to be Acting Captain whilst Commanding a Coy from 13/10/17. Temp.Lt.J.D.HARCOMBE to be Adjutant and Acting Captain whilst so employed from 3/8/17. Lieut (Temp.Captain) A.TILLETT, M.C. ceased to hold the appointment of Adjutant, 25/11/16. Captain G.A.W.MONK proceeded on 14 days Sick leave to U.K. 12/12/17. 2/Lieut.H.EDWARDS and 2/Lieut.J.P.TUCKER rejoined from Second Army School on 15/12/17.
23/12/17.		Usual Services held by the Chaplain. Draft of 25 other ranks joined the Battalion.

WAR DIARY or INTELLIGENCE SUMMARY

2nd Battalion Devonshire Regiment.

- 5 -

Date	Summary of Events and Information
23/12/17 (contd)	No.16709 Pte J.LOCK was awarded a Bar to the M.M. for gallantry and devotion to duty near PASSCHENDAELE between 29th Novr and 30th Novr.1917. No.8258 C.S.M.HOBBS awarded the D.C.M. for gallantry and devotion to duty near PASSCHENDAELE.
24/12/17.	Battalion carried out Field Firing competition which resulted in a win for "C" Coy. Captain W.L.CLEGG and 2/Lieut.J.C.HOLBERTON joined the Battalion. A Concert was held in the evening at 8 p.m.
25/12/17.	Church of England service at 9 a.m. C.O. visited men's dinners at 12.45 p.m. The Divisional Commander and Brigadier visited the Battn at 3 p.m. The final of half Coy Football Competition resulted in a win for "D" Coy versus "B" Coy by 4 goals to 2.
26/12/17	Cleaning up and preparing to move. 2/Lieut.R.C.A.CARDEW joined the Battalion on 24/12/17. Lieut.L.N.L.TINDAL, M.C. rejoined from Course of Intelligence at VIII.Corps School on 24/12/17. 2/Lieut.G.E.BAXTER "B" Coy admitted to Hospital "sick" 25/12/17. Lieut.A.J.SNOWDEN and Lieut.R.S.HOLMES proceeded on leave to U.K. Lieut.J.C.HOLBERTON proceeded for temporary duty with 23rd T.M.B.
27/12/17	Battalion paraded at 4.30 a.m. and marched to WIZERNES where it entrained for BRANDHOEK arriving at 10.30 a.m. and moved into "B" Camp.
28/12/17.	Still at "B" Camp. Lieut.G.D.FERARD temporarily took over the duties of L.G.O.

Army Form C. 2118.

WAR DIARY
or
INTELLIGENCE SUMMARY.

(Erase heading not required.)

Army Form C. 2118.

- 6 -

2nd Battalion Devonshire Regiment.

Date	Summary of Events and Information
29/12/17.	Battalion was visited at 12 noon by the Corps Commander who watched a demonstration of Bayonet Fighting. 2/Lieut F.R.BROOMAN "B" Coy proceeded on a Course of Instruction at Fourth Army School, FLIXECOURT. 2/Lieut.H.PARKER temporarily took over the Command of "B" Coy.
30/12/17.	Two Coys went to Divisional Baths at VLAMERTINGHE. Battalion moved off at 2.15 p.m. by Coys to JUNCTION CAMP, St.JEAN. 2/Lieut.G.F.THUILLIER and 2/Lieut.L.L.SMITH rejoined from Hospital. Drafts of 16 other ranks and 46 O.R's joined the Battalion. Captain J.MOYLE "D" Coy proceeded on a Lewis Gun Course at Brigade School. 2/Lieut.J.J.TALL "B" Coy proceeded on a Bombing and Rifle Bombing Course at Brigade School.
31/12/17.	Same Camp. The Commanding Officer attended a Conference at Brigade H.Q. 2/Lieut.G.L.HILEY proceeded on a Divisional Gas Course at VIII.Corps School, STEENVOORDE.
1/1/18.	

Lieut.Col.
Commanding 2nd Battalion Devonshire Regiment.

Army Form C. 2118.

WAR DIARY
or
INTELLIGENCE SUMMARY.
(Erase heading not required.)

Summary of Events and Information

2nd Battalion DEVONSHIRE REGIMENT.
++++++++++++++++++++++

Place	Date	Hour	Summary of Events and Information	Remarks and references to Appendices
	1/1/18.		Battalion at "B" Camp BRANDHOEK.	
	2/1/18.		Same camp. 2/Lieut. H.LEACH joined Battalion. Lieut. G.F.THUILLIER granted 14 days leave to U.K.	
	3/1/18.		Battalion moved off at 5.45 p.m. by Platoons to reserve position at BELLEVUE. Lieut.C.F.CHAPMAN joined the Battn. Details at Brake Camp.	
	4/1/18.		Same dispositions. 2/Lieut. E.E.DAVIS, 2/Lieut.W.J.HANNAM, 2/Lieut. R.TAPMAN and 2/Lieut. F.W.McCREA joined the Battalion. 2/Lieut. H.L.R.BAKER rejoined from leave to U.K. Lieut.W.L.CLEGG proceeded for attachment to 57th Battery R.F.A.	
	5/1/18.		Still at Bellevue. At 7 p.m. moved off by Companies to relieve the 2/Middlesex Regt in left sector front line. Dispositions "B" Coy right front, "C" Coy centre front, "D" Coy left front. Capt BURKE appointed Second in Command and was in charge of front line. Battn H.Q. 1500 yds in rear at Pill Box 83. Only communication with front line by Runner.	

Army Form C. 2118.

WAR DIARY
or
INTELLIGENCE SUMMARY.
(Erase heading not required.)

Instructions regarding War Diaries and Intelligence Summaries are contained in F. S. Regs., Part II. and the Staff Manual respectively. Title pages will be prepared in manuscript.

Place	Date	Hour	Summary of Events and Information	Remarks and references to Appendices
	6/1/18.		Same dispositions. Quiet day. Lieut.G.D.FERARD and 2/Lieut.S.T.MEARS granted 14 days leave to U.K. Major H.H.JAGO/M.C./rejoined from leave to U.K.	
	7/1/18.		Battn. relieved about 5.30 p.m. by the 1st Sherwood Foresters. Marched back to WIELTJE and entrained on a light railway and were conveyed to "B" Camp, BRANDHOEK.	
	8/1/18.		Same camp. Day spent in cleaning up. 2/Lieut.F.W.W.McCREA admitted to Hospital. 2/Lieut. E.W.BEARE proceeded for duty with 8th Division H.Q.	
	9/1/18.		Same camp. Day spent in improving and repairing huts.	
	10/1/18.		More work on huts. C.O. attended a conference at Brigade H.Q. 2/Lieut H.L.R.BAKER rejoined from duty with 21st Squadron R.F.C. Lieut.R.S.HOLMES and Lieut.A.J.SNOWDEN rejoined from leave to U.K. 2/Lieut.G.E.PARKER to be Lieut. 24/7/17. 2/Lt.G.F.THUILLIER to be Lt.1/7/17. 2/Lieut.W.H.RADCLIFFE do. 1/7/17. 2/Lieut.R.A.WYKES. do. 2/Lieut.G.D.FERARD do. 14/1/17. " A.R.NEWTON. do.	
	11/1/18.		Same camp. 12.30 p.m. Battn paraded and entrained in light railway at Haslar Siding for WIELTJE. Tea at WIELTJE, and marched left Battn	

Army Form C. 2118.

WAR DIARY
or
INTELLIGENCE SUMMARY.
(Erase heading not required.)

Instructions regarding War Diaries and Intelligence Summaries are contained in F.S. Regs., Part II. and the Staff Manual respectively. Title pages will be prepared in manuscript.

Place	Date	Hour	Summary of Events and Information	Remarks and references to Appendices
	11/1/18.		(continued)	
			Sector of Divisional front North of PASSCHENDAELE. "A", "B" and "C" Coys in front line "D" Coy in close support.	
	12/1/18.		Still in the line.	
	13/1/18.		Still in the line. Night of 13/14th relieved by 2/Middlesex Regt and moved into Brigade Reserve at BELLEVUE. During the tour in the front line "C" Coy captured 2 prisoners and "D" Coy 1. 2/Lieut.J.J. HUNTINGFORD admitted to Hospital 12/1/18.	
	14/1/18.		Still at BELLEVUE.	
	15/1/18.		Same dispositions. Night of 15/16th Battn was relieved by 2/Rifle Brigade, marched back to WIELTJE and entrained in light railway for BRANDHOEK and thence into "B" Camp. Lieut K. GATEY M.C. admitted to Hospital. 2/Lieut.E.D. DAVIS and 2/Lieut W.J. HANNAM proceeded for a Course of Instruction at VIII Corps School. Lieut. A.J. SNOWDEN proceeded for a Course of Instruction in Lewis Guns at G.H.Q. School, LE TOUQUET.	

Army Form C. 2118.

WAR DIARY
or
INTELLIGENCE SUMMARY.
(Erase heading not required.)

Instructions regarding War Diaries and Intelligence Summaries are contained in F. S. Regs., Part II. and the Staff Manual respectively. Title pages will be prepared in manuscript.

Place	Date	Hour	Summary of Events and Information	Remarks and references to Appendices
	16/1/18.		Parade at 10 a.m. and entrained at BRANDHOEK at 11 a.m. Detrained at GODEWAERSVELDE and marched to billets in the WINNEZEELE area. 2/Lieut E. F. BEARE rejoined from duty at 8th Divisional H.Q. 2/Lieut. J.J. HUNTINGFORD rejoined from Hospital.	
	17/1/18.		Reorganising and Interior economy. Captain U.B.BURKE, 2/Lt.G.L.HILEY, 2/Lt.B.W.JEFFERY, 2/Lieut.E.T.SANDFORD and 2/Lieut.J.P.TUCKER proceeded on 14 days leave to U.K., yesterday. Lieut.R.S.HOLMES took over temporary command of "C" Coy during absence of Captain U.B.BURKE, on leave.	
	18/1/18.		Interior economy and cleaning up billets. Lieut.G.F.THUILLIER M.C. takes over command of "B" Coy. 2/Lieut.R.C.A.CARDEW proceeded on a Course of Instruction in signalling at the X Corps School.	
	19/1/18.		Company training.	
	20/1/18.		Lieut.G.D.BERARD and 2/Lieut.S.T.MEARS rejoined from leave to U.K.	
	21/1/18.		Company training.	
	22/1/18.		Company training. Lt.Col C.H.M.TIMBERT-TERRY D.S.O. proceeded on 14 days leave to U.K. 2/Lt.(A/Capt) G.F.THUILLIER awarded the M.C.	

T2134. Wt. W708—776. 500000. 4/15. Sir J. C. & S.

Army Form C. 2118.

WAR DIARY
or
INTELLIGENCE SUMMARY.
(Erase heading not required.)

Instructions regarding War Diaries and Intelligence Summaries are contained in F. S. Regs., Part II. and the Staff Manual respectively. Title pages will be prepared in manuscript.

Place	Date	Hour	Summary of Events and Information	Remarks and references to Appendices
	22/1/18.		(continued) Lieut.(A/Lt.Col.) A.TILLETT M.C. awarded the D.S.O. Capt.J.MOYLE proceeded on a course of instruction in L.G. 2/Lieut.J.J.TALL proceeded on a course of Bombing.	
	23/1/18.		Specialists Training. Lieut.L.N.L.TINDAL M.C. and 2/Lieut.A.E.TITLEY M.C proceeded to U.K. on 14 days leave. Lieut.A.C.G.ROBERTS proceeded to U.K. on one months leave. Lieut.K.GATEY M.C. temporarily takes over command of "A" Coy. 2/Lieut.J.J.HUNTINGFORD was admitted to Hospital, yesterday. Lieut.K.GATEY M.C. rejoined from Hospital yesterday. 2/Lieut.A.E.TITLEY M.C is granted permission to wear badges of rank of Captain.	
	24/1/18.		Battalion Route march.	
	25/1/18.		Specialists training.	
	26/1/18.		Battalion paraded at 9.15 a.m. and marched to WINNEZEELE. to entrain for POPERINGHE where they were billeted at THE CLOISTERS. Lieut.A.L.NOON temporarily takes over duties of Quartermaster. Three companies supplied working parties at WIELTJE. Lt.Col.G.F.GREEN	
	27/1/18.		joined the Battn and took over command. Lieut.A.L.NOON and 2/Lieut H.LEACH granted leave to PARIS.	

Army Form C. 2118.

WAR DIARY
or
INTELLIGENCE SUMMARY.
(Erase heading not required.)

Instructions regarding War Diaries and Intelligence Summaries are contained in F. S. Regs., Part II. and the Staff Manual respectively. Title pages will be prepared in manuscript.

Place	Date	Hour	Summary of Events and Information	Remarks and references to Appendices
	27/1/18.		(continued). 2/Lieut.A.E.TITLEY M.C. and 2/Lieut.F.R BROOMAN to be acting Captains while commanding a Coy. Temp Lieut.(A/Capt) A.B.KITSON relinquishes the pay of acting rank on ceasing to command a Coy. C.S.M.BAUER is appointed Acting R.S.M.	
	28/1/18.		Three companies supplied working parties to WIELTJE.	
	29/1/18.		Three companies supplied working parties to WIELTJE	
	30/1/18.		Three companies supplied working parties to WIELTJE. Lieut.L.L.SMITH and 2/Lieut. A. E. RUTLEDGE proceeded to U.K. on 14 days leave. 2/Lieut.F.E.BEARE proceeded to 8th Divisional H.Q. for Intelligence duties.	
	31/1/18.		Three companies supplied working parties to WIELTJE.	

31/1/18.

G.F.Green Lieut.Col.

Commanding 2nd Batt?n. DEVONSHIRE REGT.

WAR DIARY
or
INTELLIGENCE SUMMARY.
(Erase heading not required.)

Army Form C. 2118.

2nd BATTALION DEVONSHIRE REGIMENT.
****

Date	Hour	Summary of Events and Information	Remarks and references to Appendices
1st Feby 1918.		R.S.M.Radford rejoined the Battalion from Hospital on 31/1/18. 2/Lieut.G.E.Baxter having embarked for England on 20/1/18 is struck off strength. A Rugby match between the Battn and the 25th Field Ambulance on 31/1/18 resulted in a win for the former by 11 points to 6.	
2/2/18.		Lieut.G.F.Chapman "B" Coy proceeded to the Fourth Army Musketry School on a course of instruction. Captain U.B.Burke and 2/Lieut. B.W.Jeffery M.M. rejoined from leave to the U.K.	
3/2/18.		The Battalion moved from The Glomstars POPERINGHE to billets in the WINNEZEELE Area. The following Officers rejoined from leave to the U.K. on the 2nd inst. 2/Lieut.G.L.Hiley, 2/Lieut J.P.Tucker, 2/Lieut.E.T.Sandford. Lieut.A.J.Snowden rejoined from a Course of Instruction at G.H.Q.School. 2/Lieut.E.D.Davis rejoined from a Course of Instruction at the VIII Corps School, TERDEGHEM.	
4/2/18.		No.8910 Cpl.A.J.Bowden was granted a permanent commission in the Regular Army and posted to "A" Coy. No.9415 Sgt.W. Maunder M.M. was granted a permanent commission in the Regular Army and posted to "C" Coy. No.7673 C.S.M.,J.H.Bauer was awarded the Belgian Croix de Guerre Lieut.W.L.Clegg and 2/Lieut.R.Tadman proceeded to 23rd Brigade School for courses of instruction.	
5/2/18.		Lieut.A.J.Snowden proceeded to 23rd Brigade School for duty 2/Lieut.A.E.Rutledge proceeded to England for a six months tour of duty.	

Army Form C. 2118.

WAR DIARY
or
INTELLIGENCE SUMMARY.
(Erase heading not required.)

Instructions regarding War Diaries and Intelligence Summaries are contained in F. S. Regs., Part II. and the Staff Manual respectively. Title pages will be prepared in manuscript.

Place	Date	Hour	Summary of Events and Information	Remarks and references to Appendices
	6/2/18.		Captain R.Yardle and Lieut.W.H.Radcliffe granted 14 days leave to U.K. Capt. J.Moyle temporarily took over command of "D" Coy during the absence of Capt.Yardle.	
	7/2/18.		Battalion Route March. 2/Lieut.M.G.Beck having been taken on the strength of VIII Corps School is struck off the strength of the Battn. 2/Lieut.H.L.R.Baker was admitted to Hospital. Lieut.K. Gatey M.C. proceeded on a course of instruction at the Fourth Army Infantry School, FLIXECOURT.	
	8/2/18.		Capt. A.E.Titley M.C. and Lieut.L.N.L.Tindal M.C. rejoined from leave. 2/Lieut.H.Parker proceeded for a 6 months tour of duty in England.	
	9/2/18.		The Officers and N.C.Os of the Battalion went to a demonstration in consolidating shell holes.	
	10/2/18.		Battalion paraded at 6.45 a.m. and marched to GODEWAERSVELDE where they entrained for St Jean Station and marched from there to camp at Irish Farm. On arrival Officers from the Battn went forward to see the O.Os of Battalions holding the line. Capt.A.E.Titley resumed command of "A" Coy 8/2/18. 2/Lieut.R.Tadman proceeded for duty with the 23rd T.M.Battery.	
	11/2/18.		Battalion moved off at 4 p.m. by companies to front line. "D" Coy took over right front and "C" and "A" Coys from support Coy of 1st Border Regt. "B" Coy took over from left front Coy of 1st Lancs Fus. Battn. H.Q. at Bellevue. Front line N.W. of PASSCHENDAELE Support on the GOUDBERG SPUR. Captain A.H.Cope taken on strength of the Battn.	
	12/2/18.		"D" Coy spread out and took over 3 posts to their left from the 1st Worcester Regt. Major H.H.Jago M.C. relinquishes the acting rank of Major and resumes his acting rank of Acting Capt.	

Army Form C. 2118.

WAR DIARY
or
INTELLIGENCE SUMMARY.
(Erase heading not required.)

Instructions regarding War Diaries and Intelligence Summaries are contained in F. S. Regs., Part II. and the Staff Manual respectively. Title pages will be prepared in manuscript.

Place	Date	Hour	Summary of Events and Information	Remarks and references to Appendices
	12/2/18.		(continued) Capt.A.E.Titley M.G. relinquishes the acting rank of Capt. Capt.H.H.Jago M.G. took over command of "A" Coy. 2/Lieuts. F.R.Brooman and J.J.Huntingford proceeded on 14 days leave to the U.K. Lieut.W.L.Clegg and 2/Lieut.R.Tadman rejoined from courses of instruction at the 23rd Brigade School. Lieut.Col.B.G.James D.S.O. taken on strength of the Battn.	
	13/2/18.		"D" Coy again spread out and took over 5 more posts from 1st Worcester Regt. "B" Coy took over 3 posts from right of "D" Coy.	
	14/2/18.		Still in same position in line. 2/Lieut.S.T.Mears proceeded to England for a six months tour of duty and is struck off strength. 2/Lieut.J.L.Gregory previously reported "missing", officially accepted as Prisoner of War 1/1/18.	
	15/2/18.		Battn was relieved by 2nd Rifle Brigade and moved back to "B" camp BRANDHOEK, by road as far as WIELTJE and thence by light railway to Hasler Siding. Lieut.L.L.Smith rejoined from 14 days leave to U.K.	
	16/2/18.		Interior economy.	
	17/2/18.		Church service at 11 a.m. 60 men per Coy attended. Brigadier inspected the Battn at "B" Camp at 11.30 a.m. Captain J.Moyle was admitted to Hospital "sick" 2/Lieut.J.P.Tucker temporarily took over command of "D" Coy. 2/Lieut.E.E.Beare rejoined from duty at 8th Divisional H.Q. Capt.A.H.Cope assumed the duties of Second in Command on 12th inst. Battn bathed at VLAMERTINGHE between 9 a.m. and 3 p.m.	
	18/2/18.		Draft of 1 N.C.O. and 5 men joined the Battalion.	

Army Form C. 2118.

WAR DIARY
or
INTELLIGENCE SUMMARY.
(Erase heading not required.)

Instructions regarding War Diaries and Intelligence Summaries are contained in F. S. Regs., Part II. and the Staff Manual respectively. Title pages will be prepared in manuscript.

Place	Date	Hour	Summary of Events and Information	Remarks and references to Appendices
	19/2/18.		Battalion moved off at 12.30 p.m. and proceeded by light railway to St Jean. Tea on the road and marched to Bellevue by platoons at 500 yards interval to relieve 2nd R.Berks Regt., in reserve.	
	20/2/18.		Bellevue was subjected to considerable gas shelling during day and the Battn had eight casualties from gas.	
	21/2/18.		Same dispositions.	
	22/2/18.		Lieut.R.S.Holmes proceeded on Instructors course in Lewis guns at G.H.Q.School. Lieut.W.H.Radcliffe rejoined from leave to the U.K. Lieut.A.L.Noon, 2/Lieut.H.Leach and 2/Lieut.G.L.Hiley detailed to proceed to Infantry Wing, VIII Corps School, TERDEGHEM on 23rd inst.	
	23/2/18.		Battalion was relieved in Bellevue positions at 5 p.m. by the 2nd E.Lancs Regt and returned to "B" camp Brandhoek by light railway from Wieltje.	
	24/2/18		Battn resting and cleaning up. The Chaplain held services in the camp at 8 a.m. and 10.30 a.m. also 6.30 and 7.30 p.m.	
	25/2/18.		Interior Economy.	
	26/2/18.		The Brigadier wrote complimenting the Battalion on the good work done during the tour at Bellevue. Capt.J.D.Harcombe, 2/Lieut.W. Mander and 2/Lieut.A.J.Bowden granted 14 days leave to the U.K. Capt.R.Yandle resumed command of "D" Coy on the 23rd inst. 2/Lieut.B.W.Jeffery M.M. proceeded for a course of instruction at 4th Army School.	

Army Form C. 2118.

WAR DIARY
or
INTELLIGENCE SUMMARY.

(Erase heading not required.)

Instructions regarding War Diaries and Intelligence Summaries are contained in F. S. Regs., Part II. and the Staff Manual respectively. Title pages will be prepared in manuscript.

Place	Date	Hour	Summary of Events and Information	
	27/2/18.		Battalion moved off by light railway from Hagle Siding at 1.45 p.m. to Junction Camp. From there they proceeded by road to relieve the 2/R.Berks Regt in the Passchendaele sector. "A" and "C" Coys in front line. "B" and "D" Coy on the Goudberg Spur. Battalion H.Q. at Bellevue. Lt.Col.B.C.James D.S.O. proceeded for duty at the 23rd Brigade School.	
	28/2/18.		2/Lieut.F.R.Brooman and 2/Lieut.J.J.Huntingford rejoined from leave to the U.K.	

Lieut.Colonel.

Commanding 2nd Battalion Devonshire Regiment.

23rd Inf.Bde.
8th Div.

2nd BATTN. THE DEVONSHIRE REGIMENT.

M A R C H

1 9 1 8

Army Form C. 2118.

WAR DIARY
or
INTELLIGENCE SUMMARY.
(Erase heading not required.)

Hour, Date, Place	Summary of Events and Information	Remarks and References to Appendices
	2nd BATTALION DEVONSHIRE REGIMENT.	
1/3/18.	Battalion in the line. 2/Lieut.E.E.Beare was wounded.	
2/3/18.	The Brigadier General visited the Battalion in the line.	
3/3/18.	Battalion in the line. 2/Lieut.H.L.R.Baker rejoined from Hospital. At 6 p.m. "A" and "C" Coys assisted the 2/Middlesex Regt in a raid of Teal Cotts by a dummy raid on their right. The operation was very successful and "A" and "C" Coys were thanked for their help by Lt.Col. Page M.C., commanding 2/Middlesex Regt.	
4/3/18.	The Battalion was relieved by 2/R.Berks Regt at 12.30 a.m. and returned to "B" Camp, BRANDHOEK, by usual route.	
5/3/18.	Interior economy. Lieut.A.J.Snowden rejoined from 23rd Brigade School.	
6/3/18.	Battalion furnished a working party of approx. 300 men to work on the defences round WIELTJE. Remainder of the Battalion marched to POPERINGHE and took over new billets. The working party was brought back by train and rejoined the Battalion same night.	

Army Form C. 2118.

WAR DIARY
or
INTELLIGENCE SUMMARY.
(Erase heading not required.)

Instructions regarding War Diaries and Intelligence Summaries are contained in F. S. Regs., Part II. and the Staff Manual respectively. Title pages will be prepared in manuscript.

Hour, Date, Place	Summary of Events and Information	Remarks and References to Appendices
7/3/18.	A working party of approx. 450 supplied for same work. Draft of 58 Other Ranks joined the Battn. 30 Other Ranks proceeded for duty with 8th Divisional M.G.Battn.	
8/3/18.	2/Lieut.H.Edwards proceeded on 14 days leave to U.K. Lt.Col.G.F.Green proceeded to U.K. on leave. Working party supplied as on 7th inst.	
9/3/18.	Working party again. Lieut.L.M.L.Tindal M.C. and Battn Observers proceeded to STEENVOORDE on a course of instruction under Bde.I.O.	
10/3/18.	Working party again. Lieut.Col.B.C.James D.S.O. rejoined from duty with 23rd Brigade School.	
11/3/18.	Working party again. The following is an extract from a letter from the Brigadier "The Brigadier General wishes to congratulate all ranks for the good name the Battn received for work in the forward area, and also to thank Commanding Officers for the great trouble they took to make ceremonial parades in POPERINGHE a success and credit to the Brigade.	

Army Form C. 2118.

WAR DIARY
or
INTELLIGENCE SUMMARY.
(Erase heading not required.)

Instructions regarding War Diaries and Intelligence Summaries are contained in F. S. Regs., Part II. and the Staff Manual respectively. Title pages will be prepared in manuscript.

Hour, Date, Place	Summary of Events and Information	Remarks and References to Appendices
12/3/18.	Battalion entrained at HOPOUTRE, detrained at LUMBRES and marched into billets at SETQUES. No.7286 C.Q.M.S., S.G.Carthew granted a commission in the Regular army and posted to "B" Coy. Lieut R.S.Holmes rejoined from a course of instruction at G.H.Q.Small Arms School 11/3/18. 2/Lieut.E.D.Davis proceeded for duty with 23rd Infantry Brigade.	
13/3/18.	Interior Economy. Lieut.L.N.L.Tindal M.C. and Battn Observers rejoined from course at STEENVOORDE. Lieut.H.G.Morrison proceeded on a course of instruction in Trench Mortars at VIII Corps School.	
14/3/18.	Training. Draft of 7 Other Ranks joined the Battalion.	
15/3/18.	Training and baths. The Divisional General and Brigadier inspected the Battn at their training and expressed great satisfaction with the turn out, keenness and training of all ranks. No.8021 A/C.Q.M.S. F.Lethbridge granted a commission in the regular army and posted to "B" Coy. Lieut.A.L.Noon, 2/Lieut.G.L.Hiley and 2/Lieut.H.Leach rejoined from VIII Corps School. Capt.J.D.Harcombe and 2/Lieut.	

Army Form C. 2118.

WAR DIARY
or
INTELLIGENCE SUMMARY.
(Erase heading not required.)

Instructions regarding War Diaries and Intelligence Summaries are contained in F. S. Regs., Part II. and the Staff Manual respectively. Title pages will be prepared in manuscript.

Hour, Date, Place	Summary of Events and Information	Remarks and References to Appendices
15/3/18.	W.Maunder rejoined from leave to U.K.	
16/3/18.	Training.	
17/3/18.	Sunday, was observed as a holiday with voluntary Church parades. Capt.J.D.Harcombe, 2/Lieuts.F.R.Brooman, G.L.Hiley and J.P.Tucker proceeded to England on a six months tour of duty. 2/Lieut.A.J.Bowden rejoined from leave to U.K.	
18/3/18.	Training continued. Lieut.K.Gatey M.O. rejoined from Fourth Army School.	
19/3/18.	Training continued. A demonstration was given by a platoon from the Fourth Army School. Lieut.W.L.Clegg was admitted to Hospital sick.	
20/3/18.	Training.	
21/3/18.	2/Lieut.B.W.Jeffery rejoined from Fourth Army School.	
22/3/18.	2/Lieut.A.E.Thitley M.O. proceeded on a course of instruction at the Fourth Army School, FLIXECOURT. 2/Lieut.H.Leach proceeded for a course of instruction in musketry at Fourth Army School	

Army Form C. 2118.

WAR DIARY
or
INTELLIGENCE SUMMARY.
(Erase heading not required.)

Instructions regarding War Diaries and Intelligence Summaries are contained in F. S. Regs., Part II. and the Staff Manual respectively. Title pages will be prepared in manuscript.

Hour, Date, Place	Summary of Events and Information	Remarks and References to Appendices
22/3/18 (cont'd)	MONTECOURT.	
	The Battalion marched to WIZERNES and entrained for the south.	
23/3/18.	The Battalion detrained at CHAULNES and was immediately rushed	
	into the line in front of VILLERS CARBONNEL about K.2.80.40	
	Sheet Amiens 47.	
24/3/18.	In Line. Beat off several attacks.	
25/3/18.	Withdrew to line in front of ESTREES.	
26/5/18.	A general line was to be held running N and S of ROSIERES.	
	Battalion was in Brigade Support.	
27/3/18.	Battalion was called upon to counter-attack through HARBONNIERES	
	which they did with great success. Details which were left behind	
	were also called out and successfully beat back an attack just	
	N. of ROSIERES.	
	2/Lieut.H.EDWARDS rejoined from leave and from a Composite Battn.	
28/3/18.	In line at CAIX. 2/Lieut.A.E.TITLEY, M.C. rejoined from Fourth	
	Army School.	
29/3/18.	Marched back to JUMEL in Billets.	

(9 29 6) W 2704 100,000 8/14 H W V Forms/C.2118/11.

Army Form C. 2118.

WAR DIARY
or
INTELLIGENCE SUMMARY.
(Erase heading not required.)

Instructions regarding War Diaries and Intelligence Summaries are contained in F. S. Regs., Part II. and the Staff Manual respectively. Title pages will be prepared in manuscript.

Hour, Date, Place	Summary of Events and Information	Remarks and References to Appendices
30/3/18.	Battalion moved up to hold line on east side of river at CASTEL.	
31/3/18.	Enemy attacked heavily and we withdrew in order to conform with movements of Unit on left flank.	
	Casualties :- Capt.G.F.Thuillier M.C. Killed 25/3/18, 2/Lieut.E.D. Davis killed 25/3/18, 2/Lieut.S.G.Carthew killed 25/3/18. 2/Lieut. W.J.Hannam, missing 25/3/18, Lieut.A.L.Noon, died of wounds 2/4/18 The following were wounded :- 2/Lieut.E.T.Sandford 25/3/18, 2/Lieut. J.J.Huntingford 27/3/18, Lieut.K.Gatey M.C. 25/3/18, Lieut.A.J. Snowden 27/3/18, Lieut.C.F.Chapman 27/3/18, Lieut.L.N.L.Tindal M.C. 31/3/18, Lieut.L.L.Smith 27/3/18, 2/Lieut.A.J.Bowden 27/3/18, Captain.R.Yardle 27/3/18.	
	Total :- Officers - 14. Other Ranks - 304.	
8/4/18.	R. H. Anderson-Morshead Lieut.Colonel., Commanding 2nd Battalion Devonshire Regiment.	

23rd Brigade.

8th Division

2nd BATTALION

DEVONSHIRE REGIMENT

APRIL   1918.

Army Form C. 2118.

WAR DIARY
or
INTELLIGENCE SUMMARY.
(Erase heading not required.)

Instructions regarding War Diaries and Intelligence Summaries are contained in F. S. Regs., Part II. and the Staff Manual respectively. Title pages will be prepared in manuscript.

2nd BATTALION DEVONSHIRE REGIMENT.

Place	Date	Hour	Summary of Events and Information	Remarks and references to Appendices
	1/4/18.		Formed line outside wood which we successfully held.	
	2/4/18.		Relieved by the French and came out to DUMMARTIN. Embussed at SAINS-EN-AMIENOIS at 11 a.m. and debussed at AILLY-SUR-SOMME. Marched to billets at BREILLY.	
	3/4/18.		Major G.F.Green struck off strength. Capt J.Moyle struck off strength. 2/Lieuts. P.Guy, A.L.Noon and A.J.Snowden to be Lieuts 1/7/17. There was a special order in R.Os in which the Divisional Commander expressed his sincere gratitude to all ranks for the splendid work they had done. The Commanding Officer also thanked the Battn. for the manner in which they had supported him. The following Officers (attd 23rd T.M.Battery) became casualties on the dates shewn:- Lieut. J.C.Holberton 28/3/18 (Wounded), 2/Lieut.R.Tadman 24/3/18 (missing). Men rested	
	4/4/18.		2/Lieut. H.L.R.Baker "A" Coy took over command of "D" Coy from this date. Men rested.	

(A9175) Wt W2355/P360 600,000 12/17 D.D.& L. Sch. 53a. Forms/Card8/15.

Army Form C. 2118.

WAR DIARY
or
INTELLIGENCE SUMMARY.
(Erase heading not required.)

Instructions regarding War Diaries and Intelligence Summaries are contained in F. S. Regs., Part II. and the Staff Manual respectively. Title pages will be prepared in manuscript.

Place	Date	Hour	Summary of Events and Information	Remarks and references to Appendices
	5/4/18.		Lt.Col.B.O.James D.S.O. proceeded to take command of the 22nd D.L.I. and was struck off strength. Training carried on.	
	6/4/18.		Lt.Col.C.H.M.Imbart-Terry D.S.O. struck off the strength of Battn. Training.	
	7/4/18		The Battn was inspected by the Divisional Commander who expressed his thanks and admiration to the Officers and men of the Battn for what he described as "a great achievement". Lt.Col R.H.Anderson-Morshead D.S.O. joined Battn and took over command from this day. 2/Lieut.H.Leach rejoined from course of instruction in musketry at Fourth Army School, NORTBECOURT on 5th inst. Major A.H.Cope assumed the duties of Senior Major. Capt.H.H.Jago M.C. took over command of "D" Coy. 2/Lieut.B.W. Jeffery M.M. took over command of "B" Coy from 26th ult. Training.	
	8/4/18.		Capt.M.R.M.McLeod was attached to Battn for duty from Fourth Army School.	
	9/4/18.		Training. Lieut.F.E.Harris and 2/Lieut.W.E.Dyson joined Battn. 2/Lieut R.C.A.Cardew rejoined from a course of instruction in signalling at X Corps School and assumed duties of Signalling Officer. Lieut. W.L.Clegg	

Army Form C. 2118.

WAR DIARY
or
INTELLIGENCE SUMMARY.
(Erase heading not required.)

Place	Date	Hour	Summary of Events and Information	Remarks and references to Appendices
	9/4/18.		(continued) rejoined from Hospital. Lieut.H.G.Morrison rejoined from course of instruction at VIII Corps School.	
	10/4/18.		Training. Lieut.H.G.Morrison proceeded for duty with 23rd T.M.Battery.	
	11/4/18.		Battn marched 20 kilos. to WARLUS and billeted there for the night.	
	12/4/18.		Battn marched to HANGEST-SUR-SOMME and bivouaced there for night.	
	13/4/18.		Battn entrained at HANGEST and detrained at DREUIL-LES-AMIENS, marching from there to billets in SALEUX.	
	14/4/18.		Voluntary Church parade at 6.30 p.m. 2/Lieut.F.W.W.McCrea having embarked for U.K. on 25/3/18 is struck off strength. Lieut.A.H. Noon died of wounds on 2/4/18. Lieut.W.H.Radcliffe to be A/Capt. with pay and allowances of Lieut. whilst employed as Act/g Adjutant. Major A.F.Northcote joined Battn and temporarily assumed duties of Quartermaster.	
	15/4/18.		The u/m to be Lieuts. 1st July 1917. 2/Lieut.H.H.Jago M.C.,2/Lieut.L.N.L. Tindal M.C. Capt.R.M.McLeod ceased to be attached to Battn.	
	16/4/18.		Battn training.	

Army Form C. 2118.

WAR DIARY
or
INTELLIGENCE SUMMARY.
(Erase heading not required.)

Place	Date	Hour	Summary of Events and Information	Remarks and references to Appendices
	17/4/18.		Draft of 75 O.Rs joined Battn. The u/m were awarded Parchment Certificates by Divisional Commander for gallantry and devotion to duty W. of the SOMME between 22nd March and 2nd April.	
			2/Lieut.J.J.Huntingford. 8510 C.S.M.,S.H.Taylor. 9328 Sgt.J.T.Bowden	
			30929 Pte.W.Devine. 25 650 Pte.E.W.Sizer. 8427 A/C.S.M., A.G.Small	
			8255 Pte.W.J.Marley.8648 Sgt.F.Way M.M. Continued training.	
	18/4/18.		Battn training.	
	19/4/18.		The following awarded Parchment Certificates by Divisional Commander for gallantry and devotion to duty W. of SOMME between 22nd March and 2nd Apl.	
			Lieut.(A/Capt) W.H.Radcliffe. 2/Lieut.(A/Capt).A.E.Titley M.C.	
			33124 L/C.L.Bryan. 204358 Pte.H.C.Gaskill. 89003 Pte.S.Bonetta.	
			6 9037 Pte.L.V.Smith. 7 413 C.S.M., H.W.Garnham. 267262 Pte.J.Harper.	
			33140 Pte.C.H.Knuckey. 31822 Pte.P.Joy. 9792 Pte.J.T.Durnall.	
			20380 Sgt.G.Smith. Battn marched to billets in the BLANGY TRONVILLE. Battn Details remained at GAMON.	
	20/4/18.		Moved into line and took over VILLERS BRETONNEUX defence line.	

Army Form C. 2118.

WAR DIARY
or
INTELLIGENCE SUMMARY.
(Erase heading not required.)

Instructions regarding War Diaries and Intelligence Summaries are contained in F. S. Regs., Part II. and the Staff Manual respectively. Title pages will be prepared in manuscript.

Place	Date	Hour	Summary of Events and Information	Remarks and references to Appendices
	21/4/18.		Capt.A.H.Cope to be A/Major whilst so employed 26/2/18. Battn still in line.	
	22/4/18.		Battn relieved by 2.E.Lancs Regt. and moved back to billets in BLANGY TRONVILLE.	
	23/4/18.		Battn moved into line and took over the CACHY SWITCH S.W. of VILLERS BRETONNEUX. Details moved to RIVERY on account of shelling.	
	24/4/18.		Enemy attack (see attached account)	
	25/4/18.		The u/m awarded the M.M. for gallantry and devotion to duty East N. of SOMME between 22nd March and 2nd April.	
			44137 Pte.H.F.Marshall. 14860 Sgt.H.W.Gill. 26061 Sgt.J.S.Seldon.	
			33172 Cpl.C.Greenslade. 22128 L/C. E.J.Lear. 68798 Pte.A.E.Street.	
			33155 Pte.E.Henson. 31038 Pte.W.Young. 15000 CPl.T.H.Grainger.	
			8868 L/C.C.W.Wakeham. 8553 Sgt.W.Goodyear. The u/m Officers joined Battn. Lieut.L.N.L.Tindal M.C. Lieut.S.H.Cox. Lieut.W.L.Barrett. 2/Lieut.L.D.Heppenstall. 2/Lieut.C.Wreford. 2/Lieut.A.E.Upperton 2/Lieut.W.T.Cross. 2/Lieut.S.J.Gussell. 2/Lieut.R.Lambert. 2/Lieut.	

Army Form C. 2118.

WAR DIARY
or
INTELLIGENCE SUMMARY.
(Erase heading not required.)

Instructions regarding War Diaries and Intelligence Summaries are contained in F. S. Regs., Part II. and the Staff Manual respectively. Title pages will be prepared in manuscript.

Place	Date	Hour	Summary of Events and Information	Remarks and references to Appendices
	25/4/18.		(contd) C.A.Hiller, 2/Lieut.C.H.Deeks, 2/Lieut.R.J.Matthews, 2/Lieut C.E.Pells 2/Lieut.F.Malkin.	
	26/4/18.		Battn still in line. 2/Lieut.F.D.Clarke joined Battn.	
	27/4/18.		Battn was relieved by 48th A.I.F. and marched back to billets in BLANGY TRONVILLE.	
	28/4/18.		Battn marched to PONT NOYELLES and joined Details there. Capt.U.B. Burke assumed the duties of Adjutant. Lieut.L.H.L.Tindal M.C. assumed the duties of Asst Adjutant and I.O. 2/Lieut.H.Edwards took over command of "A" Coy. Lieut. S.H.Cox "B" Coy, Lieut.W.L.Clegg "C" Coy, 2/Lieut.H.L.R.Baker "D" Coy.	
	29/4/18.		Interior economy. 2/Lieut.F.D.Clarke takes over command of Scouts Platoon.	
	30/4/18.		Interior economy and reorganisation.	

R.H. Anderson-Morshead
Lieut.Colonel,
Commanding 2nd Battn Devonshire Regiment.

May 1918

Army Form C. 2118.

WAR DIARY
or
INTELLIGENCE SUMMARY.
(Erase heading not required.)

Vol XVIII

Place	Date	Hour	Summary of Events and Information	Remarks and references to Appendices
BOUTILLERIE	May 1st		Billets. Under orders to move to ABBEVILLE AREA by bus from AMIENS.	
do	2nd		Transport moved to LE MESGES - SOUES Area. Orders were cancelled. Bn to move on 2nd May.	
			Orders again cancelled. Transport rejoined Bn from Soues Area.	
			Capt. G. OPENSHAW joined. J. MILNER M.C., Capt. E.A. MILLER + Capt. S.H. PASSLOE joined Battn.	
do	3rd		In Billets. Orders received to move early next morning	
Onthenoot	4th		Battn entrained at SAULEUX for new area	
DRAVEGNY	5th (Sunday)		Battn detrained at LA FERE EN TARDENOIS + marched to Billets in DRAVEGNY	
do	6th		In Billets - Day spent in cleaning up etc. Very wet at night	
do	7th		Training commenced	
do	8th		A Demonstration in Signal Rockets + Smoke given by French Officer	27 sheets

Army Form C. 2118.

WAR DIARY
or
INTELLIGENCE SUMMARY.
(Erase heading not required.)

Place	Date	Hour	Summary of Events and Information	Remarks and references to Appendices
DRAVEGNY	May 9th		Shewing carried on. Massed Drums of the Brigade played retreat. A Brigade concert was held in the evening.	
ROMAIN	10th		Batt.n marched Billets at ROMAIN starting 7.30 am.	
		12.30 p.m	Day very hot. (half Batt.n arrived, details Major Ouston & Capt. a Beckwith, 2/Lieuts Adam, Atherton, Preston joining Batt.n)	
do	11th		Batt.n marched from ROMAIN to CONCEVREUX QUARRY (near ROUCY). Weather still hot. 6.0 with Brigadier viewing 6.0 made a reconnaissance of the line.	
CONCEVREUX	12th		Day very wet. 23rd Bde relieved 219th French Regt of 11th Division in the left sub sector (JUVINCOURT SECTOR). The Batt.n taking over the front line trenches. Capt PAMBER granted leave to PARIS.	
Juvincourt	13th		Day very quiet. The Brigadier visited the line. Re-arrangement of Coys. 3 Coys in front line, & one in support. Enemy heavily shelled batteries.	
"	14th			
"	15th		Day very quiet. Enemy inactive. Weather still very hot. Batteries were again shelled.	

Army Form C. 2118.

WAR DIARY
or
INTELLIGENCE SUMMARY.
(Erase heading not required)

Instructions regarding War Diaries and Intelligence Summaries are contained in F. S. Regs., Part II. and the Staff Manual respectively. Title pages will be prepared in manuscript.

Place	Date	Hour	Summary of Events and Information	Remarks and references to Appendices
	May			
Zutkerke	16		Artillery quiet at both. Major Attlee DSO proceeded to duty as Comdt of IX Corps School.	
"	17th		Day quiet. Lewis Gun Battery went combined. Capt B. Miller rejoined from leave to Paris.	
"	18th		The enemy attempted to raid posts held by the Battn. A few bombs were thrown. No men missing.	
"	19th		Weather still warm. Day quiet.	
"	20th		The Battn was relieved at dusk by 2 D. Yorks Regt. On liv carried out a raid on enemy line which proved abortive no prisoners on identifications.	
Rouex	21st		Relief completed by 12.50 a.m. Battn in billets in Rouex. Lieut H.R. Baker M.C. admitted to hospital.	
"	22nd		In Billets. Bn Luning	
"	23rd		Training carried on	
"	24th		Training as usual. Lieut K. Williams admitted to hospital	

Army Form C. 2118.

WAR DIARY
or
INTELLIGENCE SUMMARY.

(Erase heading not required.)

Instructions regarding War Diaries and Intelligence Summaries are contained in F. S. Regs., Part II. and the Staff Manual respectively. Title pages will be prepared in manuscript.

Place	Date	Hour	Summary of Events and Information	Remarks and references to Appendices
ROVEY	May 25th		Joining Capt LtMillman joined Battn. 2/Lieut A.Rutledge reported Battn. from 6 months tour of duty.	
	26th		Sunday. Divine Service	
	27th		Battn arms ordered 15 minute notice. Support at BOIS DES BUTTES Enemy expected to attack. 1 am Bombardment commenced followed by enemy attack. Battn withdrew and did Bde was driven Eastward in heavy shelling & MG Fire. Lt.Col R H ANDERSON MORSHEAD D.S.O. missing. Major Ashby D.S.O. was shot in forward of Bde. H.Q. Major Musgrove & Mr. Smith Yerbugh 2/Lt Ruttor killed, Battalion again relied fighting still in progress. 2/Lt Meade L.R. de Yanes villain hunt	
	29th			
	30th		Transport and Bois by BOURSAULT Blannes ent with Bde & oft collected at NANTEUIL	
	31st		Laid fast in in Sunnent moved to CONDRES Bde Troops still in line	

DAY OF ATTACK - 24/4/18.

Disposition. Night 23/24th. Battn.H.Q. - U.4.a.(cent) - 2 Coys U.3.b. - 2 Coys 35.C. (Very scattered position)

24/4/18.

5 a.m. Heavy enemy barrage, at first chiefly gas but gradually thickened up with H.E. and some shrapnel.

7 a.m. Hostile barrage still on - a good deal of rifle and M.G. fire to front - whole front covered in smoke.(impossible to see men at 150 yds.).

7.30 a.m. No news of an attack except from 2 C.S.Ms of a London Regt saying their front had been forced by 15 tanks and the Right was coming back.

7.40 a.m. Tank appeared and passed through Bn.H.Q. posts U.4.a. - Runner for 2 left Coys reported 4 tanks in O.35.c, advancing N.W. down valley

8.30 a.m. At this time various small parties of enemy were observed approaching my centre and right - engaged with rifle fire and no organised attack came off, although small parties were continually dribbling up and M.G.Fire on our position increased.

9 a.m. Battn H.Q. re-occupied their original posts after tank had passed through. Bn.Command Post established at O.3.b,9.3. - completely out of touch with two left Coys and half Bn.H.Q. having become casualties - no reports from Bde. or 2 Front Battns.

10 a.m. Boche seen dribbling down from Railway Cutting O.34.b. - small squads 3 - 6. This continued till 2.30 p.m. when at least 150 enemy and numerous M.Gs had entered BOIS d' AQUENNE in O.34.a. and ever increasing M.G. Fire was coming from this wood then in rear of CACHY SWITCH.

1 p.m. Enemy attempted to advance on our front but were easily kept off, no enemy getting within 100 yards of our line of posts.

2.30 p.m. Enemy working West in BOIS d' AQUENNE were gradually cutting off my 2 Right Coys and also firing heavily with M.Gs into rear of Devon trenches.

3 p.m. Accompanied by Adjt. I left Command Post for Bde.H.Q. and reported situation there.

5 p.m. Collected stray Devon Parties in BOIS L'ABBEE. These were from 2 left Coys. With this force about 40 strong garrisoned reserve line and on orders of Bde. established 3 standing patrols in O.33.a. (West Edge)

25/4/18.

Dawn. On orders of Bde cleared E. edge of wood from O.34.a.8.8.(House in wood) to O.34.b,2.9. CACHY-VILLERS ROAD. The enemy abandoned numerous M.G., Light M.G. and a few L.T.Ms and on emerging into the open crossed up on to the spur in U.4.a. and O.34.d. and were well caught in so doing by rifle fire from Devon Line U.3.b. This wood-clearing party started digging in, on the E. of wood, but about 8 a.m. after meeting Bde.Major and O.C. W.Yorks ordered party to cross valley at E.edge of wood and dig in afresh on line O.34.a.9.0. to U.4.b.0.4. - 200 yds - 400 yds clear of wood. This was done with practically no casualties and I placed the wood-clearing party of Devons on the left flank of the 2 Coys of Devons that had held their ground in U.3.b. This left the Devons in a long thin line about 1200 (at least) garrisoned by 4 Officers and about 280 O.R.

10 a.m. New line well dug in and no change in positions took place till relief by 48 A.I.F on night 27/28th.

Copy of Notes called for by
B.G.C. for Bde War Diary

R.H Anderson-Morshead
Lieut Col - 2-Devon-R.

Thursday 30th May:- At midday the Battn was forced to withdraw from the ridge, owing to the fact that the enemy was working around the right flank, and commencing an enfilading movement. The platoon of Devons which was sent up to the right flank, in conjunction with units of the 19th Division successfully withdrew with very few casualties, and the whole force placed itself in the ARDRE Valley and effectively withheld all enemy thrusts in the midnight.

Friday 31st May:- About 12.30am the Battn was ordered to move to the rear, and the day was spent in re-organisation and rest.

Saturday 1st June:- The Battn moved up to the BOIS D'ECLISSE where it was joined by a party of about 80 Devons, which had been holding the position immediately south of CHAMBRECY since the 29th May.

Sunday 2nd June to night of Tuesday/Wednesday 11th/12th June, the 1st, 8th and 2nd/9th Divisional Composite Battns held the BOIS D'ECLISSE and the BOIS DE COURTON until relieved.

(sd) Nelson King 2/Lt
2 Devon Regt

3.

WAR DIARY or INTELLIGENCE SUMMARY

Army Form C. 2118.

(Erase heading not required.)

2nd Battalion Devonshire Regiment

Place	Date	Hour	Summary of Events and Information	Remarks and references to Appendices
In the field	1918 June 1st		Transport at GOMERS. Adjutant in charge of Advanced party. Brigade Inspection in line. Quarter and Quartermaster & Sergeants M.O. found Battn.	
	2nd		Sent 2 M. Officers proceeded to line as C.C. Brigade contacts by Brigade was relieved late by most early transport to ETRECHY. Brigadier Inspects the Battn.	
	3rd		O.C. other Ranks joined Battn. Details and Transport moved to ETRECHY at 6am. Brigadier Inspected the Transport. Brigade keeps still in line.	
	4th		Brigade keeps still in line. Nothing of interest this day.	
	5th		Brigade keeps still in line. Day hot. Do.	
	6th		Ditto	
	7th		Ditto Training. Day hot.	
	8th		Ditto	
	9th		O.C. fore Battn moved from ETRECHY to Billet BRUSS, starting at 3.45am and arriving at about mid-day.	

WAR DIARY or INTELLIGENCE SUMMARY.

Army Form C. 2118.

(Erase heading not required.)

Place	Date	Hour	Summary of Events and Information	Remarks and references to Appendices
Mailly	1918 June 10th		Bn billets at BROUSSY. Bath training.	AAB
	11th		Bn billets. Bn training. Weather hot.	AAB
	12th		Bn billets. Bath training. 2/Lieut J.B. Clarke & 2/Lieut McKing rejoined Bn. & Chas. Rankes	AAB
	13th		Joined from Lancashire Composite Bn. Orders received to move on morning of 14th.	AAB
	13th		Bn little training	AAB
	14th		Bn. paraded at 1.30 pm and marched to FERE CHAMPENOIS arriving at 5am	AAB
	15th		Bn. arrived at 4.30 am at HARGET-SUR-SOMME and marched to ETREJUST arriving	AAB
			at 9.30 am.	AAB
	16th		ETREJUST Bath training.	AAB
	17th		Major H.E.R. Fort M.C. joined and took over command of the Bn.	AAB
	18th		Bn "A" "B" "C" "D" "B" Coys moved to AVESNE C & D Coys remaining at	AAB
			ETREJUST. Draft of 16 Officers and 116 Other Ranks joined. Majors J. Affleck,	
			W. Walker, 2nd Lt R.W. Brown, 2nd Lt R.J. Osborne, 2nd Lt L. Taylor, 2nd Lt T.J. Batchelor	
			2nd Lt W.H. Saunders, 2nd Lt L.G. Murray, 2nd Lt A.E. Crutchley, 2nd Lt C.H. Simmonds	
			2nd Lt L. Grove, 2nd Lt A.L. Sandall, 2nd Lt G.H. Yates, 2nd Lt H.R. Williams, 2nd Lt R.E.	
			Hall, 2nd Lt J.B. Jones	AAB

Army Form C. 2118.

WAR DIARY
or
INTELLIGENCE SUMMARY.

(Erase heading not required.)

Instructions regarding War Diaries and Intelligence Summaries are contained in F. S. Regs., Part II. and the Staff Manual respectively. Title pages will be prepared in manuscript.

Place	Date	Hour	Summary of Events and Information	Remarks and references to Appendices
In the field	1916 June 19th	10 am	In billets. Batt. tracing. 52 other ranks joined from 2/5th Leicester Infantry Batt.	AB
			New 2nd Lieut C.J. Bakes	AB
20th			In billets. Batt. training. Note 58 Luimen inspected and addressed the Bat. Brigade.	AB
			At 1.00 other ranks reported as Bak.	
21st			In billets. Batt. tracing. Draft of 234 other ranks joined	AB
22nd			Batt. moved from AVESNE to CITERNE by march. Men to carrying out about 1 pm	AB
			The whole were awarded MILITARY MEDALS for gallantry in action by the C.O. Colonel the RSM	
			and the MARNE from 24th May to 2nd June 1915. 6144 Pte R. Naylor, 4th 23rd Batt. 13th	
			26,135 Pte A. Heary, 2nd 23rd Rifl Batt. 14344 Pte W. Smith, 8356 Pte W. J. Hunday	
			14202 Pte A. Dunn	
23rd			Batt. moved from CITERNE to MONTIERES CAMP by march, route starting at 8.30 am and	AB
			arrived at about 4 pm. Dinner served on march.	
24th			In camp. Batt. training and re-organising	AB
25th			In camp. Batt. training	AB
26th			In camp. Batt. training. The following Officers joined from Lantern Lieut R.L. Bolingbroke	AB
			Lieut J. Elliott, Lieut H.W. Boyde, Lieut L.J. Barker, 2/Lieut L.R.L. Lucas.	

WAR DIARY
INTELLIGENCE SUMMARY
(Erase heading not required.)

Army Form C. 2118.

Place	Date	Hour	Summary of Events and Information	Remarks and references to Appendices
In the Field	1918 June 24th	24th	In camp at MONTIERES. Bath having (Musketry Practice on open Range) The following were awarded PARCHMENT CERTIFICATES for gallantry and devotion to duty between the AISNE and the MARNE from 24th May to 2nd June 1918. 13011 Pte W.J. Jenks. 1354/4 L/Cpl G.H. Nellms att. 23rd T.M. Battery	
	25th		Bath having Capt. H.J.T. Rose returned from England and 29 Other Ranks as draft. The following were awarded MILITARY MEDALS for gallantry and devotion to duty between the AISNE and MARNE from 24th May to 2nd June 1918. 15324 Sgt W.G. Taylor. 40050 Pte W.J. Hunt 240804 Pte J. Morles. 2nd Lieut R.A.H. Nesbitt was awarded the MILITARY CROSS and shown with L. Taylor for YOS 1st 3246 L/Sgt.	AuB AuB
	29		Bath having at NOYERES Brigade Commander addressed the Bath Having over the following decorations were awarded to the Bath for gallantry and devotion to duty between the AISNE and MARNE from 24th May to 2nd June 1918. THE MILITARY CROSS 2/Lieut R.H. Nichter THE DISTINGUISHED CONDUCT MEDAL 33142 Cpl C. Brundale M.M.	AuB AuB
	30		Bath in camp. Divine Services.	

31/6/18

C.B. R---
Lieut Col.
Commanding 2nd Batt. Devonshire Regiment

23rd Inf. Bde. No. G. 12/1.

Headquarters,
    8th Division.

        I should like to bring to your especial notice the conduct soldierly and gallant conduct of the 2nd Devon. Regt., which was of unsurpassable excellence and whose discipline and fortitude were pre-eminent and much beyond the ordinary of a battalion.

        This Battalion was sent up on the night of May 26th to occupy the all important position of the BOIS DES BUTTES, with instructions to defend it to the last against all hostile attacks. When the enemy had successfully carried our forward and main defences on the morning of May 27th, long after, at a late hour of the morning, the 2nd Devon. Regt. was, though surrounded on all sides, successfully maintaining an unbroken front to the foe, and by hampering all attempts on his part to advance frontally was gaining time, which proved of the utmost value to enable us to organize our defences South of the AISNE, and assist the arrival of reinforcing troops to come up into action undisturbed.

        One eyewitness states that he saw the 2nd Devon. Regt., though they were merely an island in the midst of an innumerable and determined foe, mowing down the Germans in large numbers by the steadiness of their fire, and their unshakeable discipline.

        Another eyewitness, a Battery Commander, states as follows :-

"At a late hour of the morning those of my personnel who escaped the enemy ring of machine guns and his fearful barrage, found the Commanding Officer of the 2nd Devon. Regt. and a handful of men, holding on to the last trench before the Canal and in such a position that they were entirely without hope of help, but still fighting on. The Commanding Officer himself calmly writing his (writing) orders with a perfect hell of H.E. dropping round him. He was cross-questioned by me but said nothing could be done and advised those that could to get away. As all my artillerymen were quite unarmed he sent them off to get through if they could, refusing all their offers of help as they had no arms. His magnificent bearing and dauntless courage moved one's emotion as he had determined to carry on to the end"

        There is no doubt that this Battalion perished en masse, fighting to the end, refusing to surrender, and smiting down their country's foe until they had ceased to exist.

        On May 29th some 120 men of this Battalion, who had at the commencement of the fight been back at the Transport Lines, again proved that the exploits of their comrades, which I have already narrated, were no isolated act of valour, but was the common birthright of their regiment - the inheritance of countless years of the obedience and discipline that the soldier owes to his noble calling, and a living and bright example for all to behold of their proud regimental motto of "SEMPER FIDELIS".

        This gallant band, though they had been fighting continuously against desperate odds for 48 hours, when called upon to counter-attack and drive the enemy off the high ground he had seized about 2 miles North of SAVIGNY, at once responded to the effort required of them and by their swift and resolute advance drove the enemy off, seized and maintained their hold on a position, the retention of which was for the moment of urgent necessity to the security of our position.

        These gallant men were throughout, by their unbroken front and high moral, an inspiration to the fainthearted and despondent, and a visible sign of what an undaunted courage that springs from the unbroken corporate life of one of the most famous the most famous/

regiments of our Regular Army can accomplish when the day seems lost and there be none to help, except that saving grace of a soldier's honour, which forbids him to accept defeat, and still fight on whatever the odds against the enemies of his King and country.

8th June, 1918.
Brig.-General,
Commanding 23rd Infantry Brigade.

Record of the 2nd Bn Devonshire Regiment
in action 26th May to 12th June 1918 SOISSONS - RHEIMS Show.

Ref Map. Soissons 1/100,000.

Sunday 26th May. The Battn moved up into close support to the other two Battns of the 23rd Infantry Brigade at 9 pm in LA VILLE-AUX-BOIS.

Monday, 27th May:- At 1 am. an intense enemy barrage of gas and high explosive shells was effected against the front and support lines, followed at 4.0 am by an attack in considerable force. Almost immediately, the Battn found itself surrounded, the enemy having forced both flanks, and the result was that practically every man including the personnel of Battn Headquarters was either killed or taken prisoner. About 80 only, escaped, and this party rallied in a line of trenches in a field on the right hand side of the LA-VILLE-AUX-BOIS — PONTAVERT road.

A successful withdrawal was then made to some rising ground immediately due South of the canal south of PONTAVERT, which was held until about 6 am. This party next fell back to the trench running north of and parallel to the CONCEVREUX - CORMICY road, and in conjunction with the surviving members of other units successfully stemmed the enemy's advance until 2 pm. inflicting great casualties on him. It was then necessary expeditiously to withdraw the party once more, owing to the fact that enemy patrols were reported to be in ROUCY, and a detour around the town was made to the high ground to the South and the enemy were further kept in check until nearly midnight.

Tuesday 28th May. Early in the morning the Devons took up a new position on high ground between VENTELAY and MONTIGNY when they were compelled by renewed enemy attacks to withdraw to the river in front of JONCHERY at about 10 am. This position was held for over two hours until the left flank was forced to give way. Reinforcements of the Devons for the left flank successfully held the enemy for a further two hours.

Later a stand was made between JONCHERY and BRANSCOURT, where the Unit in co-operation with others held a strong point on the main JONCHERY-BRANSCOURT road until about 4 o'clock in the afternoon. Weight of numbers necessitated a further withdrawal to a high plateau north of SAVIGNY and here throughout the night a determined and effective resistance was maintained.

Wednesday 29th May. In the early hours of the morning it was necessary to withdraw from the plateau as the enemy again threatened the left flank and a new position was consolidated just North-east of FAVERELLE. This was held till about 4 pm when a ridge North-east of TRAMERY was lined. Later a strong position was occupied immediately south of CHAMBRECY and maintained until the night of 31st May/1st June.

Meanwhile another party of Devons and stragglers from all units of the Division concentrated on CHAMPLAT and re-organised and formed into the 1st-8th Divisional Composite Battn. The Devons were about 150 strong and composed mainly of regimentally employed men (tailors shoemakers &c.) and the drums. This Battalion moved up about midday to SARCY where it received orders to make a counter-attack on LHERY. When just about to carry out the attack at 4 pm the order was cancelled and an alternative position was taken up on the ridge north of BOULEUSE. Throughout the night a successful stand was made.

Army Form C. 2118.

WAR DIARY
or
INTELLIGENCE SUMMARY.
(Erase heading not required.)

Instructions regarding War Diaries and Intelligence Summaries are contained in F. S. Regs., Part II. and the Staff Manual respectively. Title pages will be prepared in manuscript.

Place	Date	Hour	Summary of Events and Information	Remarks and references to Appendices
			2nd DEVONSHIRE REGIMENT.	
MONTIERES.	July. 1st.		Battalion Training as before. 2/Lieut.L.ELLIOTT admitted to hospital.	
do	2nd.		Battalion Training.	
do	3rd.		Battalion Training. Lieut.W.H.BYRDE took over duties of Signalling Officer as from 1/7/18.	
do	4th.		Battalion Training.	
do	5th.		Battalion Training - Coy in attack. Capt.T.BELL joined for Attachment. 2/Lieut.D.M.ATKINSON joined for duty and posted to "B" Coy. Draft of 31 O.R. arrived.	
do	6th.		Battalion Training. - Range. Captain E.W.HORNE joined from 1st Devons and took over duties of Adjutant as from 6/7/18.	
do	7th.		Divine Service.	
do	8th.		Battalion in attack towards TILLOY-FLORIVILLE - semi-open warfare. (Training.).	
do	9th.		Battalion Training. 2/Lieut.F.D.CLARKE awarded M.C. and 9328 A/R.S.M.BOWDEN, 28796 Pte.E.STOCKMAN, the D.C.M. for gallantry and devotion to duty between the AISNE and MARNE. 2/Lieut. A.E.UPPERTON proceeded to	

Army Form C. 2118.

WAR DIARY
or
INTELLIGENCE SUMMARY.
(Erase heading not required.)

Instructions regarding War Diaries and Intelligence Summaries are contained in F. S. Regs., Part II. and the Staff Manual respectively. Title pages will be prepared in manuscript.

2nd DEVONSHIRE REGIMENT

Place	Date	Hour	Summary of Events and Information	Remarks and references to Appendices
MONTIERES.	July 10th.		Battn.Training. A.R.A.Competition for selection of best platoon in Coys. Brigade Boxing Tournament held. Capt.T.BELL proceeded to join 1/7th Bn.D.L.I.	
do	11th.		Draft of 22 O.R. joined from Base. Training in the morning. Battalion Sports held in afternoon, in field between MONTIERES and MONCHAUX. Weather wet. Battalion engaged in Brigade Attack towards GAMACHES. (Training).	
do	12th.		Battalion Training. A.R.A.Competition on Range. No. 2 Platoon "A" Coy winners and 15 Platoon "D" Coy, runners up.	
do	13th.		Divine Service. Billeting Party proceeded to BOURSEVILLE. Lieut.P.A. OSBORNE and 2/Lieut.F.D.CLARKE, M.C. proceeded to PARIS PLAGE for rest camp.	
do	14th.			
do	15th.		Battalion left MONTIERES and marched to BOURSEVILLE. In Billets by 1.15 p.m. Capt.F.A.F.BONE left for U.K. on 14 days leave. 2/Lieut.T.N.KING rejoined from PARIS PLAGE. The following officers joined from Base. 2/Lieuts. A.T.BUSH, F.D.THORNTON, J.SAYES, G.M.YOUNG, B.R.BROWN, W.H.MILLARD, G.R.TAYLOR, S.J.WILLIAMS, W.EXTON.	

WAR DIARY or INTELLIGENCE SUMMARY.

2nd DEVONSHIRE REGIMENT - (4)

Place	Date	Hour	Summary of Events and Information	Remarks and references to Appendices
TRENCHES.	July. 21st.		Canadians on the right, 2/Middlesex R. on the left, 2/W.Yorks.R. in support.	
do	22nd.		Capt. J. WELLS, M.C. joined the Battalion.	
do	23rd.		Batt'n. in line. Lieut. P. A. OSBORNE and 2/Lieut. F. D. CLARKE M.C. rejoined from PARIS PLAGE. 2/Lieut. J. DRUMMOND joined the Battalion. 1 O.R. joined. Casualties - 1 O.R. wounded.	
do	24th.		Capt. J. WELLS, M.C. took over Command of "C" Coy. Same dispositions. A patrol under command of 2/Lieut. E. A. COLLIER engaged an enemy patrol a few yards outside MONTREAL TRENCH. Enemy made off leaving in our hands 1 UNTER-OFFIZIER killed. No casualties to our patrol. Other casualties - 1 O.R. wounded.	
do	25th.		2/Lieut. A. E. UPPERTON granted leave to U.K. from 22/7/18 to 5/8/18. 2/Lieut. J. DRUMMOND posted to "D" Coy. Casualties - 1 O.R. Wounded. A.R.A. Competition. "A" Coy No 2 platoon, won 23rd Inf.Bde. competition.	
do	26th.		Same dispositions.	
do	27th.		ditto. Sgt. McCormack proceeded to England. Casualties - 2 O.R. wounded.	

Army Form C. 2118.

WAR DIARY
or
INTELLIGENCE SUMMARY.

(Erase heading not required.)

Instructions regarding War Diaries and Intelligence Summaries are contained in F. S. Regs., Part II. and the Staff Manual respectively. Title pages will be prepared in manuscript.

2nd DEVONSHIRE REGIMENT - (3).

Place	Date	Hour	Summary of Events and Information	Remarks and references to Appendices
BOURSEVILLE.	July 16th		Battalion Training in new area. 2/Lieut. B.A. COLLIER joined from Base. 5231 Ptes. E.BOND and 8213 Cpl. F.Aggett awarded the MERITORIOUS SERVICE MEDAL. Lieut. S.H.COX reported as a Prisoner of War in GERMANY. Divisional Commander addressed all Officers of Bde. at HAUTEBUT.	
do	17th.		C.O. Held Kit Inspection. Coy Training at BOURSEVILLE.	
do	18th.		2/Lieut. C.A. HELLIER and 17 O.R. joined from Base. Battalion carried out Field Training Scheme on Training Area. Divisional Sports held at WOINCOURT. 2/Lieut. C.A. KENDALL joined from Base.	
do	19th.		Warning Order to move at 5.30 p.m. Battalion in Training.	
do	20th.		Battalion left billets at BOURSEVILLE at 12.50 a.m. and marched to EU and entrained for new area. Arrived at SAVY at 4.30 p.m. and marched to camp at MONT ST ELOY, arriving at 8.15 p.m.	
MONT ST ELOY.	21st.		Battalion relieved 1/7th Royal Scots, in ACHEVILLE SECTOR. Battalion conveyed to Canadian Monument by Motor Lorries leaving at 3 p.m. Took up position on a four Coy Frontage, of Right Battalion of Right (section.	

Army Form C. 2118.

WAR DIARY
or
INTELLIGENCE SUMMARY.
(Erase heading not required.)

Instructions regarding War Diaries and Intelligence Summaries are contained in F. S. Regs., Part II. and the Staff Manual respectively. Title pages will be prepared in manuscript.

2nd DEVONSHIRE REGIMENT. - (5).

Place	Date	Hour	Summary of Events and Information	Remarks and references to Appendices
TRENCHES.	July 28th.		Same dispositions. 2/Lieut. W. EXTON "B" Coy and 2 O.R. proceeded to VIII Corps School for B Course of Instruction in Anti-Gas.	
do	29th.		Same dispositions.	
do	30th.		Battalion still in line. Same dispositions.	
do	31st.		The Battalion was relieved by 2/Middx.Regt., relief commencing at 3.30 p.m. Bn. now in support and holding the BROWN LINE. "B" Coy on R.E. Working Party with 185th Tunnelling Coy, in camp near NEUVILLE ST VAAST. Lieut. (A/Capt.) U.B.BURKE,M.C. officially accepted as prisoner of war in Germany. (W.O.List of 10/7/18.). Lieut. A.E. RUTLEDGE reported missing 27/31/5/18, officially accepted as prisoner of war in Germany. (W.O.List of 2/7/18.).	
1/8/18.				

[signature] Lieut.-Colonel.
Commanding, 2nd Battalion Devonshire Regiment.

Army Form C. 2118.

WAR DIARY
or
INTELLIGENCE SUMMARY.
(Erase heading not required.)

Place	Date	Hour	Summary of Events and Information	Remarks and references to Appendices
			2nd BATTALION DEVONSHIRE REGIMENT.	
	1st Augt. 1918.		Battalion still in BROWN LINE.	
	2/8/18.		Same dispositions. Enemy aeroplane brought down behind our lines. Our lewis gunners took active part in the operation and claim to have brought it down. 1,000 drums of gas discharged into MERICOURT from Brigade front.	
	3/8/18.		Lieut. P.A.OSBORNE proceeded to Base and is struck off strength of Battn. No.2 Platoon "A" Coy won Divisional L.R.A. competition.	
	4/8/18.		Nine other ranks joined Battn. and taken on strength.	
	5/8/18.		Battn relieved by 2nd Battn Rifle Brigade. Relief commencing at 6.30 p.m. Battn less "B" Coy proceeded to Hills Camp in NEUVILLE ST VAAST in huts. "B" Coy proceeded to Cinema Camp. Cpl. G.BUDD awarded D.C.M. on 24/3/18.	
	6/8/18.		2/Lieut. G.E.Barter joined Battalion.	
	7/8/18.		Lecture by Divisional Gas Officer in Y.M.C.A. Hut to Battn.	

Army Form C. 2118.

WAR DIARY
or
INTELLIGENCE SUMMARY.
(Erase heading not required.)

Instructions regarding War Diaries and Intelligence Summaries are contained in F. S. Regs., Part II. and the Staff Manual respectively. Title pages will be prepared in manuscript.

Place	Date	Hour	Summary of Events and Information	Remarks and references to Appendices
	7/8/18.		(contd) 2/Lieut.G.E.BAKER taken on strength and posted to "C" Coy. Extract from appointments 4/8/18, "Lieut.E.W.HORNE to be Acting Major"	
	8/8/18.		H.Q.,Coys and Transport proceeded to BERTHONVAL Farm for baths during the course of the day.	
	9/8/18.		Capt.R.J.MATTHEWS having been taken on strength of L.T.M. Battery is struck off strength of Battn.	
	10/8/18.		A football match was played against the 7th D.L.I. in the afternoon. Result – Devons 4 goals – D.L.I. 1 goal.	
	11/8/18.		Battalion training.	
	12/8/18.		Concert given in the Y.M.C.A. by the Battn concert party at 6 p.m.	
	13/8/18.		Training carried on at NEUVILLE ST VAAST.	
	14/8/18.		Battn proceeded to the trenches in a new sector at WILLERVAL and relieved the 5th Royal Scots FUSILIERS, 52nd Division.	

Army Form C. 2118.

WAR DIARY
or
INTELLIGENCE SUMMARY.
(Erase heading not required.)

Place	Date	Hour	Summary of Events and Information	Remarks and references to Appendices
	14/8/18. (contd)		Bn'tn disposed in depth on a one company front.	
	15/8/18.		Holding the line. Sector very quiet.	
	16/8/18.		Same dispositions.	
	17/8/18.		Dispositions of Bn'tn changed. "B" Coy still in BROWN LINE. Remainder one 3 Coy front. Coys disposed in depth. Front extended North to WILLERVAL ROAD. Casualties 1 Other rank wounded. Capt.W.H.Simmonds proceeded to First Army Infantry School on course of instruction. Major E.W.HORNE proceeded on leave to U.K.	
	18/8/18.		A patrol under 2/Lieut.G.N.KENDALL consisting of 1 platoon succeeded in passing enemy Observation line and entering ARLEUX through which it proceeded. No enemy were encountered. Casualties Nil. 2/Lieut.L.D.HEPPENSTALL proceeded on Gas Course to VIII Corps S. Mil.	
	19/8/18.		Projector and gas beam & tack on enemy from our sector. 2nd Middlesex Regt. relieved by 2nd West Yorks Reg. on our left. 2/Lieut.A.T.BUSH posted to 23rd T.M.Battery and struck off strength	

Army Form C. 2118.

WAR DIARY
or
INTELLIGENCE SUMMARY.
(Erase heading not required.)

Instructions regarding War Diaries and Intelligence Summaries are contained in F. S. Regs., Part II. and the Staff Manual respectively. Title pages will be prepared in manuscript.

Place	Date	Hour	Summary of Events and Information	Remarks and references to Appendices
	19/8/18. (contd)		Capt. E.H.SAVILLE joined Battn and took over command of "B" Coy.	
	20/8/18.		Another patrol under 2/Lieut. B.R.BROWN entered ARLEUX without encountering enemy. New post taped in rear of BLACK LINE.	
	21/8/18.		Patrol was sent out at 8 p.m. under 2/Lieut. A.R.WILLIAMS. Entered ARLEUX and successfully engaged the enemy, the effects of 2 dead Germans being brought back and identification (69th Res.Inf. Regt.) obtained. Patrol Commander congratulated by G.O.C. A.R.A. competition again won by No.2 Platoon "A" Coy -v- 2nd Scottish Rifles. (Corps competition) 2/Lieut. E.A.COLLIER proceeded to Army Musketry Camp, MATRINGHEM.	
	22/8/18.		3 a.m. Heavy gas shelling in neighbourhood of BLUE LINE. 2/Lieut. C.A.HELLIER and 15 Other Ranks gassed. Corps Commander and Divisional General visited the line. Capt.N.J.BRETHERTON proceeded on a Bye-products course. 2/Lieut.A.E.UPPERTON rejoined from XXII Corps School. Casualties - 2 Other Ranks wounded.	

(A9175) W1 W235/P360 600,000 12/17 D. D. & L. Sch. 82a. Forms/C118/45

Army Form C. 2118.

WAR DIARY
or
INTELLIGENCE SUMMARY.
(Erase heading not required.)

Place	Date	Hour	Summary of Events and Information	Remarks and references to Appendices
	23/8/18.		Construction of 2 new posts outside Observation line commenced.	
	24/8/18.		Battn relieved by 2nd Middlesex Regt and moved into Hills Camp, NEUVILLE ST VAAST. Casualties 2 Other Ranks wounded.	
	25/8/18.		Cleaning up and Bths. 2/Lieut. W.H.MILLARD proceeded on a Course of Instruction at VIII Corps School.	
	26/8/18.		Camp inspected by Corps Commander (VIII Corps). Battn at half hours notice to proceed to trenches owing to operations re advancing front line.	
	27/8/18.		Officers football match -v- D.L.I. Result 2/Devons. 11 - D.L.I. Nil. 24th Div. Concert Party at Y.M.C.A. Capt.F.A.F. BONE pronounced B II and struck off strength of Battn.	
	28/8/18.		Battn. medically inspected. 2/Lieut. W.Exton and 36 Other Ranks proceeded to Army Musketry Camp, HEZECQUES. Battn at 1 hours notice to move. Lieut. G.T.MARTIN M.C. to Brigade (temporarily) as Brigade I.O. 23rd Inf.Bde G.28/120. 23rd Brigade Northern Boundary :- T.30.d.6.9. - T.30.c.75.75 - T.29.d.1.5. thence along	

Army Form C. 2118.

WAR DIARY
or
INTELLIGENCE SUMMARY.
(Erase heading not required.)

Place	Date	Hour	Summary of Events and Information	Remarks and references to Appendices
	28/8/18. (contd)		WESTERN ROAD to T.27.c.0.0. - T.26.d.2.0. - B.1.d.6.9. - A.12.a.9.5. - thence westwards. 23rd Brigade N Southern Boundary. C.7.a.0.4. - B.12.s.0.4. - along MACHINE GUN TRENCH (inclusive to Left Brigade) to B.11.a.5.3. - B.10.a.6.3. - B.10.c.0.0. - along TIRED Alley (inclusive to Left Brigade) The main line of Resistance of the 23rd Inf. Bde. is the old BLACK LINE. The main line of resistance of the 24th Inf. Bde. on the right is BON SUPPORT. Following information obtained from prisoners :- Enemy main line of resistance is along FRESNOY Trench with 3 Coys in line and 1 Coy in Support in FLANDE and UNIFORM TRENCH. Bn HQ. U.19.b.4.8. Battn were expecting relief either on the night 26/27th or 27/28th. Sentry group posted in TORTOISE Trench.	
	29/8/18.		3 Platoon of "A" Coy required in line tonight for carrying Trench Mortars. To remain in BROWN LINE after work pending further orders.	

Army Form C. 2118.

WAR DIARY
or
INTELLIGENCE SUMMARY.
(Erase heading not required.)

Instructions regarding War Diaries and Intelligence Summaries are contained in F.S. Regs., Part II. and the Staff Manual respectively. Title pages will be prepared in manuscript.

Place	Date	Hour	Summary of Events and Information	Remarks and references to Appendices
	30/8/18.		Relieving 2nd West Yorks Regt in left sub-sector of Brigade front on Septr. 1st. 1 Platoon of "A" Coy returning tonight from carrying party. Instructions received from Brigade to leave "Battle Surplus" out of line. Remaining 2 Platoons of "A" Coy returned from line tonight. 11 Other Ranks more or less gassed last night. Lieut.Col.G.E.R.PRIOR M.C. and Capt. R.L.BROKENSHIRE visited West Yorks in line this afternoon. 2/Lieut. R.H.HOBERN and 2/Lieut.F.R.FOLKES joined Battn and posted temporarily to "D" Coy.	
	31/8/18.		Extract from List No.102 "Appointments,Commissions" Lieut R.W. BOWN 5/Gloucester Reg. to be Actg. Capt.whilst employed as Actg Adjutant, with pay and allowances of Lieut. The u/m to be acting Capts. whilst commanding Coys :- Lieut.R.L.BROKENSHIRE (S.R.) 29/6/18. Lieut.W.H.SIMMONDS 4th Gloucester Regt. 19/6/18. Operation Orders for relief of 2nd West Yorks Regt issued tonight.	

Army Form C. 2118.

WAR DIARY
or
INTELLIGENCE SUMMARY.
(Erase heading not required.)

Instructions regarding War Diaries and Intelligence Summaries are contained in F. S. Regs., Part II. and the Staff Manual respectively. Title pages will be prepared in manuscript.

Place	Date	Hour	Summary of Events and Information	Remarks and references to Appendices
	31/8/18.	(contd)	2/Lieut. W.H.MILLARD rejoined from a Course of Instruction at VIII Corps School.	
	1/9/18.		[signature] Lieut.Colonel, Commanding 2nd Battalion Devonshire Regiment.	

Army Form C. 2118.

WAR DIARY
or
INTELLIGENCE SUMMARY.
(Erase heading not required.)

2nd BATTALION DEVONSHIRE REGIMENT.

Place	Date	Hour	Summary of Events and Information	Remarks and references to Appendices
	1918.			
	Septr.1st.		Battalion relieved 2/West Yorks Regt in left sector. Relief complete at about 7.15 p.m. "A" Coy in Oak valley forming outposts in newly captured trench. "B" Coy in ARLEUX also newly captured Other Coys in BLACK Line. Enemy twice attempted to bomb "A" Coy post in OAK VALLEY but were driven off with bombs on both occasions. Groans heard indicating enemy casualties. Casualties nil. 2/Lieut. H.PARKER joined Battn and posted to "C"Coy	
	2/9/18.		2nd Battn Devonshire granted the "French Distinction"CITATION" in recognition of the great stand on the MARNE May 1918. The first Infantry Regt in the British Army to be granted this very rare distinction.. Post of "A" Coy bombed, 3 men being wounded, enemy driven off with bombs. Patrol under 2/Lieut.J.DRUMMOND engaged enemy patrol. Our casualties 2 wounded. Enemy reported to leave 3 dead	

Army Form C. 2118.

WAR DIARY
or
INTELLIGENCE SUMMARY.
(Erase heading not required.)

Instructions regarding War Diaries and Intelligence Summaries are contained in F. S. Regs., Part II. and the Staff Manual respectively. Title pages will be prepared in manuscript.

Place	Date	Hour	Summary of Events and Information	Remarks and references to Appendices
	2/9/18.		which they fetched in later, seen by man who became entangled in wire, returning later. Casualties 5 wounded. CROIX deGUERRE conferred on Battalion by the French.	
	3/9/18.		Holding ARLEUX LOOP. Some slight changes in dispositions of posts "A" Coy pushing two posts out into ARLEUX village. Casualties 50 O.Ranks (49 gassed 1 wounded) 2/Lieut.W.EXTON "D" Coy admitted to 51 C.C.S. from 1st Army Musketry Camp.	
	4/9/18.		Holding the line. Work on trenches. Casualties 4 Other Ranks wounded. Major E.W.HORNE rejoined from leave to U.K.	
	5/9/18.		Holding the line, work on trenches etc. Casualties nil. The following awarded Parchment Certificates by Divisional Commander for gallantry and devotion to duty in the field. 2/Lieut.A.R.WILLIAMS 32059 Pte.D.Fullerton, 32055 Pte.C.Caines, of "B" Coy.	
	6/9/18.		Holding the line, work on trenches etc. 3 Other Ranks gassed.	
	7/9/18.		Same dispositions. 1 O.Rank wounded.	
	8/9/18.		Enemy patrol bombed "C" Coy post wounding 2 Other Ranks, driven off with Lewis Gun.	

Army Form C. 2118.

WAR DIARY
or
INTELLIGENCE SUMMARY.
(Erase heading not required.)

Place	Date	Hour	Summary of Events and Information	Remarks and references to Appendices
	9/9/18.		Holding the line. Weather wet and trenches very muddy.	
	10/9/18.		Holding the line. Very wet and muddy.	
	11/9/18.		Lieut. W.L.CLEGG reported missing 27/5/18 officially accepted as Prisoner of War. 14864 Pte. G. Rockley reported missing 25/3/18 escaped from territory occupied by enemy, arrived in U.K. 22/8/18.	
	12/9/18.		Wet and muddy. Holding the line.	
	13/9/18.		Ditto. 2/Lieut. G.F.THOMAS joined Battn and posted to "A" Coy.	
	14/9/18.		Same dispositions. 2/Lieut. A.R.WILLIAMS rejoined from leave in France.	
	15/9/18.		Holding the line. Normal.	
	16/9/18.		Holding the line. Normal day.	
	17/9/18.		Battalion relieved in the trenches by 2/Middlesex Regt and proceeded to HILLS CAMP, NEUVILLE ST VAAST.	
	18/9/18.		Day spent in cleaning up and baths. Divisional Guard found by Battalion in honour of "CITATION". Mess meeting in afternoon. New "War Bond" lottery started.	
	19/9/18.		Battn proceeded for the day to VILLERS AU BOIS to take part in	

Instructions regarding War Diaries and Intelligence Summaries are contained in F. S. Regs., Part II. and the Staff Manual respectively. Title pages will be prepared in manuscript.

Army Form C. 2118.

WAR DIARY
or
INTELLIGENCE SUMMARY.
(Erase heading not required.)

Instructions regarding War Diaries and Intelligence Summaries are contained in F. S. Regs., Part II. and the Staff Manual respectively. Title pages will be prepared in manuscript.

Place	Date	Hour	Summary of Events and Information	Remarks and references to Appendices
	19/9/18.		Tank demonstration. No tanks turned up so Battn did an attack.	
	20/9/18.		Visited by the Brigadier General about noon who lunched in the mess. Platoon football in the afternoon.	
	21/9/18.		Resting at NEUVILLE ST VAAST. Inter platoon football. Show in evening at Y.M.C.A. by "The Dumplings".	
	22/9/18.		Training. Inter platoon football.	
	23/9/18.		Battn proceeded to MONT ST ELOY where it was inspected by the Divisional Commander. Medals presented. Inter platoon football.	
	24/9/18.		Resting Hills Camp. Lieut. (A/Capt) W.H.RADCLIFFE joined Battn for duty and took over 2nd in command "B" Coy.	
	25/9/18.		Final - Platoon football competition. No.6 Platoon .v. Signallers & Runners. Result a draw. Match to be played again. Funeral of Lt.Col.LOWRY 2/West Yorks Regt. Officers of Battn. attended.	
	26/9/18.		Final Platoon Football - Winners, Sigs and Runners Score 1 - 0. Battn relieved 2/West Yorks Regt in Left Sector	

Army Form C. 2118.

WAR DIARY
or
INTELLIGENCE SUMMARY.
(Erase heading not required.)

Instructions regarding War Diaries and Intelligence Summaries are contained in F. S. Regs., Part II. and the Staff Manual respectively. Title pages will be prepared in manuscript.

Place	Date	Hour	Summary of Events and Information	Remarks and references to Appendices
	26/9/18.		The following is an extract from "Special Order of the Day" published on 26th Septr 1918. " The following citations which appeared in the Orders of the Day, No.371 of the 5th French Army, on Augt. 20th 1918, on behalf of 2nd Battn Devonshire Regt, is published for the information of all ranks :-	
			' On the 27th May 1918, at a time when the British trenches were subjected to fierce attacks, the 2nd Battn the Devonshire Regt repelled successive enemy assaults with gallantry and determination and maintained an unbroken front till a late hour. The staunchness of this Battalion permitted defences South of A. to be organized and their occupation by reinforcements to be completed.	
			Inspired by the sangfroid of their gallant Commander, in the face of an intense bombardment, the few survivors of the Battalion, though isolated and without hope of assistance, held on to the trenches north of the river and fought to the last with an unhesitating obedience to orders. Thus the whole Battalion - Colonel,	

Army Form C. 2118.

WAR DIARY
or
INTELLIGENCE SUMMARY.
(Erase heading not required.)

Instructions regarding War Diaries and Intelligence Summaries are contained in F. S. Regs., Part II. and the Staff Manual respectively. Title pages will be prepared in manuscript.

Place	Date	Hour	Summary of Events and Information	Remarks and references to Appendices
	26/9/18.		28 Officers, and 552 Non-commissioned Officers and men — responded with one accord and offered their lives in ungrudging sacrifice to the sacred cause of the Allies'".	
			Night 26/27th. Battn attacked enemy's Outpost system in conjunction with 2/Middlesex Regt on the Right and 7th D.C.L.I. (20th Divn) on the Left. We captured BRITANNIA and BRANDY Trenches on both sides of the ARLEUX—FRESNOY Road, killing large numbers of the enemy and holding our gains. Full report attached.	A
			Casualties 15 killed and 15 wounded, including H.Q.Signallers and Runners who were shelled moving up to the position — also includes 1 Officer wounded 2/Lieut.G.F.THOMAS "A" Coy.	
	27/9/18.		Battn. consolidated new positions — congratulated by G.H.Q. on successful show. Pushed out patrols — One under command of 2/Lieut.W.H.MILLARD bringing in 2 prisoners. This Officer was congratulated by the Brigade Commander.	
	28/9/18.		Battalion holding whole of Brigade Outpost line. Enemy counter—	

Army Form C. 2118.

WAR DIARY
or
INTELLIGENCE SUMMARY.
(Erase heading not required.)

Place	Date	Hour	Summary of Events and Information	Remarks and references to Appendices
	28/9/18.		attacked at 2 a.m. but was repulsed. Casualties 2/Lieut. A.E. COLLIER wounded. 1, O.Rank killed, 3, O.Ranks wounded.	
	29/9/18.		Battn holding Brigade Outpost Line. Much rain has fallen within the last two days and line in consequence is in a bad condition. Casualties Nil.	
	30/9/18.		Battn still holding Outpost Line - day very quiet - strong northerly wind but no rain - Line still very wet and dirty.	
	1/10/18.		[signature] Lieut.Colonel, Commanding 2nd Battalion Devonshire Regiment.	

A

OPERATIONS.

On the night of the 26th/27th September 1918 the Battalion carried out a successful attack in conjunction with the 2nd Battalion Middlesex Regiment and the 7th Duke of Cornwall's Light Infantry.

The objectives for this Battalion were BRITANNIA and BRANDY Trenches East of ARLEUX-EN-GOHELLE (North East of ARRAS).

A, D, and 2 Platoons of C Company were the assaulting troops advancing in two waves to the assault. The Barrage was provided by Field Guns, Howitzers and Machine Guns and was excellent. ZERO hour was at midnight and within ¾ of an hour of this time the objectives had been taken all along the line. Seven prisoners were taken and a number of the enemy were found dead in the captured trenches. Two Light Machine guns and One Automatic Pistol of a new type were also captured together with numerous documents. Prisoners belonged to the 25th and 69th R.I.R..

Our casualties during the operation were 9 killed and 1 Officer and 11 Other Ranks wounded.

Two Sections of A Company advanced beyond the objective and eventually reached FRESNOY PARK, they were forced to return owing to our own barrage and captured Three prisoners (included in the above)

The Operation was entirely successful and the following wire was received from General Headquarters:- "Congratulations to battalion on successful operations".

On the afternoon of the 27th September 1918 a patrol of six Other Ranks under 2/Lieut E.H.MILLARD was sent to ascertain whether the enemy held the FRESNOY LINE as it was reported that the enemy had evacuated this trench. This patrol did exceedingly good work and returned with 2 prisoners which they captured in daylight from the enemy lines.

Lieut. Col.
Commanding 2nd Devonshire Regiment.

23rd Bde. 8th Division.

War Diary

2nd Bn: Devonshire Regt.

October 1918.

(Report on Operations. Attached)

WAR DIARY or INTELLIGENCE SUMMARY.

(Erase heading not required.)

Army Form C. 2118.

Place	Date	Hour	Summary of Events and Information	Remarks and references to Appendices
1918			**1. 2nd Battalion Devonshire Regiment.**	
October	1st.		Battalion holding Outpost Line.	
"	2nd.		Bn. relieved by D.C.L.I. and went out to STIRLING Camp, east of ST LAURENT BLANGY near ARRAS. "C" and "D" Coys in reserve forward near ATHIES.	
"	3rd.		Bn. at STIRLING CAMP.	
"	4th.		STIRLING CAMP. "A" and "B" Coys relieved "C" and "D" Coys at ATHIES.	
"	5th.		At STIRLING CAMP.	
"	6th.		Bn. relieved 6th Gordon Highlanders, 51st Division, in the line in front of FAMPOUX. Bn. to attack FRESNES-ROUVROY Line in support to 2/Middx.Regt and 2/W.Yorks.Regt tomorrow morning. "B" and "C" Coys to be under orders of above Battalions. ZERO hour fixed for dawn, 5 a.m. morning of 11th. 8 pltn "B" Coy to form Right Defensive Flank at BIACHES ST VAAST.	
"	7th.		At 5 a.m. this morning 2/W.Yorks. and 2/Middx.Regt supported by "C" and "D" Coys 2nd Devons attacked the FRESNES-ROUVROY Line on a 1000 yd front and succeeded in taking all objectives. 1 pltn. "B" Coy under 2/Lieut.J.SAYES successfully established a	

Army Form C. 2118.

WAR DIARY
or
INTELLIGENCE SUMMARY.
(Erase heading not required.)

Instructions regarding War Diaries and Intelligence Summaries are contained in F. S. Regs., Part II. and the Staff Manual respectively. Title pages will be prepared in manuscript.

Place	Date	Hour	Summary of Events and Information	Remarks and references to Appendices
1918	Oct. 7th contd.		**2. 2nd Battalion Devonshire Regiment.** defensive post on the right flank of the Right Bn. beyond the Electric Power Station, BIACHE ST VAAST taking several prisoners and a M.G. About 80 prisoners were taken by the Brigade. In the evening the new line of the 2/W.Yorks.Regt was taken by the 2nd Devons.	
	October 8th.		Late last night and early this morning our patrols cleared the village of FRESNES-LEZ-MONTAUBAN and GLOUCESTER WOOD taking a few prisoners and establishing posts to the east.	
"	9th		Active Patrolling and advancing posts in front. A shell burst outside "C" Coy H.Q. killing 2/Lieut. G.E.BAXTER and 2 O.R. and wounding 2/Lieut.G.M.YOUNG and several other ranks.	
"	10th.		"C" and "D" Coys relieved in the front line by "A" and "B" Coys. Post pushed out further and contact with enemy maintained. Patrol Encounters etc.	
"	11th.		At dawn (5.15 a.m.) this morning the 2nd Devons and 2nd Middx.Regt attacked QUEANT-DROCOURT LINE (WOTAN LINE) just N. of VITRY-EN-ARTOIS on a front of 1000 yds. No resistance on the part of the enemy who had retired an hour or so previously. A few prisoners were captured and all objectives taken	

Army Form C. 2118.

WAR DIARY
or
INTELLIGENCE SUMMARY.
(Erase heading not required.)

Place	Date	Hour	Summary of Events and Information	Remarks and references to Appendices
	1918.		**3. 2nd Battalion Devonshire Regiment.**	
	Oct. 11th contd.		About 20 casualties from our own barrage. 2nd W.Yorks Regt pushed on forward and established posts E. of QUEANT-DROCOURT Line. 2/Lieut.Folkes and 2/Lieut.Williams wounded.	
	October 12th.		In support holding QUEANT-DROCOURT Line. Excellent dug-out accomodation. Mines and booby-traps successfully removed.	
"	13th.		Bn. took over outpost line from 2nd W.Yorks.Regt extending from CORBEHEM to LA BRAVELLE FARM on a front of about 5000 yds. Enemy holding E. bank of deviation of the SCARPE with M.G. posts on W. bank. Our positions very heavily shelled and a lot of accurate M.G.fire. Ground around our left post flooded by enemy opening Canal sluice and post compelled to withdraw about 600 yds. Our line runs roughly 2000 yds W. of DOUAI.	
"	14th.		Relieved from outpost line by 2nd Bn. Middlesex Regt and returned to support in QUEANT-DROCOURT line. Relief completed at about 11 tonight.	
"	15th.		Cleaning up and resting in QUEANT-DROCOURT line. News of proposed armistice has come through but very little details.	

Army Form C. 2118.

WAR DIARY
or
INTELLIGENCE SUMMARY.
(Erase heading not required.)

Instructions regarding War Diaries and Intelligence Summaries are contained in F. S. Regs., Part II. and the Staff Manual respectively. Title pages will be prepared in manuscript.

Place	Date	Hour	Summary of Events and Information	Remarks and references to Appendices
1918.				
	16th October.		**4. 2nd Bn. Devonshire Regiment.** Resting in QUEANT-DROCOURT line. Raining and ground muddy.	
	17th "		"A" Coy practised crossing the SCARPE in pontoon boats made by the Field Coy. The u/m Officers joined the Bn. for duty. 2/Lieut. A.M.Harvey, 2/Lieut. D.J.Tuckett, 2/Lieut. A.Willis, Lieut. R.C.D.Napier, Lieut. B.A.Schooling, 2/Lieut. S.T.Mears.	
	18th "		Bn. working on roads in vicinity of billeting area and towards QUIERY-LA-MOTTE.	
	19th "		Work carried on on roads. 2/Lieut. E.R.Folkes embarked for England.	
	20th "		Battalion marched to village of RACHES via DOUAI. Good billets in village. A few civilians returned having been released by the Bosche who had deported them several days before. Bn.H.Q. in CHATEAU PLAISANT.	
	21st "		Cleaning up and working parties on roads. All Coys working 6 hours. Village structurally intact but a great deal of damage to furniture was done by the Huns. All windows and most of the ornaments were broken and village looted from end to end.	

Army Form C. 2118.

WAR DIARY
or
INTELLIGENCE SUMMARY.
(Erase heading not required.)

Place	Date	Hour	Summary of Events and Information	Remarks and references to Appendices
	1918.			
	Octr.27th contd.		**6. 2nd Bn.Devonshire Regiment.** object to establish posts to enable the success to be exploited. "A" Coy on right flank effected a crossing by 0230 over the R.Escaut, one platoon and one M.G. Section establishing post between River and Canal. "D" Coy. central Coy. were able to get 1 Officer and 2 O.R. across the river but remainder of Coy were met with heavy shelling and M.G. fire. The Brigadier ordered their withdrawal. 2/Lieut.W.Exton and 2 O.R. got back by swimming River. "C" Coy. left Coy; effected a crossing but were ordered to withdraw. Casualties 28 O.R.	
	October 28th.		"A" Coys platoon that had effected a crossing of the river and the M.G. section, were captured by the enemy at 1100 hours. L/c.Marchment and 2 men escaped. The 2 men were wounded. They reported that 2/Lieut. Harvey and the remainder had been captured, all being wounded except 2/Lieut.Harvey and 1 other rank. Casualties 1 Officer and 18 O.R. Very little shelling. 1 man of "A" Coy killed on patrol. Lt.Col.G.E.R.Prior M.C. rejoined Bn. from French Leave. Lieut. G.T.Martin M.C. admitted to Casualty Clearing Station.	

Army Form C. 2118.

WAR DIARY
or
INTELLIGENCE SUMMARY.
(Erase heading not required.)

Instructions regarding War Diaries and Intelligence Summaries are contained in F.S. Regs., Part II. and the Staff Manual respectively. Title pages will be prepared in manuscript.

Place	Date	Hour	Summary of Events and Information	Remarks and references to Appendices
1918.			**5. 2nd Bn. Devonshire Regiment.**	
October	22nd.		All Coys working 6 hours on roads towards MONTREUIL and FLINES. Many pianos found in the village added to the amusement of the men. Billets cleaned up and made very comfortable.	
"	23rd.		The Bn. marched to MARCHIENNES and occupied billets in the town. Many civilians living in the town and considerably less damage done by the Hun. News received that during their retirement the Huns deposited as many civilians as the town would hold in ST. AMAND and then proceeded to heavily shell the place.	
"	24th.		Bn. parade in the morning. Football indulged in during the afternoon. 2/Lieut. A.R. Williams proceeded on leave to the U.K.	
"	25th.		One hours notice at 1400 hours to move to ST. AMAND. Bn. moved at 1310 hours. Whole Bn. in large hospital. Town not badly damaged. No civilians in town.	
"	26th.		Bn. relieved the 2nd Northamptonshire Regt. in ODENEZ village and posts touching River Escaut. Capt. J. Wells M.C. assumed duties of 2nd in Command of 1st Bn. Sherwood Forresters.	
"	27th.		"A", "C" and "D" Coys with "B" Coy in support attempted to cross R. ESCAUT and Canal JARD with	

Army Form C. 2118.

WAR DIARY
or
INTELLIGENCE SUMMARY.
(Erase heading not required.)

Instructions regarding War Diaries and Intelligence Summaries are contained in F. S. Regs., Part II. and the Staff Manual respectively. Title pages will be prepared in manuscript.

Place	Date	Hour	Summary of Events and Information	Remarks and references to Appendices
1918.				
October	29th		**7. 2nd Bn.Devonshire Regiment.**	
			Very quiet all night.	
"	30th		Four Machine Gunners supposed captured on the 28th effected a safe crossing to our lines. The Corps, Divisional and Brigadier Generals visited the Battalion H.Q. Bn.H.Q. moved into village of ODENEZ. River L'Escaut bridged by R.Es at 2100 hours but it gave way. "A", "B" and "D" Coys effected a crossing by Jerusalem Rafts - no casualties in crossing. R.Es built a Jerusalem Pontoon Bridge. "B" Coy were heavily shelled at 2330 hours.	
"	31st		See diary of operations attached.	

Gardner
Lieut.Colonel.
Commanding, 2nd Bn.Devonshire Regiment.

Diary of operations during the forcing of the passage of the
RIVER L'ESCAUT Night of 30/31st.October1918.

1820 hours. Battn.H.Q. opened at Q4d90.60.
1935 hours. Jerusalem Pontoons arrived. "C" Coy left to take up position as covering party. Intermittent M.G.Fire.
2000 hours. Two first platoons (A & D Coys) of Bridgehead crossing by ponton Message received that R.E.are already throwing Bridge across.
2010 hours. Message received from B Coy that they are moving to Assembly position.
2020 hours. 1 Bridge in position. A & D Coys.instructed to cross immediately.
2045 hours. B Coy ordered to move up to garden wall ready to cross on D Coy reaching objective.
2115 hours. Message received that all C Coy are in position on Tow Path. Crossing by Bridge proceeding very slowly as end has collapsed. More Jerusalems arriving.
2315 hours. 14 more Jerusalems arrived. 3 Platoons across remainder crossing by Pontoons now fairly quickly.
2320 hours. Bosche patrol reported approaching copse about Q5a90.50. to Q5a&C
2350 hours Crossing proceeding with very little opposition. Message received from 23rd.Infty.Bde.to effect the crossing of the CANAL DU JARD tonight by any means possible, making Bridgehead east of CANAL when 2nd.West Yorks will push through us. 2nd.Middx.at one hours notice to move.

31/10/18.

0030 hours. B Coy commencing crossing of River. A & D Coys across and Bridgehead established.
0100 hours. Fairly heavy shelling just N.E. of River Bank and in village. Retaliation called for. 3 Platoons of B Coy across.
0150 R.E.Officer wounded in hand. 1 Prisoner (Wounded) captured by A Coy belonging to 451 Regt states 20 Bosche this side of CANAL remainder have gone back distance of 2½ miles. Appears unreliable.
0230 hours. Message received from A Coy that Bosche are massing on right for counter attack. Information confirmed by B.I.O. A Coy have had several casualties. C Coy ordered to send up Platoon to A Coy. D Coy to hold their reserve platoon in readiness to reinforce.
0310 hours. 2 M.G. ordered to report to A Coy.
0330 hours. B Coy.report Co.H.Q. at Fosse Amoury and no possible crossing of CANAL DU JARD. M.G.fire from opposite side of CANAL direction of K.34 b 1.3.
0415 hours. Bridge reported now fully repaired and dry crossing possible. Considerable gas shelling about FOSSE AMOURY.
0550 hours. Dispositions are as follows:- A Coy H.Q. Q5 c 40.90 with two weak platoons near wood and two platoons pushed forward to Q5a8050 and Q5 b 2.0. with orders to push forward to PONT JOLLY.
D Coy:- 1 Platoon at Q5 a 40.20. with Coy. H.Q. at Q.4.b.9.6. Remaining Platoons around Island at D.4.b.8.6.
"B" Coy H.Q. at K.34.d.5.0. 4 platoons around debris. Orders given to push 1 platoon to K.34.8.8. towards bridge and 1 platoon to work N. along Canal.
0605 hours. Message from "D" Coy. 4 O.R. wounded.
0815 hours. G.O.C. Brigade congratulated Battalion on successful operation last night.
0830 hours. Canadians reported Bosche massing for counter attack at Q.5.b.6.7. and on road running N.E. from there. Artillery and Brigade informed. 2/W.Yorks. relieving us tonight.
Casualties 12 O.R. wounded (through R.A.P.) 1 Killed. Probably incomplete.
0850 hours. Heavy shelling of Battn.H.Q. S.O.S. sent up from Right Front. Bde. and Artillery informed.
0910 hours. Cpl. Pope and 2 men reported at Bn..H.Q.

"A" Coy less about 5 men and Capt. Brokenshire, back across the river.. Casualties heavy.

Under pressure from exceedingly heavy barrage, "A" Coy withdrew across the river, leaving Capt. Brokenshire, Lt. Napier and 4 men behind who held on to bank with 6 Lewis Guns. 1145 hours 1 platoon of "C" Coy to reinforce Capt. Brokenshire on bank.

Lieut. Napier carried wounded man on his back across the bridge, under the bombardment.   in street

"A" Coys casualties caused chiefly/in adjacent to Bn. H.Q.

1100 hours. Report through from O.C. "B" Coy on FOSSE ARMOURY. Runner swam river and arrived minus his boots, coats etc. O.C. Coy reports 2/Lieut. Sayes killed and casualties very heavy. Out of touch with "D" Coy and unable to evacuate wounded. Previous runner drowned in attempt to get message through. Reply sent to "hold on," relief being sent tonight.

1510 hours. Fairly frequent heavy bursts of shellfire. Total casualties estimated about 80.

O.O. 297 received for relief tonight.

1640 hours. Orders received to withdraw posts immediately and proceed to billets. Situation on flanks responsible.

1730 hours. Report received from Capt Taylor that bridge has been broken. More pontoons due from R.E. Crossing progressing slowly.

1830 hours. "A" and "C" Coys clear.

1915 hours. "B" Coy all clear and all wounded across.

1930 hours. 490th Coy R.E. arrived with more Jerusalems.

1950 hours. Last of "D" Coy across and Bde. wired to this effect.

To Historical Section
Committee of Imperial Defence
(Military Branch)
Public Record Office
Chancery Lane
London. 22nd Uripadi

2nd Record.
Vol I. 4.11 — 31.12.14

121/3971   2/11/14

Bn. disembarked
Havre from England
6.11.14

Apl 1919

WAR DIARY or INTELLIGENCE SUMMARY.

Army Form C. 2118.

(Erase heading not required.)

Place	Date	Hour	Summary of Events and Information	Remarks and References to Appendices
			2nd Battalion DEVONSHIRE REGIMENT	
	1918			
	1st. Novr.		Battalion took billets in ST. AMAND. Cleaning up billets during the day. At 1700 hours shelling near "A" Coys billets. No casualties. C.S.M. J.Radford appointed A/R.S.M.	
	2/11/18.		Parades by Coys. Wet day. Concert in the evening. ST.AMAND shelled at 1600 hours. Capt. P.J.Bretherton awarded the M.C. 10027 C.S.M. C.S.Surway awarded the D.C.M. 69282 C.S.M. May M.M. awarded Bar to M.M. The u/m were awarded the Military Medal :- 8859 Sgt. J.Lorey. 9273 Pte. E.Coles. 69327 Pte. J.Watkins. 74093 Pte. A.Powell. 49009 Pte. H.Cooper. 32121 Pte. T.Midlane.	RAB
	3/11/18.		Battalion paraded for Church Service at 1000 hours. Fine day. ST.AMAND shelled at 1730 hours. Capt and Adjutant R.W.Bowen granted leave to U.K. 5-19/11/18. 4th Battalion moved at 1300 hours to WARLAING. Fine day. Men in good billets.	RAB
	4/11/18.		Very wet day, seriously hampered training. 2/Lieut.F.D.Clarke.M.C	RAB

WAR DIARY
or
INTELLIGENCE SUMMARY.
(Erase heading not required.)

Army Form C. 2118.

Place	Date	Hour	Summary of Events and Information	Remarks and references to Appendices
			2nd Battalion Devonshire Regiment.	
	5/11/18. (contd)		rejoined from First Army School.	RwB
	6/11/18.		Very wet day. Interfered with training.	RwB
	7/11/18.		Very wet day. 2/Lt.S.J.Williams embarked for U.K. wounded. Lt.W.H.Simmonds struck off and taken on establishment of 1st Army Sch.	RwB
	8/11/18.		Very wet day. Bn. parade - Organisation, Divnl.Comdr's Inspection postponed.	RwB
	9/11/18.		Bn. moved from WARLAING to ESCAUPONT. Good billets. No civilians in the town. Town not badly damaged. 2/Lt.F.D.Clarke M.C. proceeded on leave to U.K. Capt.& Adjt.R.W.Bowen granted 2 days extension of leave.	RwB
	10/11/18.		Fine day. Church Service at 1100 hours. Bn. moved at 1400 to QUIVERCHAIN.	RwB
	11/11/18.		Bn. moved at 0700 hours to TERTRE. News of the armistice received by Bn. whilst on march. Civilians shewed great pleasure on entry of Bn. TERTRE full of troops. Lt.R.H. Cummings joined Bn and posted to "D" Coy.	RwB
	12/11/18.		Bn. moved to GHLIN. Civil population shewed great enthusiasm at Bn. entry. Good billets.	RwB
	13/11/18.		Bn. Concert Party "DUMPLINGS" gave a performance. Major E.W.Horne granted local leave from 13 to 24/11/18.	RwB

Army Form C. 2118.

WAR DIARY
or
INTELLIGENCE SUMMARY.
(Erase heading not required.)

Instructions regarding War Diaries and Intelligence Summaries are contained in F. S. Regs., Part II, and the Staff Manual respectively. Title pages will be prepared in manuscript.

Place	Date	Hour	Summary of Events and Information	Remarks and references to Appendices
			2nd Bn. Devonshire Regiment.	
	14/11/18.		Bn. parades.	[sgd]
	15/11/18.		Bn. lined the streets of MONS for the formal entry of General HORNE and were the first Infantry Regt. to march past. Bn. congratulated by Divnl. Commander on its smart turn-out.	[sgd]
	16/11/18.		Bn. moved in busses from GHLIN to RUMES near TOURNAI. Billets not good.	[sgd]
	17/11/18.		Divine Services. 2/Lieut. W. Exton proceeded to 23rd Inf. Bde. as Education Officer. Lieut. G.L.Hiley joined the Bn. and posted to "B" Coy. Capt. E.H. Savill M.C. awarded Parchment Certificate for Devotion to Duty in FRESNES-ROUVROY and QUENT-DROCOURT attack.	[sgd]
	18/11/18.		Bn. moved to LA GLANERIE. Billets not good. 2/Lieuts. A.G. Sandwell and G.N.Kendall rejoined from Course.	[sgd]
	19/11/18.		Lieut. G.T.Martin M.C. struck off strength from 5th inst. 2/Lieut. J.D.Harcombe joined Bn. and posted to "B" Coy. 2/Lieut. C.H. Townsend proceeded on leave to U.K.	[sgd]
	20/11/18.		Coy parades. Reading and writing room opened for Bn. "DUMPLINGS" gave a performance. 2/Lieut. A..Tucker joined Bn. and posted to "B" Coy.	[sgd]
	21/11/18.		Capt. P.J.Bretherton M.C. rejoined from leave to U.K.	[sgd]

Army Form C. 2118.

WAR DIARY
or
INTELLIGENCE SUMMARY.
(Erase heading not required.)

Instructions regarding War Diaries and Intelligence Summaries are contained in F. S. Regs., Part II. and the Staff Manual respectively. Title pages will be prepared in manuscript.

Place	Date	Hour	Summary of Events and Information	Remarks and references to Appendices
			2nd Battalion Devonshire Regiment.	
	22/11/18.		2/Lieut. J.D.Harcombe admitted to Hospl.	RWB
	23/11/18.		2/Lieut. R.J.Cock joined Battn and posted to "B" Coy. Capt and Adjt. R.W.Bowen rejoined from leave to U.K.	RWB
	24/11/18.		Major B.W.Horne rejoined from leave in France.	RWB
	25/11/18.		Battn moved from billets in LA GLANERIE to Inf. Barracks, TOURNAI.	RWB
	26/11/18.		Battn under Major B.W.Horne practised Battn parade with a view to Bde parade. Lt.Col. G.B.R.Prior M.C. rejoined from 23rd Bde.H.Q.	RWB
	27/11/18.		Battn marched to TAIGNTINIES for Bde parade under Brig.Genl. G.W.St.G.Grogan V.C.,C.M.G.,D.S.O.	RWB
	28/11/18.		Battn parades. 2/Lieut.C.Luffman proceeded for duty as Area Comdt., ATH.	RWB
	29/11/18.		Battn parades.	RWB
	30/11/18.		2/Lieut. E.D.Clarke M.C. rejoined from leave to U.K.	RWB
	2/12/18.			RWB

J.C.Prior Lieut.Colonel;
Commanding 2nd Battalion Devonshire Regiment;

WAR DIARY or INTELLIGENCE SUMMARY.

(Erase heading not required.)

Army Form C. 2118.

Place	Date	Hour	Summary of Events and Information	Remarks and references to Appendices
TOURNAI.	December. 1st.		2nd Battalion Devonshire Regiment.	
			DIVINE SERVICES.	
do	2nd.		Battalion Parades. A concert was given by the Bn. Concert Party "The Dumplings" in the Y.M.C.A. 2/Lieut. A.R.Williams struck off strength whilst on leave (Medical Board).	
do	3rd.		Battalion Parades. A repatriated prisoner taken by the enemy near CONDE on the 28th October, visited the Batn. on his return from LIEGE.	
do	4th.		Battalion Parades.	
do	5th.		Great Ceremonial Parade on CHAMP DE MANOEUVRES, when the CROIX DE GUERRE was presented to the Batn. by the French General de Division De la Guiche.	
do	6th.		Battalion Parades.	
do	7th.		H.M. The King accompanied by the Prince of Wales and Prince Albert visited TOURNAI. The Battalion massed in the BOULEVARD, N. of the CHAMP DE MANOEUVRES.	
do	8th.		Divine Service in PALACE OF JUSTICE. Lieut. D.M.Atkinson rejoined from leave at PARIS PLAGE. 2/Lieut. C.H.Townsend rejoined from leave to U.K.	

Army Form C. 2118.

WAR DIARY
or
INTELLIGENCE SUMMARY.
(Erase heading not required.)

Instructions regarding War Diaries and Intelligence Summaries are contained in F. S. Regs., Part II. and the Staff Manual respectively. Title pages will be prepared in manuscript.

Place	Date	Hour	Summary of Events and Information	Remarks and references to Appendices
	December.		2. 2nd Battalion Devonshire Regiment.	
TOURNAI.	9th.		Battalion Parades. Battalion played the 24th Field Ambulance at Rugby and were beaten by 15 points to 8. 2/Lieuts. D.B.Baker and A.G.Sandwell granted leave to U.K.	
do	10th.		Battalion Parades. Concert given by the "Dumplings"	
do	11th.		Battalion Parades. Compulsory Education started by authorities. Wet day. 2/Lieut. F.D.Thornton granted leave to U.K. 2/Lieuts. B.R.Brown M.M. G.N.Kendall, J.Drummond granted leave to U.K. Colour Party proceeded to U.K. for Battalion Colours. Party consisted of 2/Lieut. J.J.Marchant, 2/Lieut. H.Parker, C.S.M. J.Bourne, Sgt.J.Lorey and A/c.E.Searl.	
do	12th.		Battalion Parades. Capt. W.C.D.Taylor rejoined from leave to U.K.	
do	13th.		Presentation by the G.O.C. 8th Division of Medal Ribbons and Parchment Certificates to 23rd Inf.Bde., at TAINTIGNIES.	
do	14th.		Battalion Parades. Draft of 19 O.R. joined.	

Army Form C. 2118.

WAR DIARY
or
INTELLIGENCE SUMMARY.
(Erase heading not required.)

Instructions regarding War Diaries and Intelligence Summaries are contained in F. S. Regs., Part II. and the Staff Manual respectively. Title pages will be prepared in manuscript.

Place	Date	Hour	Summary of Events and Information	Remarks and references to Appendices
	December.		3. 2nd Battalion Devonshire Regiment.	
TOURNAI	15th.		Divine Service in CINEMA. Lt.Col.G.E.R.Prior M.C. granted leave to the U.K.	
do	16th.		Battalion Parades. 2/Lieut.R.H.Hobern rejoined from Course.	
do	17th.		Battalion moved by march route to billets at BARRY.	
do & Barry	18th.		2/Lieut.E.A.Collier rejoined from Base. Battalion marched to billets at ATH.	
BARRY				
ATH	19th.		Inspection of Billets by G.O.C. 23rd Inf.Bde.	
do	20th.		Battalion Training. Military Medals awarded to 290153 Cpl. (now Sergt) G.White, 292047 Pte.T.Wickham, 71214 Pte.V.G.Hutt, Bar to Military Medal awarded to 74004 Pte.A.Dunn.	
do	21st.		Battalion Training. Tables and Forms procured for seating accomodation for Christmas Dinners. "Dumplings" gave a performance in Y.M.C.A. ATH.	
do	22nd.		Divine Service.	
do	23rd.		Colour Party rejoined from U.K. with Colours. Capt.E.H.Savill M.C. and Lt. & Qr.Mr. F.Gunn M.C. granted leave to U.K.	

Army Form C. 2118.

WAR DIARY
or
INTELLIGENCE SUMMARY.
(Erase heading not required.)

Instructions regarding War Diaries and Intelligence Summaries are contained in F.S. Regs., Part II. and the Staff Manual respectively. Title pages will be prepared in manuscript.

Place	Date	Hour	Summary of Events and Information	Remarks and references to Appendices
4TH.	December.		2nd Battalion Devonshire Regiment.	
do	24th.		Battalion Parades. Preparation for Christmas Day.	
do	25th.		XMAS DAY. Battalion had dinners in Coy Messes. C.O. visited each Coy at dinner. Church Service at 1115 hours.	
do	26.		BOXING DAY. No parades. Inter Coy Football Matches arranged.	
do	27th.		Battalion Training. Football matches in the afternoon.	
do	28th.		Battalion Training. Games & Recreational Training in afternoon.	
do	29th.		Divine Service. 2/Lieuts. D.E.Baker and G.G. Sandwell rejoined from leave to U.K.	
do	30th.		Battalion Training. Football Matches in afternoon. 2/Lieuts. B.R.Brown.M.M., G.N.Kendall and J.Drummond rejoined from leave to U.K.	
do	31st.		Adjutant's and Commanding Officer's Parades. Football in the afternoon.	

E.N.Horne. Major.

Commanding, 2nd Battalion Devonshire Regt.

Army Form C. 2118.

WAR DIARY
or
INTELLIGENCE SUMMARY.
(Erase heading not required.)

2nd Battalion Devonshire Regiment.

Place	Date	Hour	Summary of Events and Information	Remarks and references to Appendices
	1st January 1919.		Battalion Parades.	
	2/1/19.		Battalion Training.	
	3/1/19.		Ditto. Capt. Brokenshire and Lieut. W.H. Radcliffe rejoined from Base. 2/Lieut. F.D. Thornton rejoined from leave to U.K.	
	4/1/19.		Battalion Training. Football - 2/Devons 3 v. 2/Middlesex Reg. 1.	
	5/1/19.		Church Parades. in Salle des Concert, ATH.	
	6/1/19.		Battalion Training. Lieut.Col.G.E.R.Prior M.C. rejoined from leave to U.K.	
	7/1/19.		Battalion Training.	
	8/1/19.		Ditto. The u/m proceeded to U.K. as conducting Officers for demobilisation parties :- 2/Lieut.A.Willis, 2/Lieut.L.D.Heppenstall. 2/Lieut.R.S.Minton evacuated to U.K. "sick" and struck off strength.	
	9/1/19.		Battalion Training.	

Army Form C. 2118.

WAR DIARY
or
INTELLIGENCE SUMMARY.
(Erase heading not required.)

Instructions regarding War Diaries and Intelligence Summaries are contained in F. S. Regs., Part II. and the Staff Manual respectively. Title pages will be prepared in manuscript.

Place	Date	Hour	Summary of Events and Information	Remarks and references to Appendices
	10/1/19.		Battalion Training. Lieut. & Qr.Mr. F.Gunn M.C. rejoined from leave to U.K. Lieut. R.C.D.Napier proceeded on leave to U.K.	RNB
	11/1/19.		Battalion Training. 2/Lieut. J.D.Harcombe struck off strength.	RNB
	12/1/19.		Sunday. Services in the Halle des Concert, Ath.	RNB
	13/1/19.		Battalion Training.	RNB
	14/1/19.		Ditto. Lieut.J.J.Marchant proceeded to U.K. as Conducting Officer for demobilisation parties.	RNB
	15/1/19.		Battalion Training. Sgt. W.Gorman "C" Coy awarded the Chevalier de L'Ordre Leopold II.	RNB
	16/1/19.		Battalion Training.	RNB
	17/1/19.		Ditto.	RNB
	18/1/19.		Ditto. Ceremonial Parade. Reception of the Kings and Regimental Colours into the Battalion.	RNB

Army Form C. 2118.

WAR DIARY
or
INTELLIGENCE SUMMARY.
(Erase heading not required.)

Place	Date	Hour	Summary of Events and Information	Remarks and references to Appendices
	19/1/19.		Divine service at 1030 a.m.	
	20/1/19.		Battalion Parades. Concert by the Regimental Concert Party "The Dumplings" in the Halle des Concert Ath. Capt.W.C.D. Taylor proceeded to U.K. for demobilisation.	
	21/1/19.		Battalion Training.	
	22/1/19.		Ditto. Lieut.A.C.G.Roberts M.C. appointed Actg. Captain 31/12/18. vide London Gazette. 2/Lieut.B.R.Brown appointed Education Officer. 2/Lieut. C.Luffman proceeded to U.K. for demobilisation.	
	23/1/19.		Battalion Training.	
	24/1/19.		Ditto.	
	25/1/19.		Ditto.	
	26/1/19.		Divine service in Halle des Concert, ATH.	
	27/1/19.		Battalion Training.	
	28/1/19.		Ditto.	
	29/1/19.		Ditto.	

Instructions regarding War Diaries and Intelligence Summaries are contained in F. S. Regs., Part II. and the Staff Manual respectively. Title pages will be prepared in manuscript.

Army Form C. 2118.

WAR DIARY
or
INTELLIGENCE SUMMARY.
(Erase heading not required.)

Place	Date	Hour	Summary of Events and Information	Remarks and references to Appendices
	30/1/19.		Battalion Training.	
	31/1/19.		Ditto. 2/Lieut. A. Willis rejoined from leave to U.K.	

Lieut. Col.,

Commanding 2nd Battalion Devonshire Regiment.

WAR DIARY or INTELLIGENCE SUMMARY

2nd BATTALION DEVONSHIRE REGIMENT.

Date	Summary of Events and Information	Remarks
1919. Feby. 1st.	Battalion Training. 2/Lieut. A. Willis admitted to Hospital.	RWB
2/2/19.	Divine Service in Y.M.C.A., ATH.	RWB
3/2/19.	Battn. Training. Lieut. H.W. Byrde proceeded to U.K. for demobilisation.	RWB
4/2/19.	Battn. Training. Capt. S.H. Parsloe (Transport Officer, 23rd Infantry Brigade) taken on strength from 29/1/19.	RWB
5/2/19.	Battn. Training.	RWB
6/2/19.	Do. 2/Lieut. J.J. Huntingford granted permission to wear badges of rank of Lieut. pending announcement appearing in London Gazette.	RWB
7/2/19.	Battn. Training. 2/Lieut. A.G. Sandwell proceeded to U.K. for demobilisation.	RWB
8/2/19.	Battn. Training.	RWB
9/2/19.	Divine Services in Y.M.C.A., ATH.	RWB

Army Form C. 2118.

WAR DIARY
or
INTELLIGENCE SUMMARY.
(Erase heading not required.)

Instructions regarding War Diaries and Intelligence Summaries are contained in F.S. Regs., Part II. and the Staff Manual respectively. Title pages will be prepared in manuscript.

Place	Date	Hour	Summary of Events and Information	Remarks and references to Appendices
	10/2/19.		Battn. Training.	
	11/2/19.		Do.	
	12/2/19.		Do. Lieut.G.W.White (attached 8th Division) demobilised and struck off strength. Lieut.J.J.Marchant rejoined from leave to U.K.	RcB
	13/2/19.		Battn.Training. Lieut.R.C.D.Napier M.C. proceeded to U.K. for demobilisation.	RcB
	14/2/19.		Battn.Training. Capt.A.G.C.Roberts M.C. proceeded to U.K. for demobilisation. Lieut.R.H.Cumming rejoined from leave to U.K.	RcB
	15/2/19.		Battn.training. 2/Lieut.A.Willis rejoined from Hospital. 2/Lieut.A.S.Watkins proceeded to U.K. as Conducting Officer for demobilisation party. 2/Lieut.C.H.Townsend took over duties of Transport Officer.	RcB
	16/2/19.		Church parade.	RcB
	17/2/19.		Battn.Training. 2/Lieut.L.D.Heppenstall proceeded to U.K. for demobilisation.	RcB
	18/2/19.		Battn. Training. Capt.R.L.Brokenshire M.C. proceeded on special leave to U.K.	RcB

Army Form C. 2118.

WAR DIARY
or
INTELLIGENCE SUMMARY.
(Erase heading not required.)

Instructions regarding War Diaries and Intelligence Summaries are contained in F.S. Regs., Part II. and the Staff Manual respectively. Title pages will be prepared in manuscript.

Place	Date	Hour	Summary of Events and Information	Remarks and references to Appendices
	19/2/19.		Battn. Training.	
	20/2/19.		Do. 2/Lieut.R.J.Shutter rejoined from leave to U.K. Lieut.S.T.Mears proceeded to U.K. for demobilisation.	/s/
	21/2/19.		Battn.Training. 2/Lieut.A.E.Collier proceeded to U.K. as Conducting Officer for demobilisation party.	/s/
	22/2/19.		Battn. Training.	/s/
	23/2/19.		Divine Services. 2/Lieut.S.Groves proceeded to U.K. as Conducting Officer for demobilisation party.	
	24/2/19.		Battn Training.	
	25/2/19.		Do.	
	26/2/19.		Do.	
	27/2/19.		Do.	
	28/2/19.		Do. 2/Lieut.B.R.Brown proceeded on leave to U.K. 2/Lieut. R.J.Shutter proceeded for duty with D.A.D.R.T.Dunkirk and is struck off strength.	/s/

1/3/19.

(signed) Graham
Lieut.Col.,
Commanding 2nd Battalion Devonshire Regiment.

Army Form C. 2118.

WAR DIARY
or
INTELLIGENCE SUMMARY.
(Erase heading not required.)

Instructions regarding War Diaries and Intelligence Summaries are contained in F. S. Regs., Part II. and the Staff Manual respectively. Title pages will be prepared in manuscript.

Place	Date	Hour	Summary of Events and Information	Remarks and references to Appendices
	March 1919.			
ATH.	1st.		1. 2nd Battalion Devonshire Regiment.	
			Orders received that draft of 150 other ranks would be required from men retained for the Army of Occupation, to proceed to 2/8th Worcesters at CHERBOURG.	
do	2nd.		Divine Service.	
do	3rd.		Captain P.J.Bretherton M.C. demobilised on leave.	
do	4th.		Nothing of interest.	
do	5th.		Captain W.R.McLeod rejoined from Fourth Army School.	
do	6th.		Nothing of interest.	
do	7th.		do	
do	8th.		do	
do	9th.		do	
do	10th.		do	
do	11th.		Captain W.H.Savill M.C. and Lieut. B.W.Schooling demobilised whilst on leave	
do	12th.		Major E.W.Horne proceeded to U.K. for 2 month's leave prior to assuming duties of Adjt at Depot Devon Regt.	
do	13th.		Nothing of interest.	
do	14th.		2/Lieut. F.D.Clarke M.C. granted 2 month's leave to England.	
do	15th.		Nothing of interest.	
do	16th.		Lieut. D.M.Atkinson, Lieut. J.P.Tucker and 126 other ranks proceeded to join 2/8 Worcesters at CHERBOURG to form part of the Army of Occupation.	
do	17th.		Nothing of interest.	
do	18th.		7810 C.S.M. J.T.Lane awarded the "Medaille Barbatie Si Credinta - 1st Class."	

WAR DIARY
or
INTELLIGENCE SUMMARY.

(Erase heading not required.)

Army Form C. 2118.

Place	Date	Hour	Summary of Events and Information	Remarks and references to Appendices
	March 1919.		2nd Battalion Devonshire Regiment.	
ATH	19th.		Nothing of interest.	
do	20th.		24 other ranks (balance of draft of 150 other ranks ordered) proceeded to join 2/8th Worcester Regiment at CHERBOURG.	
do	21st.		2/Lieut. G.R. Taylor proceeded for duty with Chinese Labour Corps.	
do	22nd.		Nothing of interest.	
do	23rd.		do	
do	24th.		do	
do	25th.		Captain S.H. Parsloe proceeded to U.K. for demobilisation.	
do	26th.		Nothing of interest.	
do	27th.		2/Lieut. J.W. Kendall granted 14 days leave to U.K.	
do	28th.		Captain W. Exton, M.C. demobilised.	
do	29th.		Nothing of interest.	
do	30th.		Lt.Col. G.E.R. Prior, D.S.O., M.C. proceeded on leave to U.K. prior to joining 51st Devon Regt with the Army of Occupation in Germany, as Second in Command.	
do	31st.		Lieut. R.H. Cummins demobilised. 1/1st Hereford Regt arrived at ATH for the purpose of relieving the Battalion.	
	1/4/19.			

Ru Cowan Capt & adjt
for Captain
Commanding, 2nd Battalion Devonshire Regiment

Army Form C. 2118.

WAR DIARY
or
INTELLIGENCE SUMMARY.

(Erase heading not required.)

Instructions regarding War Diaries and Intelligence Summaries are contained in F.S. Regs., Part II. and the Staff Manual respectively. Title pages will be prepared in manuscript.

Place	Date	Hour	Summary of Events and Information	Remarks and references to Appendices
	APRIL 1919.		2nd Battalion Devonshire Regiment.	
ATH.	1st		2/Lieuts. D.H.BAKER and C.H.TOWNSEND departed for the U.K. and are struck off strength.	
	2nd		~~2/Lieut.R.H.COWLING departed for the U.K. and is S.O.S.~~	
	3rd		Nothing of interest.	
	4th		Nothing of interest.	
	5th		2/Lieut A.WILLIS admitted to hospital.	
	6th		Band Boys visited BRUSSELS.	
	7th		Nothing of interest.	
	8th		Nothing of interest.	
	9th		Nothing of interest.	
	10th		Lieut. H.PARKER.L.C. rejoined from Conducting Duty to the U.K.	
	11th		Nothing of interest.	
	12th		Nothing of interest.	
	13th		Lieut. F.R.BROMAN, 2/Lieuts J.DRUMMOND, S.GROVES, B.R.BROWN.M.M. A.S.WATKINS. F.D.THRONTON, R.H.HOBERN proceeded to Prisoners of War Companies and are struck off strength.	
	14th		Nothing of interest.	
	15th		2/Lieut. R.J.COOK departed for demobilization. Orders received for the Cadre to entrain on the 16th	

Army Form C. 2118.

WAR DIARY
or
INTELLIGENCE SUMMARY.
(Erase heading not required.)

Instructions regarding War Diaries and Intelligence Summaries are contained in F. S. Regs., Part II. and the Staff Manual respectively. Title pages will be prepared in manuscript.

Place	Date	Hour	Summary of Events and Information	Remarks and references to Appendices
DUNKIRK ATT.	17th 16		Cadre's Band returned at 1900 hours for Dunkirk	
DUNKIRK	17		Cadre Band arrived at 1400 hours, marched to embarkation Camp for Batt. etc	
"	18		afterwards proceeding to No 2 embarkation Camp	
"	19		for embarkation On 19th at 1100 hours Cadre of Battn embarked on SS "ANTRIM" for England	

[signature] Capt.
for Commanding 2nd Devon Regt.

www.ingramcontent.com/pod-product-compliance
Lightning Source LLC
Chambersburg PA
CBHW080836010526
44114CB00017B/2319